Winthrop's Journal, "History Of New England," 1630-1649, Volume 1

James Kendall Hosmer, John Winthrop

Nabu Public Domain Reprints:

You are holding a reproduction of an original work published before 1923 that is in the public domain in the United States of America, and possibly other countries. You may freely copy and distribute this work as no entity (individual or corporate) has a copyright on the body of the work. This book may contain prior copyright references, and library stamps (as most of these works were scanned from library copies). These have been scanned and retained as part of the historical artifact.

This book may have occasional imperfections such as missing or blurred pages, poor pictures, errant marks, etc. that were either part of the original artifact, or were introduced by the scanning process. We believe this work is culturally important, and despite the imperfections, have elected to bring it back into print as part of our continuing commitment to the preservation of printed works worldwide. We appreciate your understanding of the imperfections in the preservation process, and hope you enjoy this valuable book.

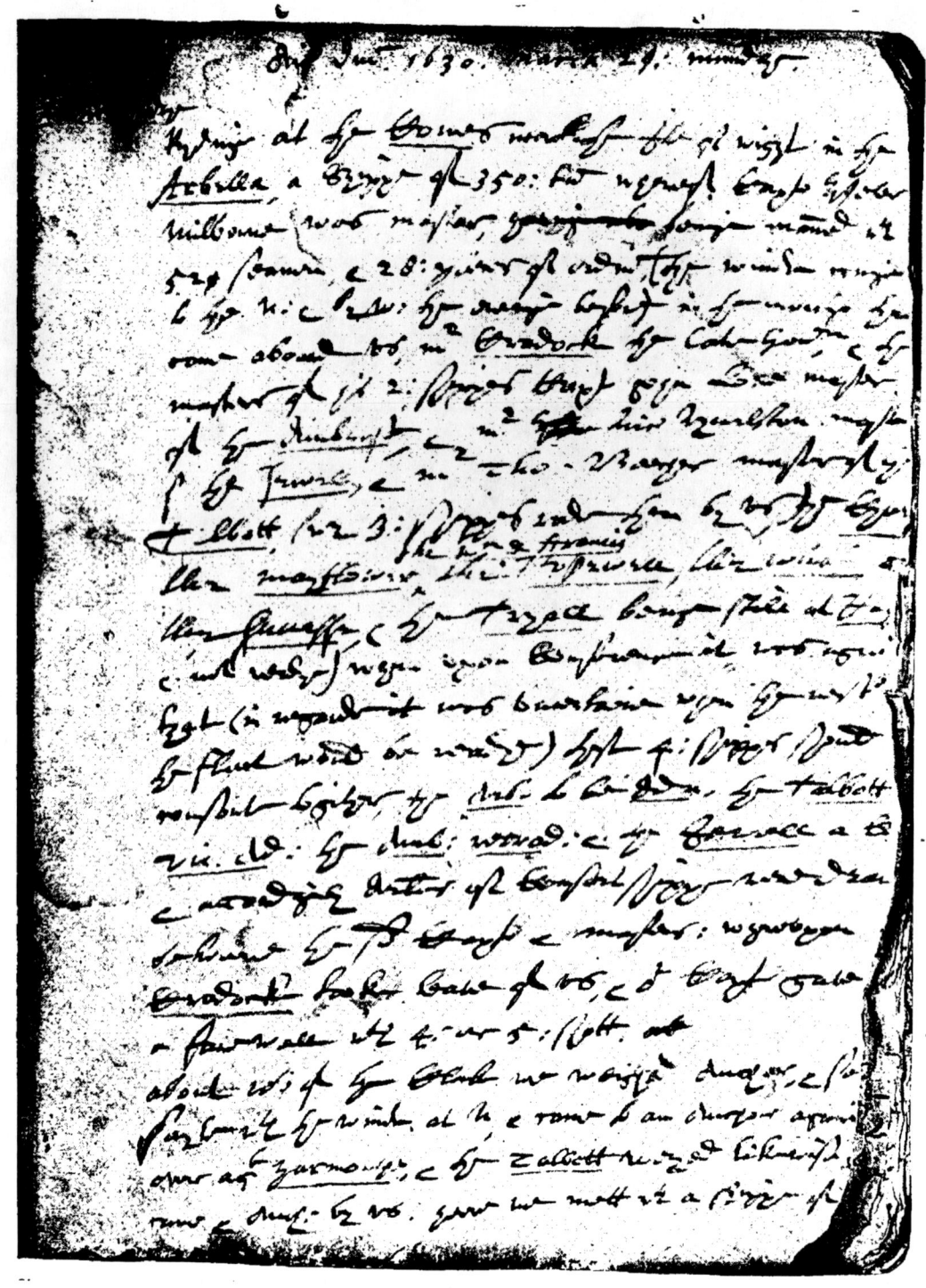

FIRST PAGE OF THE WINTHROP MANUSCRIPT
From the original in the Library of the Massachusetts Historical Society

*ORIGINAL NARRATIVES
OF EARLY AMERICAN HISTORY*

WINTHROP'S JOURNAL

"HISTORY OF NEW ENGLAND"

1630—1649

EDITED BY

JAMES KENDALL HOSMER, LL.D.

CORRESPONDING MEMBER OF THE MASSACHUSETTS HISTORICAL SOCIETY
AND OF THE COLONIAL SOCIETY OF MASSACHUSETTS

WITH MAPS AND FACSIMILES

VOLUME I

CHARLES SCRIBNER'S SONS
NEW YORK
1908

Copyright, 1908, by
CHARLES SCRIBNER'S SONS

Printed in the United States of America

All rights reserved. No part of this book may be reproduced in any form without the permission of Charles Scribner's Sons

NOTE

WHILE in this edition of Winthrop's *Journal* we have followed, as Dr. Hosmer explains in his Introduction, the text prepared by Savage, it has been thought wise to add devices which will make the dates easier for the reader to follow; but these have, it is hoped, been given such a form that the reader will have no difficulty in distinguishing added words or figures from those belonging to the original text. Winthrop makes no division into chapters. In this edition the text has, for the reader's convenience, been broken by headings representing the years. These, however, in accordance with modern usage, have been set at the beginning of January, not at the date with which Winthrop began his year, the first of March. The dates set in the inner margins of the headlines to our pages have been arranged on the same plan. Early in 1635 Winthrop abandons in his text the Roman names of the months, substituting, in accordance with Puritan sentiment, a system of numbering, beginning with March as the first month. In this edition the more familiar names of the months are inserted in italics.

With respect to the first of the illustrations, it may be mentioned that the first volume of the original manuscript has pages of about $7\frac{1}{2}$ by $5\frac{1}{2}$ inches, so that the facsimile here presented is somewhat reduced. The second facsimile exhibits the famous patent of 1629 to the Massachusetts Company, the conveyance of which to New England was of so momentous consequences to the colony. Though annulled in 1684, the original patent has remained in Massachusetts, and is now exhibited in the office of the Secretary of State, to whom we are indebted for permission to reproduce it. The next illustration, reproducing the map given in William Wood's book called *New England's Prospect*, bears date of 1634, the year in which that book was published. Wood was an intelligent traveller, whose book is of much value. It was reproduced by the Prince Society in 1634, edited by Dr. Charles Deane. Wood left New England August 15, 1633, and the map no doubt represents the state of settlement at the time of his departure. It is closely related to the map reproduced in Winsor's

Narrative and Critical History of America, III. 381, which, by whomsoever draughted, bears a marginal key in the handwriting of Governor Winthrop. Perhaps Wood depended in part on this map, now in the British Museum; perhaps both were based in greater or less degree on the same original survey. Of the two maps, Wood's has been selected for reproduction in this volume, because it is much more easily read. It is here presented in the size of the original. For the opportunity to photograph it, and also the title-page of the *Short Story*, we are indebted to Mr. Wilberforce Eames of the Lenox Library; for similar permission in the case of the precious original manuscript of Winthrop, to Dr. Samuel A. Green, Librarian of the Massachusetts Historical Society.

J. F. J.

CONTENTS

WINTHROP'S JOURNAL

"HISTORY OF NEW ENGLAND"

Edited by James Kendall Hosmer

	PAGE
Introduction	3
Journal	23

1630

Winthrop's Fleet sails from the Isle of Wight	24
A Fast kept on the Ships	25
Matthew Cradock bids Farewell to the Fleet	26
Danger feared from Hostile Ships	27
Captain Kirk encountered on the High Seas	36
Tempest strikes the Fleet	37
Mount Desert sighted	47
Arbella casts Anchor in Salem Harbor	50
Expedition to Massachusetts Bay	50
Marriage of John Endicott	51
Settlement at Charlestown	52
Death of the Lady Arbella and Isaac Johnson	52
Boston occupied and a Church organized	52
Salem, Dorchester, Watertown and Roxbury named	52
The Plantation set in Order	53
Winter Severities	55

1631

Prevalence of Illness	58
Friendly Overtures from Chickatabot and other Sachems	59
Rev. John Wilson departs for England	60
Roger Williams at Salem	61
Sir Christopher Gardiner	63
Philip Ratcliffe disciplined for traducing Church and Government	64
The *Blessing of the Bay* launched	65

CONTENTS

	PAGE
Piscataqua heard from	69
The *Lyon* arrives, with important Succor	70
Bradford of Plymouth visits Boston	71

1632

Winthrop explores the Neighborhood	73
People press for more Power	74
Winthrop reëlected Governor; Deputies chosen by the Towns	79
The French to the Eastward heard from	82
Churches consult after the Congregational Way	83
Winthrop and Dudley disagree	84
Narragansetts send Envoys	89
Return of Rev. John Wilson	91
Winthrop visits Plymouth	92
Pirates give Trouble to the Eastward	95

1633

Gorges and Mason Petition against us	99
Gardiner, Morton and Ratcliffe make Trouble	100
Thanksgiving over Friends preserved and Foes confounded	102
Arrival of John Cotton, Thomas Hooker and John Haynes	105
John Oldham goes Overland to the Connecticut	108
The *Blessing of the Bay* sails to the Connecticut and the Dutch	109
John Cotton made Teacher of the Boston Church	110
Roger Williams at Salem takes Exception	112
Two Sagamores and Most of their Folks die of Smallpox	115
The Lord directs through John Cotton the Support of the Ministers	116

1634

The Narragansetts lose Seven Hundred by Smallpox	118
Controversy as to Women's wearing Veils	120
Satan bestirs himself to Distract the Churches	121
Deputies sent from Towns to General Court	122
The Killing of Hockin	123
Thomas Dudley chosen Governor	125
Four General Courts a Year, of Magistrates and Deputies	125
News of the Founding of Maryland	126
Archbishops and Others try to stay the Ships and annul the Patent	127
Profitable Trade with Manhattan and the Kennebec Country	130
Newtown desires to Remove to Connecticut	132
Legislation against Tobacco, Costly Apparel, etc.	134
Threatenings of the Privy Council against our Patent	135
The Cross cut out of the Ensign at Salem	137
Pequots desire our Friendship	138
John Eliot, Friend of Massachusetts Indians	142
The Dutch to the Westward cause Anxiety	144

CONTENTS

1635

	PAGE
Interference from England feared	145
Military Commission established	148
John Haynes chosen Governor	149
Endicott questioned about Defacing the Ensign	149
Disturbed Relations between Magistrates and Deputies	150
Fear of the Schemes of Gorges and Mason	152
Roger Williams called to Account for Dangerous Opinions	154
The French capture Penobscot, a Plantation of Plymouth	157
Arrival of Thomas Shepard and Hugh Peter	160
Young Henry Vane, called to the Obedience of the Gospel, arrives	161
Hugh Peter's Practical Good Sense	165

1636

Roger Williams gives Trouble	166
Hugh Peter's Practical Benevolence	168
Vane and Peter set themselves up as Arbiters	169
Flag devised leaving out the Cross	174
Henry Vane elected Governor	180
The King's Colors set up at Castle Island	181
Murder of John Oldham brings on the Pequot War	183
Narragansetts remain Friendly	186
Endicott's Expedition to Block Island	187
Miantonomo received in Boston	192
Anne Hutchinson gives Trouble	195
Distraction in the New England Churches	196
The French claim most of the Maine Coast	201
General Court and the Elders take Council	203
John Cotton intervenes and is disapproved	204

1637

General Fast over the miserable Estate of the Churches	208
Wheelwright questioned on Account of his Sermon	210
Underhill sent to Connecticut with Soldiers	212
Reluctance of Plymouth to take Part in the War	213
Winthrop made Governor at stormy Session	215
Cotton and Shepard as Reconcilers	216
John Mason's Victory over the Pequots	218
Discontent of Henry Vane	219
Pequots dispersed and destroyed	221
Three hundred and sixty Immigrants in one Day	222
Sir Ferdinando Gorges wishes to be Governor-General	224
Pequot Survivors deported and enslaved	225
Henry Vane departs for England	229
A Movement toward Confederation of the Colonies	231
Synod convened to deal with the Errors	232

MAPS AND FACSIMILE REPRODUCTIONS

First Page of the Winthrop Manuscript. From the original in the
   Library of the Massachusetts Historical Society . . . *Frontispiece*

                                                                                                                PAGE

The Royal Patent or Charter of March 4, 1629, to the Governor
   and Company of the Massachusetts Bay. From the original in
   the office of the Secretary of the Commonwealth of Massachusetts . 52

William Wood's Map of the South Part of New England in 1634.
   From a copy of Wood's *New England's Prospect*, edition of 1634, in the
   New York Public Library (Lenox Building) 118

Title-page of "A Short Story of the Rise, Reign and Ruine of the
   Antinomians." From a copy of the original edition in the New York
   Public Library (Lenox Building) 242

WINTHROP'S JOURNAL
"THE HISTORY OF NEW ENGLAND"
1630–1649

Vol. I

INTRODUCTION

THE *Journal* of John Winthrop, founder of the colony of Massachusetts Bay in New England, recording the story of that colony during the first nineteen years of its existence, must always have an interest not only for New England but for America in general, and indeed for the world at large. Though a few Englishmen may have made a precarious lodgment on the New England coast before 1620, no proper settlement took place until December of that year, when the Pilgrims landed at Plymouth. Ten years later, in 1630, came Winthrop's company. After the lapse of another ten years, during which time the English in New England increased to about twenty thousand, the immigration suddenly ceased; with the opening of the Long Parliament the grievances which had driven into exile so many of the non-conformists no longer pressed heavily. For almost two hundred years the New England stock received no further accretion from home and almost no new elements. An isolated, homogeneous population, it multiplied largely within itself, and began at the end of the eighteenth century to send its children westward.[1]

What the twenty thousand Puritan Englishmen and their descendants have accomplished is worth taking note of. Almost at once, dating from the early years of the settlement, a curious reaction set back from the new world across the Atlantic: New England became the leader of Old England. As the combat deepened between Court and Parliament the "New England Way" began more and more to prevail, and the New England way was Independency. This, finding such promoters as Cromwell, Milton and Vane, at last resulted in the Commonwealth, a political construction short-lived, but

[1] Palfrey, *History of New England*, I., Preface.

under which England was indeed a mighty and puissant nation.[1]

As New England waxed in numbers her vigor and influence continued to be impressively manifest. When a hundred years had passed, the pre-natal throes of the great Federal Republic were convulsing the Thirteen Colonies which now fringed the coast of the Atlantic. In this agitation New England had the initiative: within her borders it was that a spirit of resistance to British encroachments upon freedom first awoke; it was her sons who devised most of the methods through which resistance became effective; and it was her soil which was first bloodstained when at last the clash took place. In establishing the United States, while Washington, Jefferson, Madison, Marshall, Hamilton, are figures of supreme interest, the New Englanders James Otis, Franklin, Samuel and John Adams were perhaps not less indispensable. Massachusetts, one of the thirteen, furnished probably more than one-quarter of the fighting men.[2]

In the civilized world in general during the century and a quarter that has followed our Revolution, nations everywhere have accommodated themselves more and more to a democratic basis[3] and in this vast and widespread reconstruction a live wire of influence may be traced back even to dynamos in the popularly governed communities that sprang out of the enterprises of Winthrop and Bradford.

Nor is the vigor of the twenty-thousand and their children yet spent: it may be traced at the present moment in each one of the forty-six United States and in the world beyond: in its ancient home, though wave after wave of new-comers, Celtic,

---

[1] J. Wingate Thornton, *The Historical Relations of New England to the English Commonwealth* (Boston, 1874); Charles Borgeaud, *Rise of Modern Democracy in Old and New England*, p. 37; J. K. Hosmer, *Young Sir Harry Vane*, p. 166 et seqq.

[2] For a summary of authority on which to base the claim for New England's initiative in our Revolution, see J. K. Hosmer, *Samuel Adams*, p. 11 et seqq.

[3] J. K. Hosmer, *Short History of Anglo-Saxon Freedom*, ch. XVIII.

Latin, Slav, have within the two past generations overswept the English seed which the *Mayflower* and *Arbella* with their little consorts distributed, it is the old stock that is still in the fore-front. Winthrop, Bradford, Adams, Quincy, Lowell, Hoar, Sherman, Savage, Saltonstall, Brewster, Eliot, Phillips, Brooks, Emerson, Hawthorne, Endicott, Winslow, Cushman, Higginson, and many more, are names in our own day, dominant, often brilliantly distinguished, in various ways, the same names that are borne on the lists of men who shipped for New England when the Star Chamber and the High Commission Court were pressing with heavy hand.

A stock so persistent, so virile, so widely eminent, claims attention in every period of its course, and naturally a special interest attaches to its earliest American memorials. The discovery and restoration to Massachusetts of the long-lost journal of William Bradford, governor of Plymouth, was a matter of almost national rejoicing. A reprint of this is included in the present series.[1] Scarcely less treasured is the journal of John Winthrop, governor of Massachusetts Bay, a reprint of which is here introduced;—and what of the man and his book?

The fortunes of the Winthrop family[2] were established by Adam Winthrop, whose life extended from 1498 to 1562; after a prosperous career as a clothier, he was granted the freedom of the city of London in 1526, and after 1548 was permitted to write himself *armiger*, or esquire, so attaining to the gentry. In 1544 he had obtained the manor of Groton, in Suffolk, till then belonging to the monastery of Bury St. Edmunds, thus profiting as did so many Englishmen, high and low-born, from the dissolution of the monasteries. A fine contemporary portrait presents a face marked by resolution and good sense, surmounted by such a cap as often marks the portraits of the

---

[1] Bradford's *History of Plymouth Plantation*, edited by W. T. Davis.
[2] Robert C. Winthrop, *Life and Letters of John Winthrop*; C. Harding Firth, article "John Winthrop" in *Dictionary of National Biography*.

Reformation period, the figure below attired in a rich fur-trimmed over-garment. His third son, Adam, being educated as a lawyer, reached responsibilities and distinctions that advanced the family. For fifteen years, 1594 to 1609, he was auditor of St. John's and Trinity Colleges, Cambridge. Dying in 1623, after being twice married, he left four daughters, their mother being a sister of Bishop John Still; and, by a second wife, an only son, John, who became founder of the colony of Massachusetts Bay in New England.

John Winthrop was born in 1588, his mother being Anne Browne, daughter of a well-to-do tradesman, through whom presumably the possessions of the Winthrops were enhanced. In boyhood he was admitted to Trinity College, Cambridge, but his course was interrupted by his sudden marriage, at the age of seventeen, with Mary Forth, an heiress, the mother of John Winthrop, jr., governor of Connecticut, and other sons and daughters. Mary Winthrop died in 1615, whereupon Winthrop speedily married Thomasine Clopton; who surviving only a year, he took as third wife Margaret Tyndale, daughter of Sir John Tyndale. This lady, though dying before her husband, in 1647, giving place to a fourth wife, is the Mistress Winthrop whom we know best.[1]

When John Winthrop thus in 1605 assumed, as we should say so prematurely, the responsibilities of a man, James I. had been two years on the throne. From the days of Henry VIII. the family at Groton had been devotedly Protestant, a loyalty perhaps helped by the fact that a return of England to the ancient church would impair the title to their handsome estate. As the Church of England took shape with the sovereign at its head and the establishment of an elaborate hierarchy below, no family was more zealous for the new order than the Winthrops. From the old Romanism they held strictly aloof; and on the other hand they had nothing in common with the

---

[1] Alice Morse Earle, *Margaret Winthrop* (1895); J. Anderson, *Margaret Tyndale*, in *Memorable Women of the Puritan Times*, p. 120 *et seqq.* (1862).

Separatists, the Protestants who as the sixteenth century advanced, dissatisfied with what they held to be the half-way reformation of the Established Church, broke out from its fold into various extremes of belief. Far on in life, John Winthrop was destined to show sympathy with the ideas of Robert Browne, one of the best known and perhaps least esteemed among the Separatists, the founder of certain independent congregations some of which were driven out of England for their refusal to submit to authority. But, in an earlier time, while steadfast in their allegiance to the Church of England, it was with the so-called non-conformists that the Winthrops ranged themselves, the large class who, when the sovereigns and higher prelates sought to set up a ritualistic order akin to the ecclesiasticism which the country had forsaken, declared for a ceremonial simpler and without Romish taint.

From the family memorials, which have been preserved to a remarkable extent, we know that the elder Adam Winthrop, though for the most part a man of affairs, was intellectually active; still more so was the second Adam, who, while managing the business of the Cambridge colleges, yet was a profuse inditer of letters and diaries; John Winthrop, carrying still farther the tradition, became one of the most voluminous of writers, letters, journals, tracts and books following each other abundantly from his youth to the day of his death. An atmosphere of stern Puritanism pervades the memorials of grandfather, father and son. In particular the letters of John Winthrop, even on the ordinary occasions of life, are so clouded by a Calvinistic piety that it is hard to get, through the theologizing, the simple fact he desires to convey. Yet evidence is not wanting that the Winthrops in these early generations had plenty of worldly wisdom, steering shrewdly in the public turmoil, swelling the patrimony prudently by marriage jointures, and wasting nothing in unprofitable ventures. John Winthrop in private life was certainly an excellent husband, father and householder; and as a citizen early obtained through good judgment, balance, and steadfast courage, a wide influence among the Puritan gentry.

Winthrop's plan for emigrating to America was not long entertained before it was carried out. In 1626 he became an attorney, and in 1628 a member of the Inner Temple, thus assuming positions which seem to imply an intention of fixed residence. The earliest hint of his purpose to remove is conveyed in a letter to his wife of May 15, 1629, in which his discontent with the condition of England is made plain, with an intimation of his future course. Charles I. had just dissolved Parliament, the antagonism between the High Church and Prerogative men on the one hand and those of a freer spirit on the other, having become acute. To earnest men of Winthrop's views England was becoming a place no longer fit to dwell in. He had passed into middle age and was bound by many ties to his native land, but he now embarked upon an enterprise of the boldest.

As Winthrop here turns his face toward the new world, we must note briefly the facts of its exploration and settlement up to this time.[1] The basis of the English claim to rights in North America rested on the discoveries of Cabot; since the French were equally well provided with a title through the voyage of Verrazano, a contention arose not settled until the days of Pitt and Wolfe. In the first years of the seventeenth century lived in southern England an active knight, Sir Ferdinando Gorges, who, though bearing a name of Spanish or Italian sound, was nevertheless a thorough Englishman in quality and birth. Associated with the Earl of Essex, in Elizabeth's time, he drew upon himself, and probably merited, odium, by later testifying against him. But he was persistent and courageous, and after a career against Spain in the navy received the post of governor of Plymouth.

[1] Palfrey, *History of New England*, vol. I.

INTRODUCTION

Gorges, in connection with Sir John Popham, chief-justice of the King's Bench, brought into existence in 1606 the Virginia Company, a corporation with a patent from the King, which presently, divided into two sections known as the London Company and the Plymouth Company, set forth strenuously to possess the great territory. The earliest result of the effort was Jamestown, founded in 1607. The attempts farther north were at first less successful. A colony sent to the Kennebec neighborhood by Gorges and Popham, in 1607, disheartened by misfortune and winter severities, had no success. Popham died, but Gorges continued indefatigable: his enterprises followed each other, never resulting in anything more than little groups of fishermen or traders clinging precariously to the coast. As the century proceeded and in England the strife arose between King and Parliament, Sir Ferdinando sided with the King. The successes in New England colonization were won by the Puritans, but for many a year, as Winthrop's *Journal* often evidences, the enterprises of the old cavalier, in Maine and New Hampshire, disquieted the Puritan plantations.

Of the settlement of the *Mayflower* Pilgrims no account is required here.[1] In the years following their establishment in 1620, Bradford's colonists ranged north and south making well known the coast of New England, from Manhattan, where the Dutch had fixed themselves in 1613, to the region of Maine, where they met the French from Port Royal and its outposts. Adventurers from Plymouth, or brought in by the ships which now frequented these waters, settled around Massachusetts Bay. Thomas Weston attempted a post at Wessagusset, now Weymouth, in 1622; Thomas Morton in 1625, was at Merry Mount; John Oldham at Hull or Natascott; William Blackstone built a house on the peninsula of Trimount, as did Thomas Walford at Mishawum, now Charlestown, and Samuel Maverick at Winnisimmet, now Chelsea. A few years after the *May-*

[1] See Bradford's *History*, edited by W. T. Davis.

flower's coming, an enterprise more markedly Puritan than before sought to gain a footing on Cape Ann. Its ruling spirit was John White, minister of Dorchester in England. Forsaking the bleak promontory for Naumkeag, now Salem, and receiving reinforcements, among whom John Endicott in 1628 and Francis Higginson in 1629 were the leaders, these planters were the immediate precursors of the settlement with which at present we have to deal.

The London Company, the part of the Virginia Company designed to exploit the southern field, falling into difficulties and incurring the royal displeasure, Gorges and his friends obtained, in 1620, a new incorporation, the Council for New England. Its membership was distinguished, and the territory which it was authorized to administer extended from sea to sea between the fortieth and forty-eighth parallels. In 1628 this Council for New England granted to Sir Henry Roswell, Sir John Young, Thomas Southcote, John Humfrey, John Endicott, and Simon Whitcomb, Massachusetts, a strip running from sea to sea, with its northward limit three miles north of the Merrimac, and its southward limit three miles south of the Charles. That this grant became something more than a mere voluntary partnership without corporate powers, is due especially to the agency of John White, of Dorchester. He was zealous and widely influential among the Puritans, and it is attributed to him that, the company having been much enlarged by royal charter, a corporation was sanctioned, under the title of "The Governor and the Company of the Massachusetts Bay in New England." The charter gave power forever to the freemen of the company to elect each year a governor, deputy-governor, and eighteen assistants, on the last Wednesday of Easter term, and to make laws consistent with those of England. Four meetings were to be regularly held, with provision also for special occasions. The magistrates were empowered to administer the oaths of supremacy and allegiance; new associates might be admitted, and the corporation was empowered to defend itself against attack by sea or land. As to religious liberty the charter has nothing to say.[1]

Under this charter a new government was now organized, April 30, 1629. Thirteen councillors were elected, to hold office for a year, of whom seven beside the governor were to be appointed by the company at home; these eight were to appoint three others; the two remaining were to be elected by the "old planters," the men on the spot, the pioneers of the colony. Matthew Cradock, a London merchant of repute, who appears later in the Long Parliament, being named as governor, instructs Endicott, who had gone over the previous year, and is agent, that the propagation of the gospel is "the thing they do profess above all other aims;" the colonists are to be carefully watched and restrained. Tobacco is to be cultivated only under severe restrictions; Massachusetts Bay, by which was then understood Boston harbor and its neighborhood, is to be secured; persons who may prove "not conformable to their government" shall not be allowed to remain within the limits of their grant.

Six vessels were now dispatched containing three hundred men, eighty women and maids, twenty-six children, one hundred and forty head of cattle, and forty goats, with all needful furnishings and appliances. Francis Higginson, the most interesting figure of this large and well-provided company, was a Cambridge scholar, of Emmanuel College, and later had been rector of a church in Leicester. Cotton Mather, writing in 1697, gives a tradition of Higginson which perhaps may be accepted:[2]

"They sailed from the Isle of Wight about the 1st of May, 1629, and when they came to the Land's End, Mr. Higginson, calling up his children and other passengers to the stern of the ship to take their last sight of England, said: We will not say, as the Separatists were wont to say at their leaving of

---

[1] The venerable document is still preserved in the office of the Secretary of State in Massachusetts. The text is given in Poore's *Charters and Constitutions*, and elsewhere.

[2] *Magnalia Christi Americana*, Book III., part 2, chap. II., section 12.

England, Farewell Babylon, farewell Rome! but we will say, farewell dear England! farewell the Church of God in England, and all the Christian friends there! We do not go to New England as Separatists from the Church of England, though we cannot but separate from the corruptions in it, but we go to practise the positive part of church reformation, and propagate the gospel in America." He concluded with a fervent prayer for the King and church and state in England and all the Christian friends there.

The six ships, though not sailing together, all arrived in June, and at once the plantation, till then but an unorganized knot of adventurous people, became established as a proper community. Steps were taken to form a church with Samuel Skelton for teacher and Higginson for pastor.[1] Even thus early can be noted a drifting away from old moorings. Whereas Higginson in his affectionate leavetaking, just quoted, disclaimed sympathy with the Separatists and spoke with love of the Church of England, now the Plymouth Separatists were invited to the ordination, Bradford and other delegates taking pains to come. Though the Plymouth men did not arrive in time to take part they gave their sanction to the ceremonies, which showed a wide departure from church methods—a laying-on of hands and other forms of consecration, more than foreshadowing the Congregationalism that was about to prevail.

At once appeared disapproval of such departures from the old order. The brothers John and Samuel Browne, prominent among the councillors, took exception to the new religious methods, setting up worship with the *Book of Common Prayer* and leading a group faithful to the old Church. These men were promptly seized and sent back to England, Endicott being the leader, and here began the policy of intolerance, so marked a feature of early New England.

[1] In important churches the heavy duty made two ministers necessary, whose functions seem to have differed little, though one was called pastor and the other teacher. See Mr. Davis's note in Bradford, p. 26.

Since the seventeenth century the civilized world has come to see in toleration one of the first virtues of a community. The narrowness of the founders of New England has received heavy condemnation. It was a marked trait and Winthrop's *Journal* illustrates its prevalence in the record of each year. But the intolerance of our forefathers has found apologists in authorities whom we must respect. Says Palfrey: "Religious intolerance is criminal wherever it is not necessary to the public safety; it is simply self-defense whenever tolerance would be public ruin. . . . It is an idle casuistry which condemns the earlier comer and the stronger possessor for insisting on the unshared occupation of his place of residence. . . . It is preposterous to maintain that the right to exclude is not his, or that its exercise is not his bounden duty."[1] Of the early New England intolerance, first plainly shown in the persecution of the Brownes, and so often appearing during the period with which we have to do, against Antinomians, Familists, Baptists, Quakers, Catholics, this may certainly be said, that although unamiable, repulsive indeed to the modern spirit, it preserved the colony from being wiped out of existence.

The first enterprise after the plantation had been, so to speak, set on its feet after Higginson's arrival, was the dispatching of a party to survey and occupy Mishawum, now Charlestown, on Massachusetts Bay, an undertaking enjoined by the heads of the company, who feared a forestalling by Englishmen not of their Company who might assert rights under a supposed patent issued to Gorges. Before the summer of 1629 closed, therefore, the Salem men, for the Indian name of Naumkeag was now exchanged for a Hebrew title, occupied a point on what is now Boston harbor, which henceforth becomes the centre of interest in the story of New England.

[1] Palfrey, I. 300. See also H. M. Dexter, *As to Roger Williams*, and John A. Vinton, *The Antinomian Controversy of* 1637. For strong arraignments of the Puritans, see Peter Oliver, *Puritan Commonwealth*, and Brooks Adams, *Emancipation of Massachusetts*. See also an interesting passage in C. F. Adams, *Three Episodes of Massachusetts History*, I. 248.

Meantime important events were taking place in England. The public trouble, becoming always more acute, caused many men to despair of England; and on August 26 a company of such persons, possessing means and good position, meeting at Cambridge, resolved as follows:

"We will be ready in our persons, and with such of our several families that are to go with us, to embark (for New England) by the 1st of March next, . . . provided always that before the last of September next the whole government, together with the patent for the said plantation, be first legally transferred."[1] The first suggestion of a transfer of the government and patent came from Matthew Cradock. Such a transference was pronounced legal by the lawyers consulted, though since that time the transformation of a license for a trading corporation into a charter for a political establishment has been pronounced fraudulent and without color of the law.[2] These twelve considerable men, of most of whom Winthrop's *Journal* has much to record, were Sir Richard Saltonstall, Thomas Dudley, William Vassall, Nicholas West, John Winthrop, Kellam Browne, Isaac Johnson, John Humfrey, John Sharpe, Increase Nowell, William Pinchon, and William Colbron.[3] On September 19, 1629, Winthrop's presence, on a committee, at a court of the company is recorded, on which date, therefore, began his active part in the momentous undertaking.

Winthrop writes July 28, 1629, "My brother Downing and myself, riding into Lincolnshire by Ely, my horse fell under me in a bogge in the fennes so as I was almost to the waist in water; but the Lord preserved me from further danger, Blessed be his name."[4]

Winthrop here had a narrow escape, perhaps from death,

[1] *Hutchinson Papers*, Prince Society ed., I. 28.
[2] Oliver, *Puritan Commonwealth*, 19 *et seqq.* See Palfrey's argument and citations, I. 306.
[3] Winthrop, *Life and Letters*, I. 347.
[4] *Ibid.*, I. 304.

on the threshold of his New England service. Emanuel Downing, his companion, we shall often encounter hereafter. The two rode out of Suffolk to meet at Sempringham Isaac Johnson, son-in-law of the Earl of Lincoln. Another son-in-law was John Humfrey; both men embarked in the New England experiment. This visit of Winthrop, which so nearly proved disastrous, had no doubt an important relation to his decision. On October 20, at a court held at the house of Thomas Goffe, Winthrop was elected governor, Humfrey deputy-governor, and eighteen others assistants. Humfrey's departure from England being delayed, Thomas Dudley became deputy-governor in his place.

Winthrop, now forty-two years old, had gone through experiences to ripen him thoroughly. He had thrice married, had many children and grandchildren. He had a property of six or seven hundred pounds a year, perhaps equivalent to eight times as much at the present day. In administering this, and in discharging the functions of the legal profession which he had followed many years, he had gained a wide knowledge of affairs and exhibited abilities which made him conspicuous.[1] All efforts were now bent toward the equipment and despatch of an expedition such as had never before left England for America. When things were ready Reverend John Cotton, selected probably as being the most noted of the non-conformist divines of the times, proceeded to Southampton to the assembling fleet and performed the same office which had been performed ten years before by John Robinson, on the departure of the Plymouth pilgrims from Delfshaven. Cotton's sermon, *God's Promise to his Plantation*, is still extant.[2]

Leaving Winthrop to tell the further story of the Massachusetts settlement, it is now in place to describe the venerable manuscript and the fortunes that have befallen it. The *Journal* was contained in three note-books, which appear to

[1] Winthrop, *Life and Letters*, I. 348.
[2] *Old South Leaflet*, no. 53.

have been cared for after Winthrop's death in 1649 by his Connecticut descendants. The first note-book has no title, but the second and third were inscribed by him "Continuation of the History of New England,"—a misnomer certainly, for of New England outside of Massachusetts Bay it is a most imperfect account. The three manuscripts were in the hands of the older New England historians, William Hubbard, Cotton Mather and Thomas Prince. In our revolutionary period, Governor Jonathan Trumbull of Connecticut became interested in the *Journal*. But two note-books, however, had come back to the Connecticut Winthrops, the third manuscript for a time being lost.

Governor Trumbull and his intelligent secretary, John Porter, carefully deciphered and copied the two documents, and the transcript coming to the notice of Noah Webster, of dictionary fame, he caused it to be printed at Hartford in 1790, himself furnishing a short introduction and a few notes. The value of the *Journal* was generally recognized, and much regret was felt that the work was incomplete. It was an occasion of rejoicing therefore, when in 1816 the long-lost third book of the manuscript was discovered in the tower of the Old South Church, in Boston. Its publication, as an addition to the Hartford book of 1790, was at once undertaken by the Massachusetts Historical Society, the work being committed to the editorship of James Savage, a young and zealous member. Savage was a man most accurate and indefatigable: having transcribed the third note-book, he proceeded to compare the 1790 publication with the first and second note-books which it reproduced. He found that the work of his predecessors, though in general correct, contained many minor inaccuracies. He concluded that a new transcription of the two note-books was necessary, and planned to supplement the text with an elaborate body of notes. The Massachusetts Historical Society having secured legislative aid, the work was vigorously prosecuted, and in 1825–1826 the entire *Journal* appeared, profusely annotated, in two substantial well-printed volumes, entitled *The History of New England from 1630 to 1649, by John Winthrop, Esq., First Governour of the Colony of the Massachusetts Bay.*

The *Winthrop* of 1825–1826 took its place at once in the minds of men as the foundation of Massachusetts history, and the importance of the services of Savage was universally recognized: he became henceforth a man of mark, attained to the position of president of the Massachusetts Historical Society, and devoted himself to the genealogical and antiquarian work into which he had been led through his labors upon Winthrop. When, after twenty-five years, the edition of 1825–1826 was out of print, he revised his work, made some additions to his notes, and gave to the world in 1853 a new edition. This, too, after having served a most excellent purpose for more than half a century, is out of print, making necessary still another reproduction.

Savage having long since passed, greatly honored, to his account, the present editor, with the approval of the general editor of the series, has proceeded as follows: First, he has adopted without change the transcript of the text made by Savage. Careful tests of the accuracy of Savage's work here have been made, a comparison having been instituted in many parts between the original and the copy. It is plain that Savage was in the highest degree painstaking, and the examination renders it certain that the transcript could not well be more correct. Savage, as many think unfortunately, modernized Winthrop's spelling, and wrote out in full abbreviated words. It is desirable that the manuscript as it lies in the archives of the Massachusetts Historical Society should be carefully photographed. Some day perhaps it will be worth while to transcribe and reprint *verbatim et literatim.* As regards historical ends, however, Winthrop's record is satisfactorily rendered by Savage, and to make a new transcript is unnecessary. It must be said that the second note-book of the original, while in Savage's hands, was through ill-luck in 1825 destroyed by fire; this portion of the record therefore is extant only in the copies.

Secondly, as to the annotation, the work of Savage has been replaced in the present reprint by a scheme much more compendious and simple. The former editor had peculiarities of character making him personally racy and interesting, but impairing the excellence of his commentary. His successor in the presidency of the Massachusetts Historical Society, Mr. Charles Francis Adams, aptly compares him to Dr. Samuel Johnson. Like Johnson, Savage while most laborious, scrupulously honest, and always resolute and unshrinking, was testy, prejudiced and opinionated; he was prone to measure by small local standards. These peculiarities constantly appear in his notes, which are often in a high degree prolix, in some portions of the books largely exceeding in bulk the text. They are encumbered with genealogies of unimportant people and details as to trivial events and obscure localities. While possessed thus by the spirit of the county antiquary rather than by the broad temper of the proper historian, his hates and loves, equally undiscriminating, are curiously, often amusingly, manifest: he has his *bêtes noires*, like William Hubbard, Thomas Welde and Cotton Mather, whom he cannot mention without dealing a stout Johnsonian cuff; and also his favorites, of whose shortcomings he is always blandly unconscious. It will be worth while some day to reprint the vast body of Savage's notes not only because they are a mine of learning, (bearing often upon trifles, but often too upon important things), but also because the annotation has much interest as a "human document," pleasantly tart from the individuality of a quaintly provincial but sincere and vigorous mind.[1]

---

[1] In 1906 a fine bust of Savage was placed in the rooms of the Massachusetts Historical Society, on which occasion he was elaborately and happily characterized by the president, Mr. Charles Francis Adams. See *Proceedings* of the Society for that year.

In making the notes to the present edition the point of view sought has been that of a student of history in a large sense. The Anglo-Saxon race is but one of the races of the world; the United States forms but one of the English-speaking nations; Massachusetts is one of forty-six commonwealths, the story of each of which is an essential part of the story of our country. There were many other settlements upon our shores beside those made by Englishmen, and several other English settlements beside that guided by Winthrop, which have affected powerfully America and the world. Winthrop's *Journal* is only one among a group of interesting records, an important one of the group, but the incidents it relates must not be unduly magnified; just proportioning must not be neglected in the perspective. In the notes nothing more has been attempted than to make plain the language of the narrative, to fill out the story when too meagrely related, and to describe more at length the principal personages. Winthrop's work is rough and hurried; he probably intended to base upon it an account more carefully written; it needs to be supplemented, but the attempt has been made to do no more than is necessary to a clear understanding.

The work of preparing this edition has been done in the Boston Public and Harvard Libraries, with some use also of the Boston Athenæum, and especially of the original manuscripts in the archives of the Massachusetts Historical Society. Nearly all the literature extant bearing upon the topic has been at hand. Winthrop and his circle left many letters and documents that are illuminative, which are contained in the appendix to Savage's edition, in Robert C. Winthrop, *Life and Letters of John Winthrop*, and in the *Collections of the Massachusetts Historical Society*, fourth series, vols. VI., VII. (1863, 1865), and fifth series, vol. I. (1871); the manuscripts of the Winthrop family, extant to a remarkable degree, are also preserved by the Society. The *Massachusetts Colonial Records*, complete from the year 1630, the records of the First Church in Boston, and of the neighboring churches, now in general printed, letters of Thomas Dudley, and of other companions, Johnson's *Wonder-Working Providence*, Ward's *Simple Cobler of Aggawam*, Thomas Morton's *New English Canaan*, the narrative of Bradford, governor of Plymouth, tracts and sermons of John Cotton and other ministers—these and many more contemporary documents throw light on the time.

Of the general histories of New England and Massachusetts, written since Winthrop's time, may be mentioned as secondary authorities of more or less value, Hubbard, *General History of New England from 1620 to 1680*, published about the latter date, Cotton Mather, *Magnalia Christi Americana* (1702); Prince, *Chronological History of New England* (1736); Hutchinson, *History of Massachusetts Bay* (1764); Barry, *History of Massachusetts* (1855); Palfrey, *History of New England* (1858); Justin Winsor, *Narrative and Critical History of America*, vol. III., and *Memorial History of Boston*, vol. I. Special phases of Massachusetts history, including aspects of Winthrop's community, are treated in C. F. Adams, *Three Episodes of Massachusetts History* (1892); Oliver, *The Puritan Commonwealth* (1856); Brooks Adams, *The Emancipation of Massachusetts* (1893); Ellis, *The Puritan Age and Rule* (1888); M. C. Tyler, *History of American Literature*, vol. I. (1878, 1897), and J. A. Doyle, *English in America*, vol. II. (1887). The biographical dictionaries of John Eliot and William Allen, both published in 1809, and the *Genealogical Dictionary* of Savage, relating especially to New England, are valuable. All these have aided the present editor in his work. In the case of many notes, however, the information has been condensed from the learning of Savage, and sometimes his work has been quoted in full.

JAMES KENDALL HOSMER.

WINTHROP'S JOURNAL

"THE HISTORY OF NEW ENGLAND"

1630–1649

WINTHROP'S JOURNAL

"THE HISTORY OF NEW ENGLAND"

1630–1649

ANNO DOMINI 1630, MARCH 29, MONDAY.

Easter Monday.][1] RIDING at the Cowes, near the Isle of Wight, in the *Arbella*,[2] a ship of three hundred and fifty tons, whereof Capt. Peter Milborne was master, being manned with fifty-two seamen, and twenty-eight pieces of ordnance, (the wind coming to the N. by W. the evening before,) in the morning there came aboard us Mr. Cradock,[3] the late governor, and

---

[1] The use of the designation "Easter Monday" is significant. Winthrop has not yet broken from the Church of England, and retains the ecclesiastical name. After reaching New England came a sudden dropping of all reference to church holidays. Note that in Winthrop's chronology, March is the first month of the year, and February the twelfth,—September, October, November and December becoming thus literally the seventh, eighth, ninth and tenth months. As to New Year's Day an awkward diversity prevailed in the seventeenth century; it was sometimes the 1st, sometimes the 25th of March. In the *Journal* New Year's Day is generally March 1st, but not always. Winthrop gives dates sometimes by means of two numerals, the first denoting the month, the second the day; for instance, "7, 6" is the 6th of September; more rarely the day precedes; sometimes "Mo." stands before the figure denoting a month; when but one number precedes an entry, it usually denotes the day, the month number having been given previously once for all, when the month begins.

[2] The ship was named for the Lady Arbella Johnson, who was of the company.

[3] Matthew Cradock, a rich London merchant, the first head of the Massachusetts Company, who, however, never came to the colony. A noteworthy service of Cradock's was the proposal, July 28, 1629, to transfer the government by the company from London to the colony itself, a measure fraught with important consequences. Cradock maintained a small plantation on the Mystic River. He was a member of the Long Parliament, and is believed to have died about 1644.

the masters of his two ships, Capt. John Lowe, master of the *Ambrose*, and Mr. Nicholas Hurlston, master of the *Jewel*, and Mr. Thomas Beecher, master of the *Talbot*, (which three ships rode then by us,—the *Charles*, the *Mayflower*,[1] the *William and Francis*, the *Hopewell*, the *Whale*, the *Success* and the *Trial* being still at Hampton[2] and not ready,) when, upon conference, it was agreed, that (in regard it was uncertain when the rest of the fleet would be ready) these four ships should consort together; the *Arbella* to be admiral,[3] the *Talbot* vice-admiral, the *Ambrose* rear-admiral, and the *Jewel* a captain; and accordingly articles of consortship were drawn between the said captains and masters; whereupon Mr. Cradock took leave of us, and our captain gave him a farewell with four or five shot.

About ten of the clock we weighed anchor and set sail, with the wind at N., and came to an anchor again over against Yarmouth, and the *Talbot* weighed likewise, and came and anchored by us. Here we met with a ship of Hampton, called the *Plantation*, newly come from Virginia. Our captain saluted her, and she us again; and the master, one Mr. [*blank*] Graves [?], came on board our ship, and stayed with us about two or three hours, and in the meantime his ship came to an anchor by us.

Tuesday, 30.] In the morning, about ten of the clock, the wind being come to the W. with fair weather, we weighed and rode nearer Yarmouth. When we came before the town, the castle put forth a flag; our captain saluted them, and they answered us again. The *Talbot*, which rode farther off, saluted the castle also.

Here we saw, close by the shore of the Isle of Wight, a Dutch ship of one thousand tons, which, being bound to the East Indies, about two years since, in passing through the Needles, struck upon a rock, and being forced to run ashore

---

[1] This has been supposed to be the *Mayflower* of the Plymouth Pilgrims.
[2] Southampton.
[3] In modern phrase, flag-ship.

to save her men, could never be weighed since, although she lies a great height above the water, and yet she hath some men aboard her.

Wednesday, 31.] The wind continued W. and S. W. with rain. Our captain and some of our company went to Yarmouth for supply of wood and other provisions; (our captain was still careful to fill our empty casks with water).

Thursday, April 1.] The wind continued very strong at W. and by S. with much rain.

Friday, 2.] We kept a fast aboard our ship and the *Talbot*. The wind continued still very high at W. and S. and rainy. In the time of our fast, two of our landmen pierced a rundlet of strong water, and stole some of it, for which we laid them in bolts all the night, and the next morning the principal was openly whipped, and both kept with bread and water that day.

Saturday, 3.] The wind continued still at W. and with continual storms and rain.

Sunday, 4.] Fair, clear weather. In the morning the wind W. and by N., but in the afternoon S. S. W. This evening the *Talbot* weighed and went back to the Cowes, because her anchor would not hold here, the tide set with so strong a race.

Monday, 5.] The wind still W. and S. with fair weather. A maid of Sir Richard Saltonstall[1] fell down at the grating by the cook-room, but the carpenter's man, who occasioned her fall unwittingly, caught hold of her with incredible nimbleness, and saved her; otherwise she had fallen into the hold.

Tuesday, 6.] Capt. Burleigh, captain of Yarmouth castle, a grave, comely gentleman, and of great age, came aboard us and stayed breakfast, and, offering us much courtesy, he departed, our captain giving him four shot out of the forecastle for his farewell. He was an old sea captain in Queen Elizabeth's time, and, being taken prisoner at sea, was kept prisoner

[1] Sir Richard Saltonstall, son of a lord mayor of London, was founder of a family prominent in every generation of Massachusetts history, and still well maintained. The knight himself returned to England, leaving sons to transmit the name.

in Spain three years. Himself and three of his sons were captains in Roe's voyage.[1]

The wind was now come about to N. E. with very fair weather.

In the afternoon Mr. Cradock came aboard us, and told us, that the *Talbot, Jewel* and *Ambrose* were fallen down into Stoke's Bay, intending to take their way by St. Helen's Point, and that they desired we could come back to them. Hereupon we came to council, and wrote unto them to take the first opportunity of the wind to fall down to us, and Mr. Cradock presently went back to them, our captain giving him three shot out of the steerage for a farewell.

Our captain called over our landmen, and tried them at their muskets, and such as were good shot among them were enrolled to serve in the ship, if occasion should be.

The lady Arbella and the gentlewomen, and Mr. Johnson[2] and some others went on shore to refresh themselves.

Wednesday, 7.][3] Fair weather, the wind easterly, in the morning a small gale, but in the afternoon it came about to the south. This afternoon our other consorts came up to us, and about ten or twelve Flemings, and all anchored by us, and the masters of the *Jewel* and of the *Ambrose* came aboard us, and our captain and they went on shore.

Towards night there came from the W. a Fleming, a small man-of-war, with a Brazil man which he had taken prize, and came to anchor by us.

Thursday, 8.] About six in the morning (the wind being

---

[1] Doubtless the voyage which Sir Thomas Roe made to Guiana in 1610.

[2] Mr. Isaac Johnson and his wife, Lady Arbella, daughter of the Earl of Lincoln, were in position and wealth the most important members of the ship's company. Johnson, a gentleman of Rutlandshire, contributed to the enterprise more liberally than any other, and was very zealous. It was a severe blow to the colony that the death of the Lady Arbella occurred in August, but two months after the arrival, followed next month by that of her husband.

[3] On this day the *Farewell to the Church of England* was addressed from the *Arbella*, lying at Yarmouth. See Hutchinson, *History of Massachusetts Bay*, I., Appendix 1. The Congregationalism of a later day finds no expression here.

E. and N. and fair weather) we weighed anchor and set sail, and before ten we gat through the Needles, having so little wind as we had much to do to stem the tide, so as the rest of our fleet (we being nine in all, wherof some were small ships, which were bound for Newfoundland) could not get out all then till the ebb. In the afternoon the wind came S. and W. and we were becalmed, so as being not able to get above three or four leagues from the Needles, our captain tacked about, and putting his fore-sheets aback stays, he stayed for the rest of the fleet, and as they came by us we spake to them, and about eight in the evening we let fall an anchor, intending to stop till the ebb. But before ten at night the wind came about to the N. a good gale; so we put up a light in the poop, and weighed and set sail, and by daylight, Friday 9, we were come to Portland; but the other ships being not able to hold up with us, we were forced to spare our mainsail, and went on with a merry gale. In the morning we descried from the top eight sail astern of us, (whom Capt. Lowe told us he had seen at Dunnose in the evening). We supposing they might be Dunkirkers,[1] our captain caused the gunroom and gundeck to be cleared; all the hammocks were taken down, our ordnance loaded, and our powder-chests and fireworks made ready, and our landmen quartered among the seamen, and twenty-five of them appointed for muskets, and every man written down for his quarter.

The wind continued N. [blank] with fair weather, and afternoon it calmed, and we still saw those eight ships to stand towards us; having more wind than we, they came up apace, so as our captain and the masters of our consorts were more occasioned to think they might be Dunkirkers, (for we were told at Yarmouth, that there were ten sail of them waiting for us;) whereupon we all prepared to fight with them, and took down some cabins which were in the way of our ordnance, and out of every ship were thrown such bed matters as were subject to

[1] Dunkirk was then a possession of Spain, at that time at war with England.

take fire, and we heaved out our long boats, and put up our waste cloths, and drew forth our men, and armed them with muskets and other weapons, and instruments for fireworks; and for an experiment our captain shot a ball of wild-fire fastened to an arrow out of a cross-bow, which burnt in the water a good time. The lady Arbella and the other women and children were removed into the lower deck, that they might be out of danger. All things being thus fitted, we went to prayer upon the upper deck. It was much to see how cheerful and comfortable all the company appeared; not a woman or child that showed fear, though all did apprehend the danger to have been great, if things had proved as might well be expected, for there had been eight against four, and the least of the enemy's ships were reported to carry thirty brass pieces; but our trust was in the Lord of Hosts; and the courage of our captain, and his care and diligence, did much encourage us. It was now about one of the clock, and the fleet seemed to be within a league of us; therefore our captain, because he would show he was not afraid of them, and that he might see the issue before night should overtake us, tacked about and stood to meet them, and when we came near we perceived them to be our friends,—the *Little Neptune*, a ship of some twenty pieces of ordnance, and her two consorts, bound for the Straits; a ship of Flushing, and a Frenchman, and three other English ships bound for Canada and Newfoundland. So when we drew near, every ship (as they met) saluted each other, and the musketeers discharged their small shot; and so (God be praised) our fear and danger was turned into mirth and friendly entertainment. Our danger being thus over, we espied two boats on fishing in the channel; so every of our four ships manned out a skiff, and we bought of them great store of excellent fresh fish of divers sorts.

Saturday, 10.] The wind at E. and by N. a handsome gale with fair weather. By seven in the morning we were come over against Plymouth.

About noon the wind slacked, and we were come within sight of the Lizard, and towards night it grew very calm and a great fog, so as our ships made no way.

This afternoon Mr. Hurlston, the master of the *Jewel*, came aboard our ship, and our captain went in his skiff aboard the *Ambrose* and the *Neptune*, of which one Mr. Andrew Cole was master. There he was told, that the bark *Warwick* was taken by the Dunkirkers, for she came single out of the Downs about fourteen days since, intending to come to us to the Wight, but was never heard of since. She was a pretty ship of about eighty tons and ten pieces of ordnance, and was set out by Sir Ferdinando Gorges, Capt. Mason,[1] and others, for discovery of the great lake in New England,[2] so to have intercepted the trade of beaver. The master of her was one Mr. Weatherell, whose father was master of one of the cattle ships, which we left at Hampton.

This day two young men, falling at odds and fighting, contrary to the orders which we had published and set up in the ship, were adjudged to walk upon the deck till night with their hands bound behind them, which accordingly was executed; and another man, for using contemptuous speeches in

---

[1] Sir Ferdinando Gorges, already described in the Introduction, an important figure in the settlement of New England. He failed in Maine, in 1607, nor were other enterprises more successful. The success of the Leyden Pilgrims in 1620 encouraged further trial. In 1622 he became connected with Captain John Mason, an adventurous London merchant, and the two obtained a patent for a tract bounded by the Merrimac and Kennebec rivers and running back to the lakes which were the sources. In 1623 Gorges made an establishment at the mouth of the Piscataqua. In 1629 Mason obtained a new patent for New Hampshire, and Mason and Gorges and others a patent for "Laconia," farther inland. Through Gorges and Mason, Winthrop's colony was embarrassed from the first, and soon brought close to ruin. A scheme was attempted for organizing a colony to extend from the St. Croix to Maryland, which would have involved an abrogation of the Massachusetts charter. This fell through by reason of the commotions at home preceding the Civil War. But in 1639 Gorges was confirmed as lord-palatine of Maine, and taking the royal side, vexed to his life's end his Puritan neighbors. He died soon after the beginning of the Civil War.

[2] The Lake of the Iroquois, or Lake Champlain. The *Warwick* sailed for the Laconia Company under the Laconia patent of November 17, 1629.

our presence, was laid in bolts till he submitted himself, and promised open confession of his offence.

I should have noted before, that the day we set sail from the Cowes, my son Henry Winthrop went on shore with one of my servants to fetch an ox and ten wethers, which he had provided for our ship, and there went on shore with him, Mr. Pelham and one of his servants. They sent the cattle aboard, but returned not themselves. About three days after, my servant and a servant of Mr. Pelham's came to us to Yarmouth, and told us they were all coming to us in a boat the day before, but the wind was so strong against them, as they were forced on shore in the night, and the two servants came to Yarmouth by land, and so came on ship-board, but my son and Mr. Pelham (we heard) went back to the Cowes and so to Hampton. We expected them three or four days after, but they came not to us, so we have left them behind, and suppose they will come after in Mr. Goffe's ships.[1] We were very sorry they had put themselves upon such inconvenience, when they were so well accommodated in our ship. This was not noted before, because we expected daily their return; and upon this occasion I must add here one observation, that we have many young gentlemen in our ship, who behave themselves well, and are conformable to all good orders.

About ten at night it cleared up with a fresh gale at N. and by W., so we stood on our course merrily.

Sunday, 11.] The wind at N. and by W. a very stiff gale.

About eight in the morning, being gotten past Scilly, and standing to the W. S. W. we met two small ships, which falling in among us, and the Admiral coming under our lee, we let him pass, but the *Jewel* and *Ambrose*, perceiving the other to be a Brazil man, and to take the wind of us, shot at them and made them stop and fall after us, and sent a skiff aboard

---

[1] Thomas Goffe, a London merchant, was one of the patentees of Massachusetts.

them to know what they were. Our captain, fearing lest some mistake might arise, and lest they should take them for enemies which were friends, and so, through the unruliness of the mariners some wrong might be done them, caused his skiff to be heaved out, and sent Mr. Graves [?], one of his mates and our pilot, (a discreet man,) to see how things were, who returned soon after, and brought with him the master of one of the ships and Mr. Lowe and Mr. Hurlston. When they were come aboard us, they agreed to send for the captain, who came and showed his commission from the Prince of Orange. In conclusion he proved to be a Dutchman, and his a man-of-war of Flushing, and the other ship was a prize he had taken laden with sugar and tobacco; so we sent them aboard their ships again, and held on our course. In this time (which hindered us five or six leagues) the *Jewel* and the *Ambrose* came foul of each other, so as we much feared the issue, but, through God's mercy, they came well off again, only the *Jewel* had her foresail torn, and one of her anchors broken. This occasion, and the sickness of our minister and people, put us all out of order this day, so as we could have no sermons.

Monday, 12.] The wind more large to the N. a stiff gale, with fair weather. In the afternoon less wind, and our people began to grow well again. Our children and others, that were sick, and lay groaning in the cabins, we fetched out, and having stretched a rope from the steerage to the mainmast, we made them stand, some of one side and some of the other, and sway it up and down till they were warm, and by this means they soon grew well and merry.

Tuesday, 13.] The night before it was calm, and the next day calm and close weather, so as we made little way, the wind with us being W.

Wednesday, 14.] The wind S. W., rainy weather, in the morning.

About nine in the forenoon the wind came about to N. N. W. a stiff gale; so we tacked about and steered our course W. S. W.

This day the ship heaved and set more than before, yet we had but few sick, and of these such as came up upon the deck, and stirred themselves, were presently well again; therefore our captain set our children and young men to some harmless exercises, which the seamen were very active in, and did our people much good, though they would sometimes play the wags with them. Towards night we were forced to take in some sail to stay for the vice-admiral, which was near a league astern of us.

Thursday, 15.] The wind still at N. N. W. fair weather, but less wind than the day and night before, so as our ship made but little way.

At noon our captain made observation by the cross-staff,[1] and found we were in forty-seven degrees thirty-seven minutes north latitude.

All this forenoon our vice-admiral was much to leeward of us; so after dinner we bare up towards her, and having fetched her up and spoken with her, the wind being come to S. W. we tacked about and steered our course N. N. W. lying as near the wind as we could, and about four of the clock, with a stiff gale, we steered W. and by N. and at night the wind grew very strong, which put us on to the W. amain.

About ten at night the wind grew so high, and rain withal, that we were forced to take in our topsail, and having lowered our mainsail and foresail, the storm was so great as it split our foresail and tore it in pieces, and a knot of the sea washed our tub overboard, wherein our fish was a-watering. The storm still grew, and it was dark with clouds, (though otherwise moonlight,) so as (though it was the *Jewel's* turn to carry the light this night, yet) lest we should lose or go foul one of another, we hanged out a light upon our mizzen shrouds, and before midnight we lost sight of our vice-admiral.

[1] The cross-staff was a simple instrument of observation, which preceded the quadrant. It was a cross the intersection of which was surrounded by a graduated circle, the periphery being thus broken into four equal arcs.

Our captain, so soon as he had set the watch, at eight in the evening called his men, and told them he feared we should have a storm, and therefore commanded them to be ready upon the deck, if occasion should be; and himself was up and down the decks all times of the night.

Friday, 16.] About four in the morning the wind slacked a little, yet it continued a great storm still, and though in the afternoon it blew not much wind, yet the sea was so high as it tossed us more than before, and we carried no more but our mainsail, yet our ship steered well with it, which few such ships could have done.

About four in the afternoon, the wind still W. and by S. and rainy, we put on a new foresail and hoisted it up, and stood N W. All this day our rear-admiral and the *Jewel* held up with us.

This night was very stormy.

All the time of the storm few of our people were sick, (except the women, who kept under hatches,) and there appeared no fear or dismayedness among them.

Saturday, 17.] The wind S. W. very stormy and boisterous. All this time we bore no more sail but our mainsail and foresail, and we steered our course W. and by N.

This day our captain told me, that our landmen were very nasty and slovenly, and that the gundeck, where they lodged, was so beastly and noisome with their victuals and beastliness, as would much endanger the health of the ship. Hereupon, after prayer, we took order, and appointed four men to see to it, and to keep that room clean for three days, and then four others should succeed them, and so forth on.

The wind continued all this day at S. W. a stiff gale. In the afternoon it cleared up, but very hazy. Our captain, about four of the clock, sent one to the top to look for our vice-admiral, but he could not descry him, yet we saw a sail about two leagues to the leeward, which stood toward the N. E.

We were this evening (by our account) about ninety

leagues from Scilly, W. and by S. At this place there came a swallow and lighted upon our ship.

Sunday, 18.] About two in the morning the wind N. W.; so we tacked about and steered our course S. W. We had still much wind, and the sea went very high, which tossed our ship continually.

After our evening sermon, about five of the clock, the wind came about to S. E. a good gale, but rainy; so we steered our course W. S. W. and the ship's way was about nine leagues a watch; (a watch is four hours).

This day the captain sent to top again to discover our vice-admiral. We descried from thence to the eastward a sail, but we knew not what she was.

About seven of the clock the *Jewel* bare up so near as we could speak each to other, and after we bated some sail; so she went ahead of us, and soon after eight put forth her light.

Monday, 19.] In the morning the wind was come about to the N. W. a good gale and fair weather; so we held our course, but the ship made not so good way as when the wind was large.

This day, by observation and account, we found ourselves to be in forty-eight degrees north latitude, and two hundred and twenty leagues W. from the meridian of London.

Here I think good to note, that all this time since we came from the Wight, we had cold weather, so as we could well endure our warmest clothes. I wish, therefore, that all such as shall pass this way in the spring have care to provide warm clothing; for nothing breeds more trouble and danger of sickness, in this season, than cold.

In the afternoon the wind came to S. W. a stiff gale, with rain; so we steered westerly, till night; then the wind came about to N. W. and we tacked again and stood S. W.

Our rear-admiral being to leeward of us, we bare up to him. He told us all their people were in health, but one of their cows was dead.

Tuesday, 20.] The wind southerly, fair weather, and little

wind. In the morning we stood S. and by E., in the afternoon W. and by N.

Wednesday, 21.] Thick, rainy weather; much wind at S. W.

Our captain, over night, had invited his consorts to have dined with him this day, but it was such foul weather as they could not come aboard us.

Thursday, 22.] The wind still W. and by S. fair weather; then W. N. W.

This day at noon we found ourselves in forty-seven degrees and forty-eight minutes, and having a stiff gale, we steered S. W. about four leagues a watch, all this day and all the night following.

Friday, 23.] The wind still W. N. W. a small gale, with fair weather. Our captain put forth his ancient[1] in the poop, and heaved out his skiff, and lowered his topsails, to give sign to his consorts that they should come aboard us to dinner, for they were both a good way astern of us, and our vice-admiral was not yet seen of us since the storm, though we sent to the top every day to descry her.

About eleven of the clock, our captain sent his skiff and fetched aboard us the masters of the other two ships, and Mr. Pynchon,[2] and they dined with us in the round-house, for the lady and gentlewomen[3] dined in the great cabin.

This day and the night following we had little wind, so as the sea was very smooth, and the ship made little way.

Saturday, 24.] The wind still W. and by N., fair weather and calm all that day and night. Here we made observation again, and found we were in forty-five degrees twenty minutes, north latitude.

Sunday, 25.] The wind northerly, fair weather, but still

[1] *Ancient* was often used for *ensign* in old times, whether denoting the flag or the flag-bearer.

[2] William Pynchon, founder of Roxbury and afterwards of Springfield, Mass.

[3] The Lady Arbella Johnson, the daughters of Sir Richard Saltonstall, and the wives of several of the more prominent men.

calm. We stood W. and by S. and saw two ships ahead of us as far as we could descry.

In the afternoon the wind came W. and by S. but calm still. About five of the clock, the rear-admiral and the *Jewel* had fetched up the two ships, and by their saluting each other we perceived they were friends, (for they were so far to windward of us as we could only see the smoke of their pieces, but could not hear them). About nine of the clock, they both fell back towards us again, and we steered N. N. W. Now the weather begins to be warm.

Monday, 26.] The wind still W. and by S. close weather, and scarce any wind.

The two ships, which we saw yesterday, were bound for Canada. Capt. Kirk[1] was aboard the admiral. They bare up with us, and falling close under our lee, we saluted each other, and conferred together so long till his vice-admiral was becalmed by our sails, and we were foul one of another; but there being little wind and the sea calm, we kept them asunder with oars, etc., till they heaved out their boat, and so towed their ship away.

They told us for certain, that the king of France had set out six of his own ships to recover the fort from them.

About one of the clock Capt. Lowe sent his skiff aboard us, (with a friendly token of his love to the governor,) to desire our captain to come aboard his ship, which he did, and there met the masters of the other ships and Capt. Kirk, and before night they all returned to their ships again, Capt. Lowe bestowing some shot upon them for their welcome.

The wind now blew a pretty gale, so as our ship made some way again, though it were out of our right course N. W. by N.

Tuesday, 27.] The wind still westerly, a stiff gale, with close weather. We steered W. N. W. About noon some rain, and all the day very cold. We appointed Tuesdays

---

[1] A brother of Sir David Kirk, Savage surmises, who the year before had, with Sir David, been concerned in the capture of Quebec.

and Wednesdays to catechize our people, and this day Mr. Phillips[1] began it.

Wednesday, 28.] All the night, and this day till noon, the wind very high at S. W., close weather, and some rain. Between eleven and twelve, in a shower, the wind came W. N. W., so we tacked about and stood S. W.

Thursday, 29.] Much wind all this night at W. and by N. and the sea went very high, so as the ship rolled very much, because we sailed but with one course; therefore, about twelve, our captain arose and caused the foretopsail to be hoisted, and then the ship went more steady. He caused the quartermaster to look down into the hold to see if the cask lay fast and the . . . . [*illegible*].

In the morning the wind continued with a stiff gale; rainy and cold all the day.

We had been now three weeks at sea, and were not come above three hundred leagues, being about one third part of our way, viz., about forty-six north latitude, and near the meridian of the Terceras.[2]

This night Capt. Kirk carried the light as one of our consorts.

Friday, 30.] The wind at W. N. W., a strong gale all the night and day, with showers now and then.

We made observation, and found we were in forty-four north latitude. At night the wind scanted towards the S. with rain; so we tacked about and stood N. W. and by N.

Saturday, May 1.] All the night much wind at S. S. W. and rain. In the morning the wind still strong, so as we could bear little sail, and so it continued a growing storm all the day, and towards night so much wind as we bore no more sail but so much as should keep the ship stiff. Then it grew a very great tempest all the night with fierce showers of rain intermixed, and very cold.

[1] The first pastor of Watertown, ancestor of a numerous and distinguished line. Phillips was one of the first to urge Congregationalism as an ecclesiastical basis. See Hubbard, *General History of New England*, 186.   [2] The Azores.

Lord's day, 2.] The tempest continued all the day, with the wind W. and by N., and the sea raged and tossed us exceedingly; yet, through God's mercy, we were very comfortable, and few or none sick, but had opportunity to keep the Sabbath, and Mr. Phillips preached twice that day. The *Ambrose* and *Jewel* were separated far from us the first night, but this day we saw them again, but Capt. Kirk's ships we saw not since.

Monday, 3.] In the night the wind abated, and by morning the sea was well assuaged, so as we bare our foresail again, and stood W. S. W.; but all the time of the tempest we could make no way, but were driven to the leeward, and the *Ambrose* struck all her sails but her mizzen, and lay a hull. She brake her main yard. This day we made observation, and found we were in forty-three and a half north latitude. We set two fighters in the bolts till night, with their hands bound behind them. A maid-servant in the ship, being stomach-sick, drank so much strong water, that she was senseless, and had near killed herself. We observed it a common fault in our young people, that they gave themselves to drink hot waters very immoderately.

Tuesday, 4.] Much wind at S. W., close weather. In the morning we tacked about and stood N. W. and about ten in the morning W. N. W., but made little way in regard of the head sea.

Wednesday, 5.] The wind W. and by S. thick, foggy weather, and rainy; so we stood N. W. by W. At night the Lord remembered us, and enlarged the wind to the N.; so we tacked about and stood our course W. and by S. with a merry gale in all our sails.

Thursday, 6.] The wind at N. a good gale, and fair weather. We made observation and found we were forty-three and a half north latitude; so we stood full west, and ran, in twenty-four hours, about thirty leagues.

Four things I observed here. 1. That the declination of the pole star was much, even to the view, beneath that it is in

England. 2. That the new moon, when it first appeared, was much smaller than at any time I had seen it in England. 3. That all the way we came, we saw fowls flying and swimming, when we had no land near by two hundred leagues. 4. That wheresoever the wind blew, we had still cold weather, and the sun did not give so much heat as in England.

Friday, 7.] The wind N. and by E. a small gale, very fair weather, and towards night a still calm. This day our captain and Mr. Lowe dined aboard the *Jewel*.

Saturday, 8.] All the night calm. In the morning the wind S. W. a handsome gale; so we tacked and stood N. W. and soon after, the wind growing more large, we stood W. N. W. with a good gale. About four of the clock we saw a whale, who lay just in our ship's way, (the bunch of his back about a yard above water). He would not shun us; so we passed within a stone's cast of him, as he lay spouting up water.

Lord's day, 9.] The wind still S. W. a good gale, but close weather and some rain; we held on our course W. N. W. About nine it cleared up, and towards night a great fog for an hour or two.

We were now in forty-four and a half north latitude, and a little west of Corvos.[1]

Monday, 10.] The wind S. S. W. a good gale and fair weather; so we stood W. and by N. four or five leagues a watch, all this day. The wind increased, and was a great storm all the night. About midnight our rear-admiral put forth two lights, whereby we knew that some mischance had befallen her. We answered her with two lights again, and bare up to her, so near as we durst, (for the sea went very high, and she lay by the lee) and having hailed her, we thought she had sprung aleak; but she had broken some of her shrouds; so we went a little ahead of her, and, bringing our foresail aback stays, we stayed for her, and, about two hours after, she filled her sails, and we stood our course together, but our

[1] One of the Azores.

captain went not to rest till four of the clock, and some others of us slept but little that night.

Tuesday, 11.] The storm continued all this day, till three in the afternoon, and the sea went very high, so as our ship could make no way, being able to bear no more but our mainsail about midmast high. At three there fell a great storm of rain, which laid the wind, and the wind shifting into the W. we tacked and stood into the head sea, to avoid the rolling of our ship, and by that means we made no way, the sea beating us back as much as the wind put us forward.

We had still cold weather, and our people were so acquainted with storms as they were not sick, nor troubled, though we were much tossed forty-eight hours together, viz., twenty-four during the storm, and as long the next night and day following, Wednesday, 12, when as we lay as it were a hull,[1] for want of wind, and rolled continually in a high grown sea. This day was close and rainy.

Complaint was made to our captain of some injury that one of the under officers of the ship had done to one of our landmen. He called him and examined the cause, and commanded him to be tied up by the hands, and a weight to be hanged about his neck; but, at the intercession of the governor, (with some difficulty,) he remitted his punishment.

At night the wind blew at S. E. a handsome gale, with rain; so we put forth our sails and stood W. and by S.

Thursday, 13.] Toward morning the wind came to the south-westerly, with close weather and a strong gale, so as before noon we took in our topsails, (the rear-admiral having split her fore-topsail) and we stood west-southerly.

Friday, 14.] The wind W. S. W., thick, foggy weather, and in the afternoon rainy. We stood W. and by S. and after W. and by N. about five leagues a watch. We were in forty-four and a half. The sun set N. W. and by N. one third northerly. And towards night we stood W.

[1] A-hull means drifting without sail.

Saturday, 15.] The wind westerly all this day; fair weather. We tacked twice to small purpose.

Lord's day, 16.] As the 15 was.

Monday, 17.] The wind at S. a fine gale and fair weather. We stood W. and by S. We saw a great drift; so we heaved out our skiff, and it proved a fir log, which seemed to have been many years in the water, for it was all overgrown with barnacles and other trash. We sounded here and found no ground at one hundred fathom and more. We saw two whales. About nine at night the wind grew very strong at S. W. and continued so, with much rain, till one of the clock; then it ceased raining, but the wind came to the W. with more violence. In this storm we were forced to take in all our sails, save our mainsail, and to lower that so much as we could.

Tuesday, 18.] In the morning the wind slacked, but we could stand no nearer our course than N. and we had much wind all this day. In the afternoon we tacked and stood S. by E. Towards night (our rear-admiral being near two leagues to leeward of us) we bare up, and drawing near her, we descried, some two leagues more to leeward, two ships, which we conceived were those two of Capt. Kirk's, which parted from us in the storm, May 2. We had still cold weather.

Wednesday, 19.] The wind S. S. W.; close and rainy; little wind. We tacked again and stood W.; but about noon the wind came full W. a very strong gale; so we tacked again and stood N. by E. and at night we took off our main bonnet, and took in all our sails, save our main-course and mizzen. We were now in forty-four degrees twelve minutes north, and by our account in the midway between the false bank and the main bank.[1] All this night a great storm at W. by N.

Thursday, 20.] The storm continued all this day, the wind as it was, and rainy. In the forenoon we carried our fore-course and stood W. S. W., but in the afternoon we took

[1] Grand Banks.

it in, the wind increasing, and the sea grown very high; and lying with the helm a-weather, we made no way but as the ship drove. We had still cold weather.

[Fast] in the great cabin, at nine at night, etc., and the next day again, etc. The storm continued all this night.

Friday, 21.] The wind still N. W.; little wind, and close weather. We stood S. W. with all our sails, but made little way, and at night it was a still calm.

A servant of one of our company had bargained with a child to sell him a box worth 3d. for three biscuits a day all the voyage, and had received about forty, and had sold them and many more to some other servants. We caused his hands to be tied up to a bar, and hanged a basket with stones about his neck, and so he stood two hours.

Saturday, 22.] The wind S. S. W. much wind and rain.

Our spritsail laid so deep in as it was split in pieces with a head sea at the instant as our captain was going forth of his cabin very early in the morning to give order to take it in. It was a great mercy of God, that it did split, for otherwise it had endangered the breaking of our bowsprit and topmasts at least, and then we had no other way but to have returned for England, except the wind had come east. About ten in the morning, in a very great fret of wind, it chopt suddenly into the W. as it had done divers times before, and so continued with a small gale and [we] stood N. and by W. About four in the afternoon there arose a sudden storm of wind and rain, so violent as we had not a greater. It continued thick and boisterous all the night.

About seven we descried a sail ahead of us, towards the N. and by E. which stood towards us. Our captain, supposing it might be our vice-admiral, hoisted up his mainsail, which before was struck down aboard, and came up to meet her. When we drew near her we put forth our ancient, and she luffed up to get the wind of us; but when she saw she could not, she bare up, and hoisting up her foresail, stood away before the wind; yet we made all the signs we could, that we meant her no harm, but she would not trust us. She was within shot of us, so as we perceived she was a small Frenchman, which we did suppose had been driven off the bank. When she was clear of us, she stood her course again, and we ours.

This day at twelve we made observation, and were about forty-three, but the storm put us far to the N. again. Still cold weather.

Lord's day, 23.] Much wind, still westerly, and very cold weather.

Monday, 24.] The wind N. W. by N. a handsome gale, and close weather and very cold. We stood S. W. About noon we had occasion to lie by the lee to straighten our mizzen shrouds, and the rear-admiral and *Jewel*, being both to windward of us, bare up and came under our lee, to inquire if anything were amiss with us; so we heard the company was in health in the *Jewel*, but that two passengers were dead in the *Ambrose*, and one other cow.

Tuesday, 25.] The wind still N. W.; fair weather, but cold. We went on with a handsome gale, and at noon were in forty-three and a half; and the variation of the compass was a point and one-sixth. All this day we stood W. S. W. about five or six leagues a watch, and towards night the wind enlarged, with a cold dash of snowy rain, and then we ran in a smooth sea about eight or nine leagues a watch, and stood due W.

Wednesday, 26.] The wind still N. W. a good gale and fair weather, but very cold still; yet we were about forty-three. At night we sounded, but found no ground.

Thursday, 27.] The wind N. W. a handsome gale; fair weather. About noon it came about to the S. W. and at night rain, with a stiff gale, and it continued to rain very hard till it was near midnight.

This day our skiff went aboard the *Jewel* for a hogshead of meal, which we borrowed, because we could not come by our own, and there came back in the skiff the master of the *Jewell* and Mr. Revell;[1] so our captain stayed them dinner, and sent for Capt. Lowe; and about two hours after dinner, they went aboard their own ships, our captain giving Mr. Revell three shot, because he was one of the owners of our ship.

We understood now, that the two which died in the *Ambrose* were Mr. Cradock's servants, who were sick when they came to sea; and one of them should have been left at Cowes, if any house would have received him.

In the *Jewel*, also, one of the seamen died—a most profane fellow, and one who was very injurious to the passengers, though much against the will of the master.

At noon we tacked about and stood W. and by N. and so continued most part of that day and night following, and had much rain till midnight.

Friday, 28.] In the morning the wind veered to the W. yet we had a stiff gale, and steered N. W. and by N. It was so great a fog all this day, as we had lost sight of one of our ships, and saw the other sometimes much to leeward. We had many fierce showers of rain throughout this day.

At night the wind cleared up, and we saw both our consorts fair by us; so that wind being very scant, we tacked and stood W. and by S. A child was born in the *Jewel* about this time.

Saturday, 29.] The wind N. W. a stiff gale, and fair weather, but very cold; in the afternoon full N. and towards night N. and by E.; so we stood W.

Lord's day, 30.] The wind N. by E. a handsome gale, but close, misty weather, and very cold; so our ship made good way in a smooth sea, and our three ships kept close together. By our account we were in the same meridian with Isle Sable, and forty-two and a half.

[1] One of the assistants.

Monday, 31.] Wind N. W. a small gale, close and cold weather. We sounded, but had no ground. About noon the wind came N. by E., a stiff, constant gale and fair weather, so as our ship's way was seven, eight, and sometimes twelve leagues a watch. This day, about five at night, we expected the eclipse, but there was not any, the sun being fair and clear from three till it set.

June 1, Tuesday.] The wind N. E. a small gale, with fair, clear weather; in the afternoon full S., and towards night a good gale. We stood W. and by N. A woman in our ship fell in travail, and we sent and had a midwife out of the *Jewel*. She was so far ahead of us at this time, (though usually we could spare her some sail,) as we shot off a piece and lowered our topsails, and then she brailed her sails and stayed for us.

This evening we saw the new moon more than half an hour after sunset, being much smaller than it is at any time in England.

Wednesday, 2.] The wind S. S. W., a handsome gale; very fair weather, but still cold; in the evening a great fog. We stood W. and by N. and W. N. W.

Our captain, supposing us now to be near the N. coast, and knowing that to the S. there were dangerous shoals, fitted on a new mainsail, that was very strong, and double, and would not adventure with his old sails, as before, when he had sea-room enough.

Thursday, 3.] The wind S. by W. a good steady gale, and we stood W. and by N. The fog continued very thick, and some rain withal. We sounded in the morning, and again at noon, and had no ground. We sounded again about two, afternoon, and had ground about eighty fathom, a fine gray sand; so we presently tacked and stood S. S. E., and shot off a piece of ordnance to give notice to our consorts, whom we saw not since last evening.

The fog continued all this night, and a steady gale at S. W.

Friday, 4.] About four in the morning we tacked again

(the wind S. W.) and stood W. N. W. The fog continued all this day, so as we could not see a stone's cast from us; yet the sun shone very bright all the day. We sounded every two hours, but had no ground. At night we tacked again and stood S. In the great cabin, fast.

Saturday, 5.] In the morning the wind came to N. E. a handsome gale, and the fog was dispersed; so we stood before the wind W. and by N., all the afternoon being rainy. At night we sounded, but had no ground. In the great cabin, thanksgiving.

It rained most part of this night, yet our captain kept abroad, and was forced to come in in the night to shift his clothes.

We sounded every half watch, but had no ground.

Lord's day, 6.] The wind N. E. and after N., a good gale, but still foggy at times, and cold. We stood W. N. W., both to make Cape Sable, if we might, and also because of the current, which near the west shore sets to the S., that we might be the more clear from the southern shoals, viz., of Cape Cod.

About two in the afternoon we sounded and had ground at about eighty fathom, and the mist then breaking up, we saw the shore to the N. about five or six leagues off, and were (as we supposed) to the S. W. of Cape Sable, and in forty-three and a quarter. Towards night it calmed and was foggy again, and the wind came S. and by E. We tacked and stood W. and by N., intending to make land at Aquamenticus, being to the N. of the Isles of Shoals.

Monday, 7.] The wind S. About four in the morning we sounded and had ground at thirty fathom, and was somewhat calm; so we put our ship a-stays, and took, in less than two hours, with a few hooks, sixty-seven codfish, most of them very great fish, some a yard and a half long, and a yard in compass. This came very seasonably, for our salt fish was now spent, and we were taking care for victuals this day (being a fish day).

After this we filled our sails, and stood W. N. W. with a small gale. We hoisted out a great boat to keep our sounding the better. The weather was now very cold. We sounded at eight, and had fifty fathoms, and, being calm, we heaved out our hooks again, and took twenty-six cods; so we all feasted with fish this day. A woman was delivered of a child in our ship, stillborn. The woman had divers children before, but none lived, and she had some mischance now, which caused her to come near a month before her time, but she did very well. At one of the clock we had a fresh gale at N. W. and very fair weather all that afternoon, and warm, but the wind failed soon.

All the night the wind was W. and by S. a stiff gale, which made us stand to and again, with small advantage.

Tuesday, 8.] The wind still W. and by S., fair weather, but close and cold. We stood N. N. W. with a still gale, and, about three in the afternoon, we had sight of land to the N. W. about ten leagues, which we supposed was the Isles of Monhegan, but it proved Mount Mansell.[1] Then we tacked and stood W. S. W. We had now fair sunshine weather, and so pleasant a sweet air as did much refresh us, and there came a smell off the shore like the smell of a garden.

There came a wild pigeon into our ship, and another small land bird.

Wednesday, 9.] In the morning the wind easterly, but grew presently calm. Now we had very fair weather, and warm. About noon the wind came to S. W.; so we stood W. N. W. with a handsome gale, and had the main land upon our starboard all that day, about eight or ten leagues off. It is very high land, lying in many hills very unequal. At night we saw many small islands, being low land, between us and the main, about five or six leagues off us; and about three

[1] Named by Champlain, in 1604, Mount Desert. The name Mount Mansell came, Savage presumes, from Sir Robert Mansell, at one time the highest naval officer of England, who was interested in the New England settlements.

leagues from us, towards the main, a small rock a little above water. At night we sounded and had soft oozy ground at sixty fathom; so, the wind being now scant at W. we tacked again and stood S. S. W. We were now in forty-three and a half. This high land, which we saw, we judged to be at the W. cape of the great bay, which goeth towards Port Royal, called Mount Desert, or Mount Mansell, and no island, but part of the main. In the night the wind shifted oft.

Thursday, 10.] In the morning the wind S. and by W. till five. In the morning a thick fog; then it cleared up with fair weather, but somewhat close. After we had run some ten leagues W. and by S. we lost sight of the former land, but made other high land on our starboard, as far off as we could descry, but we lost it again.

The wind continued all this day at S. a stiff, steady gale, yet we bare all our sails, and stood W. S. W. About four in the afternoon we made land on our starboard bow, called the Three Turks' Heads, being a ridge of three hills upon the main, whereof the southmost is the greatest. It lies near Aquamenticus. We descried, also, another hill, more northward, which lies by Cape Porpus. We saw, also, ahead of us, some four leagues from shore, a small rock, called Boone Isle, not above a flight shot over, which hath a dangerous shoal to the E. and by S. of it, some two leagues in length. We kept our luff and weathered it, and left it on our starboard about two miles off. Towards night we might see the trees in all places very plainly, and a small hill to the southward of the Turks' Heads. All the rest of the land to the S. was plain, low land. Here we had a fine fresh smell from shore. Then, lest we should not get clear of the ledge of rocks, which lie under water from within a flight shot of the said rock, (called Boone Isle,) which we had now brought N. E. from us, towards Pascataquac, we tacked and stood S. E. with a stiff gale at S. by W.

Friday, 11.] The wind still S. W., close weather. We stood to and again all this day within sight of Cape Ann. The

Isles of Shoals were now within two leagues of us, and we saw a ship lie there at anchor, and five or six shallops under sail up and down.

We took many mackerels, and met a shallop, which stood from Cape Ann towards the Isles of Shoals, which belonged to some English fishermen.

Saturday, 12.] About four in the morning we were near our port. We shot off two pieces of ordnance, and sent our skiff to Mr. Peirce his ship (which lay in the harbor, and had been there [*blank*] days before). About an hour after, Mr. Allerton[1] came aboard us in a shallop as he was sailing to Pemaquid. As we stood towards the harbor, we saw another shallop coming to us; so we stood in to meet her, and passed through the narrow strait between Baker's Isle and Little Isle, and came to an anchor a little within the islands.

After Mr. Peirce came aboard us, and returned to fetch Mr. Endecott,[2] who came to us about two of the clock, and with him Mr. Skelton[3] and Capt. Levett. We that were of the assistants, and some other gentlemen, and some of the women, and our captain, returned with them to Nahumkeck,[4] where we supped with a good venison pasty and good beer, and at night we returned to our ship, but some of the women stayed behind.

---

[1] William Peirce, an experienced sailor, and Isaac Allerton, a leading man of Plymouth, were at this time in the service of that colony. Their names will often recur hereafter. Pemaquid lies some fifteen miles east of the Kennebec.

[2] "This distinguished father of Massachusetts had, near two years before, been sent to found the plantation in the settlement of Salem, the oldest town in the colony. He had a commission, in 1629, from the company to act as governor, which was, of course, superseded by the arrival of Winthrop with the charter. With the history of his adopted country, that of Endecott is interwoven, till the time of his death, 15 March, 1655. He served four years as deputy governor, and sixteen years as governor." (Note by Savage.)

[3] "Samuel Skelton, pastor of Salem, came the year before in the same fleet with Higginson. The notices of his history are very brief; that of his death will be found in this volume, 2 August, 1634. His wife died 15 March, 1631, as we learn from Dudley, who says, 'she was a godly and helpful woman; she lived desired, and died lamented, and well deserves to be honorably remembered.'" Savage.)

[4] Naumkeag, the Indian name of Salem.

In the mean time most of our people went on shore upon the land of Cape Ann, which lay very near us, and gathered store of fine strawberries.

An Indian came aboard us and lay there all night.

Lord's day, 13.] In the morning, the sagamore of Agawam[1] and one of his men came aboard our ship and stayed with us all day.

About two in the afternoon we descried the *Jewel*; so we manned out our skiff and wafted them in, and they went as near the harbor as the tide and wind would suffer.

Monday, 14.] In the morning early we weighed anchor, and the wind being against us, and the channel so narrow as we could not well turn in, we warped in our ship, and came to an anchor in the inward harbor.

In the afternoon we went with most of our company on shore, and our captain gave us five pieces.

Thursday, 17.] We went to Mattachusetts,[2] to find out a place for our sitting down. We went up Mistick River about six miles.

We lay at Mr. Maverick's, and returned home on Saturday. As we came home, we came by Nataskott, and sent for Capt. Squib ashore—(he had brought the west-country people, viz., Mr. Ludlow, Mr. Rossiter, Mr. Maverick, etc., to the bay, who were set down at Mattapan,)[3]—and ended a difference between him and the passengers; wherupon he sent his boat to his ship, (the *Mary and John*,) and at our parting gave us five pieces. At our return we found the *Ambrose* in the harbor at Salem.

Thursday, July 1.] The *Mayflower* and the *Whale* arrived

[1] Agawam, meaning river, given as a name to Ipswich (as here), to Springfield and other places.

[2] Boston harbor, where the Blue Hills, from which Massachusetts ultimately derives its name, were in sight. Samuel Maverick had already established himself at the mouth of the Mystic, at Winnisimmet, now Chelsea. Blaxton or Blackstone, too, was at Shawmut, about to become Boston, while Morton and Weston, as described in the Introduction, were at points in the same bay farther south. [3] These were the settlers of Dorchester.

safe in Charlton harbor.[1] Their passengers were all in health, but most of their cattle dead, (whereof a mare and horse of mine). Some stone horses came over in good plight.

Friday, 2.] The *Talbot* arrived there. She had lost fourteen passengers.

My son, Henry Winthrop, was drowned at Salem.[2]

Saturday, 3.] The *Hopewell* and *William and Francis* arrived.

Monday, 5.] The *Trial* arrived at Charlton, and the *Charles* at Salem.

Tuesday, 6.] The *Success* arrived. She had [blank] goats and lost [blank] of them, and many of her passengers were near starved, etc.

Wednesday, 7.] The *Lion* went back to Salem.

Thursday, 8.] We kept a day of thanksgiving in all the plantations.

Thursday, August 18.] Capt. Endecott and [blank] Gibson were married by the governor and Mr. Wilson.[3]

Saturday, 20.] The French ship called the *Gift*, came into the harbor at Charlton. She had been twelve weeks at sea, and lost one passenger and twelve goats; she delivered six.

Monday we kept a court.[4]

Friday, 27.] We, of the congregation, kept a fast, and

[1] Charlestown harbor. Charlestown replaced at once the Indian name, Mishawum. The form Charlton is derived from Captain John Smith's map of New England.

[2] The affliction disposed of here in such brief terms was a sad blow to Winthrop. See his first letters to his wife and son in England. R. C. Winthrop, *Life and Letters of John Winthrop*, II. 36, 39.

[3] The second marriage of Endicott introduces the Rev. John Wilson, the noted pastor of the Boston church. He was grand-nephew of Grindal, archbishop of Canterbury, had much energy and was powerfully befriended. He was now a man of forty-two. John Wilson is one of Cotton Mather's heroes, described in *Magnalia Christi Americana*, book III. "entituled Polybius," with other "divines by whose evangelical ministry the churches of New England have been illuminated."

[4] Court means general meeting of the company. Either through affliction or absorption in business, Winthrop's record is in these days very meagre. Supplying from other sources necessary details, we may note as most important, the

chose Mr. Wilson our teacher, and Mr. Nowell an elder, and Mr. Gager and Mr. Aspinwall, deacons. We used imposition of hands, but with this protestation by all, that it was only as a sign of election and confirmation, not of any intent that Mr. Wilson should renounce his ministry he received in England.

September 20.] Mr. Gager died.

30.] About two in the morning, Mr. Isaac Johnson died; his wife, the lady Arbella, of the house of Lincoln, being dead about one month before. He was a holy man, and wise, and died in sweet peace, leaving some part of his substance to the colony.[1]

rapid process of separation from old religious ties. Some of the Massachusetts emigrants, before leaving England, practically adopted Congregationalism. A band from the southern shires, sailing a few weeks before Winthrop, practised the new way at Plymouth before departure, which was countenanced by the Rev. John White of Dorchester. These emigrants, landing at Nantasket a fortnight before Winthrop's arrival, presently proceeded to Mattapan and founded Dorchester (Palfrey, I. 318 n.) Before the summer ended Winthrop's company organized as a Congregational church with John Wilson for its minister, definitely cutting loose from the Church of England, and seeking fellowship with the Separatists. June 28 of this year, Samuel Fuller, of Plymouth, then visiting the newcomers, wrote Bradford that the Rev. Mr. Phillips openly discarded his old ties, and that Winthrop sought aid and countenance from Plymouth. Endicott was a "dear friend," while Coddington, an assistant, declared that John Cotton, at Southampton, had counselled "that they should take advice of them at Plymouth, and should do nothing to offend them." (*Mass. Hist. Soc. Coll.*, first series, III. 74.)

The first Court of Assistants on this side of the water was held at Charlestown, August 23, 1630, followed by others at short intervals. (*Mass. Colonial Records*, under date.) Theocracy asserted itself at once, the first business being to provide for the ministers. Captains Patrick and Underhill, military heads, were also taken care of; measures were adopted to keep firearms from the Indians, for the husbanding of corn, and the prevention of drunkenness. Discipline was vigorous and most impartial, whipping and the "bilbowes" often being resorted to. Not only did Thomas Morton, of Merry Mount, and many an obscure servant suffer, but the Brownes, important men, were sent back to England for maintaining prelacy, and even Sir Richard Saltonstall was twice fined. Charlestown proving unhealthy, as was believed through bad water, the river was crossed to Shawmut where there were good springs, and where Blaxton, who had perhaps come over with Robert Gorges in 1623, had settled. Here, October 18, was held the first formal quarterly General Court, provided or in the charter. Boston, Dorchester and Watertown received the names which they have ever since borne.

[1] The loss of these high-born and generous friends was a severe blow.

The wolves killed six calves at Salem, and they killed one wolf.

Thomas Morton adjudged to be imprisoned, till he were sent into England, and his house burnt down, for his many injuries offered to the Indians, and other misdemeanors. Capt. Brook, master of the *Gift*, refused to carry him.[1]

Finch [?], of Watertown, had his wigwam burnt and all his goods.

Billington executed at Plymouth for murdering one.

Mr. Phillips, the minister of Watertown, and others, had their hay burnt.

The wolves killed some swine at Saugus.

A cow died at Plymouth, and a goat at Boston,[2] with eating Indian corn.

October 23.] Mr. Rossiter, one of the assistants, died.

25.] Mr. Colburn (who was chosen deacon by the congregation a week before) was invested by imposition of hands of the minister and elder.

The governor, upon consideration of the inconveniences which had grown in England by drinking one to another, restrained it at his own table, and wished others to do the like, so as it grew, by little and little, to disuse.

29.] The *Handmaid* arrived at Plymouth, having been twelve weeks at sea, and spent all her masts, and of twenty-eight cows she lost ten. She had about sixty passengers, who came all well; John Grant, master.

Mr. Goffe wrote to me, that his shipping this year had utterly undone him.

---

[1] Thomas Morton, whose performances at Merry Mount, or Mount Wollaston, brought down upon his head the vengeance both of Plymouth and of Massachusetts Bay, now returned to England, where he posed as a Church of England martyr, and in 1637 published at Amsterdam *The New English Canaan*, a most curious book, reprinted in 1883 by the Prince Society under the editorship of Mr. Charles Francis Adams. For an interesting and elaborate account of this picturesque reprobate, see C. F. Adams, *Three Episodes of Massachusetts History*, I., chaps. x. and xi.

[2] Here for the first time Winthrop uses the designation "Boston," the town in England most familiar to the settlers in general affording the name.

She brought out twenty-eight heifers, but brought but seventeen alive.

November 11.] The master came to Boston with Capt. Standish and two gentlemen passengers, who came to plant here, but having no testimony, we would not receive them.

10.] [*blank*] Firmin, of Watertown, had his wigwam burnt. Divers had their hay-stacks burnt by burning the grass.

27.] Three of the governor's servants were from this day to the 1 of December abroad in his skiff among the islands, in bitter frost and snow, being kept from home by the N. W. wind, and without victuals. At length they gat to Mount Wollaston, and left their boat there, and came home by land. Laus Deo.

December 6.] The governor and most of the assistants, and others, met at Roxbury, and there agreed to build a town fortified upon the neck between that and Boston, and a committee was appointed to consider of all things requisite, etc.

14.] The committee met at Roxbury, and upon further consideration, for reasons, it was concluded, that we could not have a town in the place aforesaid: 1. Because men would be forced to keep two families. 2. There was no running water; and if there were any springs, they would not suffice the town. 3. The most part of the people had built already, and would not be able to build again. So we agreed to meet at Watertown that day sen'night, and in the meantime other places should be viewed.

Capt. Neal[1] and three other gentlemen came hither to us. He came in the bark *Warwick*, this summer, to Pascataqua, sent as governor there for Sir Ferdinando Gorges and others.

21.] We met again at Watertown, and there, upon view of a place a mile beneath the town, all agreed it a fit place for a fortified town, and we took time to consider further about it.

Walter Neal, of whom we shall have several mentions, came to the Piscataqua in the interest of Sir Ferdinando Gorges, having promised that he would make available the "lakes," either Champlain or Winnepesaukee and the headwaters of the Merrimac, where beaver were abundant.

24.] Till this time there was (for the most part) fair, open weather, with gentle frosts in the night; but this day the wind came N. W., very strong, and some snow withal, but so cold as some had their fingers frozen, and in danger to be lost. Three of the governor's servants, coming in a shallop from Mistick, were driven by the wind upon Noddle's Island, and forced to stay there all that night, without fire or food; yet through God's mercy, they came safe to Boston next day, but the fingers of two of them were blistered with cold, and one swooned when he came to the fire.

26.] The rivers were frozen up, and they of Charlton could not come to the sermon at Boston till the afternoon at high water.

Many of our cows and goats were forced to be still abroad for want of houses.

28.] Richard Garrett, a shoemaker of Boston, and one of the congregation there, with one of his daughters, a young maid, and four others, went towards Plymouth in a shallop, against the advice of his friends; and about the Gurnett's Nose the wind overblew so much at N. W. as they were forced to come to a killock[1] at twenty fathom, but their boat drave and shaked out the stone, and they were put to sea, and the boat took in much water, which did freeze so hard as they could not free her; so they gave themselves for lost, and, commending themselves to God, they disposed themselves to die; but one of their company espying land near Cape Cod, then made shift to hoist up part of their sail, and, by God's special providence, were carried through the rocks to the shore, where some gat on land, but some had their legs frozen into the ice, so as they were forced to be cut out. Being come on shore they kindled a fire, but, having no hatchet, they could get little wood, and were forced to lie in the open air all night, being extremely cold. In the morning two of their company went towards Plymouth, (supposing it had been

[1] A rude anchor consisting of a stone enclosed within a frame of wood.

within seven or eight miles, whereas it was near fifty miles from them). By the way they met with two Indian squaws, who, coming home, told their husbands that they had met two Englishmen. They thinking (as it was) that they had been shipwrecked, made after them, and brought them back to their wigwam, and entertained them kindly; and one of them went with them the next day to Plymouth, and the other went to find out their boat and the rest of their company, which were seven miles off, and having found them, he holp them what he could, and returned to his wigwam, and fetched a hatchet, and built them a wigwam and covered it, and gat them wood (for they were so weak and frozen, as they could not stir;) and Garrett died about two days after his landing; and the ground being so frozen as they could not dig his grave, the Indian hewed a hole about half a yard deep, with his hatchet, and having laid the corpse in it, he laid over it a great heap of wood to keep it from the wolves. By this time the governor of Plymouth had sent three men to them with provisions, who being come, and not able to launch their boat, (which with the strong N. W. wind was driven up to the high water mark,) the Indian returned to Plymouth and fetched three more; but before they came, they had launched their boat, and with a fair southerly wind were gotten to Plymouth, where another of their company died, his flesh being mortified with the frost; and the two who went towards Plymouth died also, one of them being not able to get thither, and the other had his feet so frozen as he died of it after. The girl escaped best, and one Harwood, a godly man of the congregation of Boston, lay long under the surgeon's hands; and it was above six weeks before they could get the boat from Plymouth; and in their return they were much distressed; yet their boat was very well manned, the want whereof before was the cause of their loss.

1631

January.] A house at Dorchester was burnt down.

February 11.] Mr. Freeman's house at Watertown was burned down, but, being in the daytime, his goods were saved.

5.] The ship *Lyon*, Mr. William Peirce, master, arrived at Nantasket. She brought Mr. Williams,[1] (a godly minister,) with his wife, Mr. Throgmorton, [blank] Perkins, [blank] Ong, and others, with their wives and children, about twenty passengers, and about two hundred tons of goods. She set sail from Bristol, December 1. She had a very tempestuous passage, yet, through God's mercy, all her people came safe, except Way his son, who fell from the spritsail yard in a

[1] Here enters upon our stage Roger Williams, one of the most illustrious and important characters concerned with early New England. During his life of eighty years (1603–1683) he affected the course of history in both the old and the new world as a conspicuous pioneer in vindicating freedom of conscience. Born probably in London, he was connected as a boy with Sir Edward Coke, the great lawyer, through whom he became a scholar of the Charterhouse, and afterwards of Pembroke College, Cambridge. He appears to have taken orders, and served as chaplain in the household of Sir W. Masham, in Essex, whose wife was a cousin of Cromwell. Fine opportunities lay before him, but he early became a zealous non-conformist, and when twenty-seven years old landed, as here related, from the *Lyon*, at Nantasket, to take part with the exiles. His name frequently recurs in the *Journal*, and his eventful career, so far as it affects Massachusetts Bay, will be touched upon in subsequent notes. Though outspoken for toleration, Roger Williams in his later years made it plain that he was ready to repress anarchy by force, and in secular affairs to maintain proper subordination; a memorable utterance of his views is contained in a letter of 1655, which has his oft-quoted comparison of a distressed commonwealth to a laboring ship (*Narragansett Club Publications*, VI. 278). With all his nobleness a certain extravagance must be noted in Roger Williams. Probably the best contemporary judgment is that of Bradford, governor of Plymouth: "a man godly and zealous, having many precious parts, but very unsettled in judgment." (*History of Plymouth Plantation*, p. 299 of the edition in the present series.) That the Massachusetts General Court acted unjustly in the banishment of Roger Williams in 1635 is by no means universally admitted. See Henry M. Dexter, *As to Roger Williams and his Banishment from the Massachusetts Plantation* (Boston, 1876).

tempest, and could not be recovered, though he kept in sight near a quarter of an hour. Her goods also came all in good condition.

8.] The governor went aboard the *Lyon,* riding by Long Island.

9.] The *Lyon* came to an anchor before Boston, where she rode very well, notwithstanding the great drift of ice.

10.] The frost brake up; and after that, though we had many snows and sharp frost, yet they continued not, neither were the waters frozen up as before. It hath been observed, ever since this bay was planted by Englishmen, viz., seven years, that at this day the frost hath broken up every year.

The poorer sort of people (who lay long in tents, etc.) were much afflicted with the scurvy, and many died, especially at Boston and Charlestown; but when this ship came and brought store of juice of lemons, many recovered speedily. It hath been always observed here, that such as fell into discontent, and lingered after their former conditions in England, fell into the scurvy and died.

18.] Capt. Welden, a hopeful young gentleman, and an experienced soldier, died at Charlestown of a consumption, and was buried at Boston with a military funeral.

Of the old planters, and such as came the year before, there were but two, (and those servants,) which had the scurvy in all the country. At Plymouth not any had it, no not of those, who came this year, whereof there were above sixty. Whereas, at their first planting there, near the half of their people died of it.

A shallop of Mr. Glover's was cast away upon the rocks about Nahant, but the men were saved.

Of those which went back in the ships this summer, for fear of death or famine, etc., many died by the way and after they were landed, and others fell very sick and low, etc.

The *Ambrose,* whereof Capt. Lowe was master, being new masted at Charlton, spent all her masts near Newfoundland,

and had perished, if Mr. Peirce, in the *Lyon*, who was her consort, had not towed her home to Bristol. Of the other ships which returned, three, viz., the *Charles*, the *Success*, and the *Whale*, were set upon by Dunkirkers, near Plymouth in England, and after long fight, having lost many men, and being much torn, (especially the *Charles*,) they gat into Plymouth.

The provision, which came to us this year, came at excessive rates, in regard of the dearness of corn in England, so as every bushel of wheat-meal stood us in fourteen shillings, peas eleven shillings, etc. Tonnage was at £6.11.

22.] We held a day of thanksgiving for this ship's arrival, by order from the governor and council, directed to all the plantations.

March 16.] About noon the chimney of Mr. Sharp's house in Boston took fire, (the splinters being not clayed at the top,)[1] and taking the thatch burnt it down, and the wind being N. W., drove the fire to Mr. Colburn's house, being [blank] rods off, and burnt that down also, yet they saved most of their goods.

23.] Chickatabot[2] came with his sannops and squaws, and presented the governor with a hogshead of Indian corn.

After they had all dined, and had each a small cup of sack and beer, and the men tobacco, he sent away all his men and women, (though the governor would have stayed them, in regard of the rain and thunder). Himself and one squaw and one sannop stayed all night, and, being in English clothes, the governor set him at his own table, where he behaved himself as soberly, etc., as an Englishman. The next day after dinner he returned home, the governor giving him cheese and peas and a mug and some other small things.

---

[1] The chimney was plainly after the backwoods fashion of later times, of sticks, the interstices filled by mud.

[2] Chickatabot's domain was on the Neponset River. For "sannop" the modern frontiersman would write "buck."

26.] John[1] Sagamore and James his brother, with divers sannops, came to the governor to desire his letter for recovery of twenty beaver skins, which one Watts in England had forced [?] him of. The governor entertained them kindly, and gave him his letter with directions to Mr. Downing[2] in England, etc.

The night before, alarm was given in divers of the plantations. It arose through the shooting off some pieces at Watertown, by occasion of a calf, which Sir Richard Saltonstall had lost; and the soldiers were sent out with their pieces to try the wilderness from thence till they might find it.

29.] Sir Richard Saltonstall and his two daughters, and one of his younger sons, (his two eldest sons remained still in the country,) came down to Boston, and stayed that night at the governor's, and the next morning, by seven of the clock, accompanied with Mr. Peirce and others in two shallops, they departed to go to the ship riding at Salem. The governor gave them three drakes[3] at their setting sail, the wind being N. W. a stiff gale and full sea. Mr. Sharp went away at the same time in another shallop.

About ten of the clock, Mr. Coddington[4] and Mr. Wilson, and divers of the congregation, met at the governor's, and there Mr. Wilson, praying and exhorting the congregation to love, etc., commended to them the exercise of prophecy[5] in his absence, and designed those whom he thought most fit for it, viz., the governor, Mr. Dudley,[6] and Mr. Nowell the elder.

---

[1] The sway of this sachem extended from the Charles River near Watertown, toward the Mystic River.

[2] Emanuel Downing, brother-in-law of Winthrop, a man of wealth and influence, was an immigrant of a later time. He was father of Sir George Downing, a man of great but not always savory reputation, who will be mentioned later. [3] Salutes from cannon so denominated.

[4] William Coddington, a leading man through wealth and high character, for several years treasurer of Massachusetts Bay. He was driven forth at a later time during the "antinomian excitement", and became founder and governor of the Rhode Island or Aquidneck plantation, as Roger Williams was of Providence.

[5] "Prophecy," the Puritan equivalent of preaching.

[6] Thomas Dudley, now deputy-governor, afterward governor, stood second only to Winthrop among the lay citizens of the colony. Savage's judgment of him

Then he desired the governor to commend himself and the rest to God by prayer; which being done, they accompanied him to the boat, and so they went over to Charlestown to go by land to the ship. This ship set sail from Salem, April 1, and arrived at London (all safe) April 29.

April.] The beginning of this month we had very much rain and warm weather. It is a general rule, that when the wind blows twelve hours in any part of the east, it brings rain or snow in great abundance.

4.] Wahginnacut, a sagamore upon the River Quonehtacut[1] which lies west of Naragancet, came to the governor at Boston, with John Sagamore, and Jack Straw, (an Indian, who had lived in England and had served Sir Walter Raleigh [?], and was now turned Indian again,) and divers of their sannops, and brought a letter to the governor from Mr. Endecott to this effect: That the said Wahginnacut was very desirous to have some Englishmen to come plant in his country, and offered to find them corn, and give them yearly eighty skins of beaver, and that the country was very fruitful, etc., and wished that there might be two men sent with him to see the country. The governor entertained them at dinner, but would send none with him. He discovered after, that the said sagamore is a very treacherous man, and at war with the Pekoath[2] (a far greater sagamore). His country is not above five days' journey from us by land.

12.] At a court holden at Boston, (upon information to the governor, that they of Salem had called Mr. Williams to the office of a teacher,)[3] a letter was written from the court to Mr.

is harsh, and has been controverted of late years. See Augustine Jones, *Life of Thomas Dudley*. He was undoubtedly a worthy and serviceable character, though severely Puritan, and was the ancestor of a long and distinguished line. Before the immigration, as steward of the Earl of Lincoln he became a well trained man of affairs, in touch with the great world. In early life he served as a soldier under Henry IV. of France. His figure in the story is only less prominent than that of Winthrop.

[1] Connecticut.
[2] Pequot.
[3] Roger Williams, who reached New England in 1631, was soon invited to

Endecott to this effect: That whereas Mr. Williams had refused to join with the congregation at Boston, because they would not make a public declaration of their repentance for having communion with the churches of England, while they lived there; and, besides, had declared his opinion, that the magistrate might not punish the breach of the Sabbath, nor any other offence, as it was a breach of the first table; therefore, they marvelled they would choose him without advising with the council; and withal desiring him, that they would forbear to proceed till they had conferred about it.

13.] Chickatabot came to the governor, and desired to buy some English clothes for himself. The governor told him, that English sagamores did not use to truck; but he called his tailor and gave him order to make him a suit of clothes; whereupon he gave the governor two large skins of coat beaver, and, after he and his men had dined, they departed, and said he would come again three days after for his suit.

14.] We began a court of guard upon the neck between Roxbury and Boston, whereupon should be always resident an officer and six men.

An order was made last court, that no man should discharge a piece after sunset, except by occasion of alarm.

15.] Chickatabot came to the governor again, and he put him into a very good new suit from head to foot, and after he set meat before them; but he would not eat till the governor had given thanks, and after meat he desired him to do the like, and so departed.

---

fill the place of John Wilson, who had gone to England on a visit. Finding fault with his congregation as "unseparated" from the Church of England, or not formally withdrawn, and disliking the control assumed by the Boston church over the individual conscience, he went in April to Salem, succeeding there as teacher Francis Higginson, who had lately died. The passage makes plain the disapproval by those in power of the haste of the Salem church. Williams continued uncompromising in his opposition. "The first table", breaches of which the magistrates, in his idea, had no right to punish, included the four commandments of the decalogue first in order. In a few months, he left Salem for the more congenial atmosphere of Plymouth.

21.] The house of John Page of Watertown was burnt by carrying a few coals from one house to another: a coal fell by the way and kindled in the leaves.

One Mr. Gardiner, (calling himself Sir Christopher Gardiner,[1] knight of the golden melice,) being accused to have two wives in England, was sent for; but he had intelligence, and escaped, and travelled up and down among the Indians about a month; but, by means of the governor of Plymouth, he was taken by the Indians about Namasket,[2] and brought to Plymouth, and from thence he was brought, by Capt. Underhill[3] and his Lieut. Dudley, May 4, to Boston.

16] There was an alarm given to all our towns in the night, by occasion of a piece which was shot off, (but where could not be known,) and the Indians having sent us word the day before, that the Mohawks were coming down against them and us.

17.] A general court at Boston.[4] The former governor was chosen again, and all the freemen of the commons were sworn to this government. At noon, Cheeseborough's house was burnt down, all the people being present.

[1] As to Sir Christopher Gardiner's true character and purposes much doubt prevails. He is surmised to have been a spy or agent of Sir Ferdinando Gorges. His life was not reputable, nor did he avoid giving occasion for suspicion. Probably it was not treatment unduly harsh to send him out of the country, but it was impolitic. Together with Thomas Morton and Ratcliffe (presently to be mentioned, an humbler associate, who had suffered the New England discipline), he bitterly denounced in England the administration of Massachusetts Bay. See Adams, *Three Episodes*, 250 et seqq.

[2] Namasket, later Middleborough. See Bradford, *History of Plymouth Plantation*, in this series, pp. 286-288.

[3] Captain John Underhill often appears in Winthrop's narrative—a forceful personality sometimes serviceable, as in the Pequot war, but often troublesome and dangerous. We find him hypocritical and licentious, under a religious mask practising evil. He was subjected to merited punishment, and in later years played a part in New Hampshire, Connecticut, and Long Island.

[4] The General Court was the annual meeting of the members or stockholders of the Massachusetts Company. According to the charter a general court for elections should take place April 18 [not 17], 1631. The General Court was at the beginning, and until 1634, a primary assembly; but by recent and temporary legislation the choice of governor was entrusted to the assistants.

27.] There came from Virginia into Salem a pinnace of eighteen tons, laden with corn and tobacco. She was bound to the north, and put in there by foul weather. She sold her corn at ten shillings the bushel.

June 14.] At a court, John Sagamore and Chickatabot being told at last court of some injuries that their men did to our cattle, and giving consent to make satisfaction, etc., now one of their men was complained of for shooting a pig, etc., for which Chickatabot was ordered to pay a small skin of beaver, which he presently paid.

At this court one Philip Ratcliff,[1] a servant of Mr. Cradock, being convict, ore tenus, of most foul, scandalous invectives against our churches and government, was censured to be whipped, lose his ears, and be banished the plantation, which was presently executed.

25.] There came a shallop from Pascataqua, which brought news of a small English ship come thither with provisions and some Frenchmen to make salt. By this boat, Capt. Neal, governor of Pascataqua, sent a packet of letters to the governor, directed to Sir Christopher Gardiner, which, when the governor had opened, he found it came from Sir Ferdinando Gorges, (who claims a great part of the Bay of Massachusetts). In the packet was one letter to Thomas Morton, (sent prisoner before into England upon the lord chief justice's warrant:) by both which letters it appeared, that he had some secret design to recover his pretended right, and that he reposed much trust in Sir Christopher Gardiner.

These letters we opened, because they were directed to one, who was our prisoner, and had declared himself an ill willer to our government.[2]

27.] There came to the governor Capt. Southcot [?] of

[1] However Ratcliffe may have offended, the barbarity of his punishment is very shocking. Savage cites evidence that it excited notice in England.

[2] The fact that this paragraph was inserted at a later time into the margin of the *Journal*, suggests, thinks Savage, that the governor felt some compunction here.

Dorchester, and brought letters out of the *White Angel*, (which was lately arrived at Sauco). She brought [blank] cows, goats, and hogs, and many provisions, for the bay and for Plymouth. Mr. Allerton returned in this ship, and by him we heard, that the *Friendship*, which put out from Barnstable [blank] weeks before the *Angel*, was forced home again by extremity of foul weather, and so had given over her voyage. This ship, the *Angel*, set sail from [blank].[1]

July 4.] The governor built a bark at Mistick, which was launched this day, and called the *Blessing of the Bay*.

6.] A small ship of sixty tons arrived at Natascott, Mr. Graves master. She brought ten passengers from London. They came with a patent to Sagadahock, but, not liking the place, they came hither. Their ship drew ten feet, and went up to Watertown, but she ran on ground twice by the way. These were the company called the Husbandmen, and their ship called the *Plough*. Most of them proved familists[2] and vanished away.

13.] Canonicus' son, the great sachem of Naraganset, came to the governor's house with John Sagamore. After they had dined, he gave the governor a skin, and the governor requited him with a fair pewter pot, which he took very thankfully, and stayed all night.

---

[1] From Bristol. The *Friendship* and the *White Angel* figure largely in Bradford's pages, under this year.

[2] Through ignorance and fanaticism many strange and even dangerous doctrines prevailed in the seventeenth century, as the old repression relaxed. Edwards, a Presbyterian, a little later than this when the Independents were enforcing toleration, wrote a book called *Gangraena*, in which are enumerated one hundred and seventy-six forms of false belief, some of which certainly were of a character to disquiet the friends of law and order. The Familists professed the principle that religion lay in love irrespective of faith, a tenet no doubt harmless when intelligently held, but liable in rude minds to run into licentious extremes. The magistrates can hardly be blamed for looking askance at the "Husbandmen" who arrived in the *Plough*. The "Plough patent" which this forlorn company were designed to occupy, lay in Maine, between Capes Porpoise and Elizabeth: it was sometimes called Lygonia. The title was soon held to have no validity, and Lygonia "vanished away." For an account of its fortunes, see Charles Deane in Winsor, *Narrative and Critical History of America*, III. 322, and *The Genealogist*, new series, XIX. 270.

14.] The ship called the *Friendship*, of Barnstable, arrived at Boston, after she had been at sea eleven weeks, and beaten back again by foul weather. She set sail from Barnstable again about the midst of May. She landed here eight heifers, and one calf, and five sheep.

21.] The governor, and deputy, and Mr. Nowell, the elder of the congregation at Boston, went to Watertown to confer with Mr. Phillips, the pastor, and Mr. Brown, the elder of the congregation there, about an opinion, which they had published, that the churches of Rome were true churches. The matter was debated before many of both congregations, and, by the approbation of all the assembly, except three, was concluded an error.

22.] The *White Angel* came into the bay. She landed here twenty-one heifers.

26.] A small bark of Salem, of about twelve tons, coming towards the bay, John Elston and two of Mr. Cradock's fishermen being in her, and two tons of stone, and three hogsheads of train oil, was overset in a gust, and, being buoyed up by the oil, she floated up and down forty-eight hours, and the three men sitting upon her, till Henry Way his boat, coming by, espied them and saved them.

29.] The *Friendship* set sail for the Christopher Islands,[1] and ran on ground behind Conant's Island.

30.] The *White Angel* fell down for Plymouth, but, the wind not serving, she came to an anchor by Long Island, and ran on ground a week after, near Gurnett's Nose.

Mr. Ludlow, in digging the foundation of his house at Dorchester, found two pieces of French money: one was coined in 1596. They were in several places, and above a foot within the firm ground.

August 8.] The Tarentines, to the number of one hundred, came in three canoes, and in the night assaulted the wigwam of the sagamore of Agawam,[2] by Merimack, and slew seven

---

[1] St. Christopher, in the West Indies.   [2] Later, Ipswich.

men, and wounded John Sagamore, and James, and some others, (whereof some died after,) and rifled a wigwam where Mr. Cradock's men kept to catch sturgeon, took away their nets and biscuit, etc.

19.] The *Plough* returned to Charlestown, after she had been on her way to the Christopher Islands about three weeks, and was so broke she could not return home.

31.] The governor's bark, called the *Blessing of the Bay*, being of thirty tons, went to sea.

September 6.] The *White Angel* set sail from Marble Harbor.

About this time last year the company here set forth a pinnace to the parts about Cape Cod, to trade for corn, and it brought here above eighty bushels. This year again the Salem pinnace, being bound thither for corn, was, by contrary winds, put into Plymouth, where the governor, etc., fell out with them, not only forbidding them to trade, but also telling them they would oppose them by force, even to the spending of their lives, etc.; whereupon they returned, and acquainting the governor of Massachusetts with it, he wrote to the governor of Plymouth this letter, here inserted, with their answer, which came about a month after.[1]

The wolves did much hurt to calves and swine between Charles River and Mistick.

At the last court, a young fellow was whipped for soliciting an Indian squaw to incontinency. Her husband and she complained of the wrong, and were present at the execution, and very well satisfied.

At the same court, one Henry Linne was whipped and banished, for writing letters into England full of slander against our government and orders of our churches.

17.] Mr. Shurd of Pemaquid sent home James Sagamore's wife, who had been taken away at the surprise at Aga-

---

[1] These documents are not in the manuscripts of the *Journal*, and have disappeared.

wam, and writ that the Indians demanded [*blank*] fathom of wampampeague and [*blank*] skins for her ransom.

27.] At a court, one Josias Plaistowe and two of his servants were censured for stealing corn from Chickatabot and his men, (who were present,) the master to restore two fold, and to be degraded from the title of a gentleman, and fined five pounds, and his men to be whipped.[1]

October 4.] The *Blessing* went on a voyage to the eastward.

11.] The governor, being at his farm house at Mistick, walked out after supper, and took a piece in his hand supposing he might see a wolf, (for they came daily about the house, and killed swine and calves, etc.;) and, being about half a mile off, it grew suddenly dark, so as, in coming home, he mistook his path, and went till he came to a little house of Sagamore John, which stood empty. There he stayed, and having a piece of match in his pocket, (for he always carried about him match and a compass, and in summer time snake-weed,) he made a good fire near the house, and lay down upon some old mats, which he found there, and so spent the night, sometimes walking by the fire, sometimes singing psalms, and sometimes getting wood, but could not sleep. It was (through God's mercy) a warm night; but a little before day it began to rain, and, having no cloak, he made shift by a long pole to climb up into the house. In the morning, there came thither an Indian squaw, but perceiving her before she had opened the door, he barred her out; yet she stayed there a great while essaying to get in, and at last she went away, and he returned safe home, his servants having been much perplexed

---

[1] "Copying exactly the sentence of the court, appears to me the best explanation of this passage: 'It is ordered, that Josias Plastowe shall (for stealing four baskets of corn from the Indians) return them eight baskets again, be fined £5, and hereafter to be called by the name of Josias and not Mr. as formerly he used to be; and that William Buckland and Thomas Andrew shall be whipped for being accessory to the same offence.' We must conclude, therefore, that our fathers thought the whipping of the servants a lighter punishment than the degradation of the master." (Savage.)

for him, and having walked about, and shot off pieces, and hallooed in the night, but he heard them not.

22.] The governor received a letter from Capt. Wiggin[1] of Pascataquack, informing him of a murder committed the third of this month at Richman's Isle, by an Indian sagamore, called Squidrayset, and his company, upon one Walter Bagnall, called Great Watt, and one John P——, who kept with him. They, having killed them, burnt the house over them, and carried away their guns and what else they liked. He persuaded the governor to send twenty men presently to take revenge; but the governor, advising with some of the council, thought best to sit still awhile, partly because he heard that Capt. Neal, etc., were gone after them, and partly because of the season, (it being then frost and snow,) and want of boats fit for that expedition. This Bagnall was sometimes servant to one in the bay, and these three years had dwelt alone in the said isle, and had gotten about £400 most in goods. He was a wicked fellow, and had much wronged the Indians.

25.] The governor, with Capt. Underhill and others of the officers, went on foot to Sagus,[2] and next day to Salem, where they were bountifully entertained by Capt. Endecott, etc., and, the 28th, they returned to Boston by the ford at Sagus River, and so over at Mistick.

A plentiful crop.

30.] The governor, having erected a building of stone at Mistick, there came so violent a storm of rain, for twenty-four hours, from the N. E. and S. E. as (it being not finished, and laid with clay for want of lime) two sides of it were washed

---

[1] "Thomas Wiggin was agent, or governor, of the upper plantation, as Neal was of the lower. He was a worthy man, without doubt; for the Puritan peers, Say and Brooke, employed him as their representative, and he gave evidence in favor of our people against Gorges and Mason. In 1650, after the union of New Hampshire with our colony, he became one of the assistants, Hutch. I. 150, and, two years later, was among the commissioners to receive the submission of the inhabitants of Maine." (Savage.) Bagnall had been one of Morton's men at Merry Mount. Richmond Island is on the coast of Maine, just south of Cape Elizabeth. [2] Sagus or Saugus, later Lynn.

down to the ground; and much harm was done to other houses by that storm.

Mr. Pynchon's boat, coming from Sagadahock, was cast away at Cape Ann, but the men and chief goods saved, and the boat recovered.

November 2.] The ship *Lyon*, William Peirce master, arrived at Natascot.[1] There came in her the governor's wife, his eldest son, and his wife, and others of his children, and Mr Eliot,[2] a minister, and other families, being in all about sixty persons, who all arrived in good health, having been ten weeks at sea, and lost none of their company but two children, whereof one was the governor's daughter Ann, about one year and a half old, who died about a week after they came to sea.

3.] The wind being contrary, the ship stayed at Long Island, but the governor's son came on shore, and that night the governor went to the ship, and lay aboard all night; and the next morning, the wind coming fair, she came to an anchor before Boston.

4.] The governor, his wife and children, went on shore, with Mr. Peirce, in his ship's boat. The ship gave them six or seven pieces. At their landing, the captains, with their companies in arms, entertained them with a guard, and divers vollies of shot, and three drakes; and divers of the assistants and most of the people, of the near plantations, came to welcome them, and brought and sent, for divers days, great store of provisions, as fat hogs, kids, venison, poultry, geese, par-

---

[1] Captain Peirce and the *Lyon*, so serviceable to the new colony, brought over on this trip, beside much-needed supplies, important people. Margaret Winthrop, third wife of the governor, was a most worthy matron. Her piety, affection, and helpfulness, appear in her many letters, preserved in R. C. Winthrop, *Life and Letters of John Winthrop*, where also are abundant genealogical details as to the governor's family. John Winthrop, jr., stepson of Margaret, became the honored governor of Connecticut, and is only less distinguished in New England history than his father.

[2] John Eliot, born in 1604, and educated at Jesus College, Cambridge, became in 1632 teacher at Roxbury, and later the famous apostle to the Indians. There will be mention of him hereafter.

tridges, etc., so as the like joy and manifestation of love had never been seen in New England. It was a great marvel, that so much people and such store of provisions could be gathered together at so few hours' warning.

11.] We kept a day of thanksgiving at Boston.

17.] The governor of Plymouth[1] came to Boston, and lodged in the ship.

23.] Mr. Peirce went down to his ship, which lay at Nantascot. Divers went home with him into England by Virginia, as Sir Richard Saltonstall his eldest son and others; and they were six weeks in going to Virginia.

The congregation at Watertown (whereof Mr. George Phillips was pastor) had chosen one Richard Brown for their elder, before named, who, persisting in his opinion of the truth of the Romish church, and maintaining other errors withal, and being a man of a very violent spirit, the court wrote a letter to the congregation, directed to the pastor and brethren, to advise them to take into consideration, whether Mr. Brown were fit to be continued their elder or not; to which, after some weeks, they returned answer to this effect: That if we would take the pains to prove such things as were objected against him, they would endeavor to redress them.

December 8.] The said congregation being much divided about their elder, both parties repaired to the governor for assistance, etc.; whereupon he went to Watertown, with the deputy governor and Mr. Nowell, and the congregation being assembled, the governor told them, that being come to settle peace, etc., they might proceed in three distinct respects: 1. As the magistrates, (their assistance being desired). 2. As members of a neighboring congregation. 3. Upon the answer which we received of our letter, which did no way satisfy us. But the pastor, Mr. Phillips, desired us to sit with them as members of a neighboring congregation only, whereto the governor, etc., consented.

[1] William Bradford.

Then the one side, which had first complained, were moved to open their grievances; which they did to this effect: That they could not communicate with their elder, being guilty of errors, both in judgment and conversation. After much debate of these things, at length they were reconciled, and agreed to seek God in a day of humiliation, and so to have a solemn uniting; each party promising to reform what hath been amiss, etc.; and the pastor gave thanks to God, and the assembly brake up.

1632

January 27.] The governor, and some company with him, went up by Charles River about eight miles above Watertown, and named the first brook, on the north side of the river, (being a fair stream, and coming from a pond a mile from the river,) Beaver Brook, because the beavers had shorn down divers great trees there, and made divers dams across the brook. Thence they went to a great rock, upon which stood a high stone, cleft in sunder, that four men might go through, which they called Adam's Chair, because the youngest of their company was Adam Winthrop. Thence they came to another brook, greater than the former, which they called Masters' Brook, because the eldest of their company was one John Masters. Thence they came to another high pointed rock, having a fair ascent on the west side, which they called Mount Feake, from one Robert Feake, who had married the governor's daughter-in-law. On the west side of Mount Feake, they went up a very high rock, from whence they might see all over Neipnett, and a very high hill due west, about forty miles off, and to the N. W. the high hills by Merrimack, above sixty miles off.[1]

February 7.] The governor, Mr. Nowell, Mr. Eliot, and others, went over Mistick River at Medford, and going N. and by E. among the rocks about two or three miles, they came to a very great pond, having in the midst an island of about one acre, and very thick with trees of pine and beech; and the pond had divers small rocks, standing up here and there in it, which they therefore called Spot Pond.[2] They went all about

---

[1] It is easy to-day to trace the governor's routes. Beaver Brook still retains its name; the mountain seen to the west was Wachusett; the spurs of Monadnoc are the highlands northward.   [2] It is still "Spot Pond."

it upon the ice. From thence (towards the N. W. about half a mile,) they came to the top of a very high rock, beneath which, (towards the N.) lies a goodly plain, part open land, and part woody, from whence there is a fair prospect, but it being then close and rainy, they could see but a small distance. This place they called Cheese Rock, because, when they went to eat somewhat, they had only cheese, (the governor's man forgetting, for haste, to put up some bread).

14.] The governor and some other company went to view the country as far as Neponsett, and returned that night.

17.] The governor and assistants called before them, at Boston, divers of Watertown; the pastor and elder by letter, and the others by warrant. The occasion was, for that a warrant being sent to Watertown for levying of £8, part of a rate of £60, ordered for the fortifying of the new town,[1] the pastor and elder, etc., assembled the people and delivered their opinions, that it was not safe to pay moneys after that sort, for fear of bringing themselves and posterity into bondage. Being come before the governor and council, after much debate, they acknowledged their fault, confessing freely, that they were in an error, and made a retractation and submission under their hands, and were enjoined to read it in the assembly the next Lord's day. The ground of their error was, for that they took this government to be no other but as of a mayor and aldermen, who have not power to make laws or raise taxations without the people; but understanding that this government was rather in the nature of a parliament, and that no assistant could be chosen but by the freemen, who had power likewise to remove the assistants and put in others, and therefore at every general court (which was to be held once every year) they had free liberty to consider and propound anything concerning the same, and to declare their grievances, without being

---

[1] Newtown, later Cambridge. Old willows still exist which perhaps descend from stocks in the ancient palisade. Jones, *Life of Dudley*, gives an interesting picture of a group till lately standing in Holmes Field.

subject to question, or, etc., they were fully satisfied; and so their submission was accepted, and their offence pardoned.[1]

March 5.] The first court after winter. It was ordered, that the courts (which before were every three weeks) should now be held the first Tuesday in every month.

Commissioners appointed to set out the bounds of the towns.

14.] The bark *Warwick* arrived at Natascott, having been at Pascataquack and at Salem to sell corn, which she brought from Virginia. At her coming into Natascott, with a S. E. wind, she was in great danger, by a sudden gust, to be cast away upon the rocks.

19.] She came to Winysemett.

Mr. Maverick, one of the ministers of Dorchester, in drying a little powder, (which took fire by the heat of the fire pan,) fired a small barrel of two or three pounds, yet did no other harm but singed his clothes. It was in the new meeting-house, which was thatched, and the thatch only blacked a little.

April 3.] At a court at Boston, the deputy, Mr. Dudley, went away before the court was ended, and then the secretary

---

[1] The new government was changing essentially, and Winthrop's account being meagre, Savage's note may be quoted. "In the objection of these gentlemen of Watertown, there was much force, for no power was by the charter granted to the governor and assistants to raise money by levy, assessment or taxation. Indeed, the same may be said of the right of making general orders or laws; for the directors of the company, or court of assistants, could only be executive. The company, or great body of the corporation, however, submitted at first to the mild and equal temporary usurpation of the officers, chosen by themselves, which was also justified by indisputable necessity. So simply patriarchal was the government, and so indifferent was the majority of the settlers to retain their full charter rights, that, at the first general court, or meeting of the whole company, held at Boston, 19 October after their arrival, 'for the establishing of the government, it was propounded, if it were not the best course, that the freemen should have the power of choosing assistants, when there are to be chosen, and the assistants, from amongst themselves, to choose a governor and deputy governor, who, with the assistants, should have the power of making laws and choosing officers to execute the same. This was fully assented unto by the general vote of the people and erection of hands.' *Col. Rec.*, I. 62. Such an extraordinary surrender of power proves, that no jealousy was excited by the former assumption, by the governor and assistants, of the legislative, in addition to the executive and judicial functions, with which the charter seems to invest them."

delivered the governor a letter from him, directed to the governor and assistants, wherein he declared a resignation of his deputyship and place of assistant; but it was not allowed.

At this court an act was made expressing the governor's power, etc., and the office of the secretary and treasurer, etc.

9.] The bark *Warwick*, and Mr. Maverick's pinnace, went out towards Virginia.

12.] The governor received letters from Plymouth, signifying, that there had been a broil between their men at Sowamset and the Naraganset Indians, who set upon the English house there to have taken Owsamequin,[1] the sagamore of Packanocott,[2] who was fled thither with all his people for refuge; and that Capt. Standish, being gone thither to relieve the three English, which were in the house, had sent home in all haste for more men and other provisions, upon intelligence that Canonicus, with a great army, was coming against them. Withal they writ to our governor for some powder to be sent with all possible speed, (for it seemed they were unfurnished). Upon this the governor presently despatched away the messenger with so much powder as he could carry, viz., twenty-seven pounds.

16.] The messenger returned, and brought a letter from the governor, signifying, that the Indians were retired from Sowams to fight with the Pequins, which was probable, because John Sagamore and Chickatabott were gone with all their men, viz., John Sagamore with thirty, and Chickatabott with [blank] to Canonicus, who had sent for them.

A wear was erected by Watertown men upon Charles River, three miles above the town, where they took great store of shads.

A Dutch ship brought from Virginia two thousand bushels of corn, which was sold at four shillings sixpence the bushel.

May 1.] The governor and assistants met at Boston to

---

[1] Osamequin, better known as Massasoit, was a friend of the English and father of the more famous Metacom, or King Philip.   [2] Pokanoket.

consider of the deputy his deserting his place.[1] The points discussed were two. The 1st, upon what grounds he did it: 2d, whether it were good or void. For the 1st, his main reason was for public peace; because he must needs discharge his conscience in speaking freely; and he saw that bred disturbance, etc. For the 2d, it was maintained by all, that he could not leave his place, except by the same power which put him in; yet he would not be put from his contrary opinion, nor would be persuaded to continue till the general court, which was to be the 9th of this month.

Another question fell out with him, about some bargains he had made with some poor men, members of the same congregation, to whom he had sold seven bushels and an half of corn to receive ten for it after harvest, which the governor and some others held to be oppressing usury, and within compass of the statute; but he persisted to maintain it to be lawful, and there arose hot words about it, he telling the governor, that, if he had thought he had sent for him to his house to give him such usage, he would not have come there; and that he never knew any man of understanding of other opinion; and that the governor thought otherwise of it, it was his weakness. The governor took notice of these speeches, and bare them with more patience than he had done, upon a like occasion, at another time. Upon this there arose another question, about his house. The governor having formerly told him, that he did not well to bestow such cost about wainscotting and adorning his house, in the beginning of a plantation, both in regard of the necessity of public charges, and for example, etc., his answer now was, that it was for the warmth of his house, and the charge was little, being but clapboards nailed to the wall in the form of wainscot. These and other speeches passed before dinner. After dinner, the governor told them, that he had heard, that the people intended, at the next

---

[1] Dudley's dissatisfaction with the Winthrop régime will before long manifest itself more violently.

general court, to desire, that the assistants might be chosen anew every year, and that the governor might be chosen by the whole court, and not by the assistants only. Upon this, Mr. Ludlow grew into passion, and said, that then we should have no government, but there would be an interim, wherein every man might do what he pleased, etc. This was answered and cleared in the judgment of the rest of the assistants, but he continued stiff in his opinion, and protested he would then return back into England.

Another business fell out, which was this. Mr. Clark[1] of Watertown had complained to the governor, that Capt. Patrick, being removed out of their town to Newtown, did compel them to watch near Newtown, and desired the governor, that they might have the ordering within their own town. The governor answered him, that the ordering of the watch did properly belong to the constable; but in those towns where the captains dwelt, they had thought fit to leave it to them, and since Capt. Patrick was removed, the constable might take care of it; but advised him withal to acquaint the deputy with it, and at the court it should be ordered. Clark went right home and told the captain, that the governor had ordered, that the constable should set the watch, (which was false;) but the captain answered somewhat rashly, and like a soldier, which being certified to the governor by three witnesses, he sent a warrant to the constable to this effect, that whereas some difficulty was fallen out, etc., about the watch, etc., he should, according to his office, see due watch should be kept till the court had taken order in it. This much displeased the captain, who came to this meeting to have it redressed. The governor told the rest what he had done, and upon what ground; whereupon they refused to do anything in it till the court.

While they were thus sitting together, an Indian brings a

[1] John Clark, as constable of Watertown, was a civil official, while Patrick belonged to the class of whom Miles Standish, John Mason, and John Underhill were types, veteran soldiers who trained to good purpose the planters, exposed to many perils.

letter from Capt. Standish, then at Sowams, to this effect, that the Dutchmen (which lay for trading at Anygansett or Naragansett) had lately informed him, that many Pequins (who were professed enemies to the Anagansetts) had been there divers days, and advised us to be watchful, etc., giving other reasons, etc.

Thus the day was spent and no good done, which was the more uncomfortable to most of them, because they had commended this meeting to God in more earnest manner than ordinary at other meetings.

May 8.] A general court at Boston. Whereas it was (at our first coming) agreed, that the freemen should choose the assistants, and they the governor, the whole court agreed now, that the governor and assistants should all be new chosen every year by the general court, (the governor to be always chosen out of the assistants;) and accordingly the old governor, John Winthrop, was chosen; accordingly all the rest as before, and Mr. Humfrey[1] and Mr. Coddington also, because they were daily expected.

The deputy governor, Thomas Dudley, Esq., having submitted the validity of his resignation to the vote of the court, it was adjudged a nullity, and he accepted of his place again, and the governor and he being reconciled the day before, all things were carried very lovingly amongst all, etc., and the people carried themselves with much silence and modesty.

John Winthrop, the governor's son, was chosen an assistant.

A proposition was made by the people, that every company of trained men might choose their own captain and officers; but the governor giving them reasons to the contrary, they were satisfied without it.

Every town chose two men to be at the next court, to advise with the governor and assistants about the raising of a public stock, so as what they should agree upon should bind all, etc.

[1] Humfrey did not arrive until 1634 nor Coddington till 1633—noteworthy men, accounts of whom are deferred for the present.

This court was begun and ended with speeches for the, etc., as formerly.

The governor, among other things, used this speech to the people, after he had taken his oath: That he had received gratuities from divers towns, which he received with much comfort and content; he had also received many kindnesses from particular persons, which he would not refuse, lest he should be accounted uncourteous, etc.; but he professed, that he received them with a trembling heart, in regard of God's rule, and the consciousness of his own infirmity; and therefore desired them, that hereafter they would not take it ill, if he did refuse presents from particular persons, except they were from the assistants, or from some special friends; to which no answer was made; but he was told after, that many good people were much grieved at it, for that he never had any allowance towards the charge of his place.

24.] The fortification upon the Corn Hill at Boston was begun.

25.] Charlestown men came and wrought upon the fortification.

Roxbury the next, and Dorchester the next.

26.] The *Whale* arrived with Mr. Wilson, Mr. Dummer,[1] and about thirty passengers, all in health; and of seventy cows lost but two. She came from Hampton, April 8th. Mr. Graves was master.

June 5.] The *William and Francis*, Mr. Thomas master, with about sixty passengers, whereof Mr. Welde[2] and old

[1] John Wilson, who had been much missed, now returns with a wife. Richard Dummer will appear hereafter as an engaging character. He was ancestor of Jeremy and William Dummer, eminent citizens of a later time. The name of the family is still commemorated in Dummer Academy, Newbury.

[2] Thomas Welde, coming from Essex, at once became pastor at Roxbury, as John Eliot was teacher. He will appear often as one of the ablest and strictest upholders of the theocracy, being particularly active against Anne Hutchinson. Savage and others have wrongly ascribed to him the authorship of a book really written by Winthrop, *A Short Story of the Rise, Reign, and Ruin of the Antinomians, Familists, and Libertines that infested the Churches of New England*, portions of which are included in this volume. Welde returned to England in

Mr. Batchelor[1] (being aged 71) were, with their families, and many other honest men; also, the *Charles* of Barnstable, with near eighty cows and six mares, Mr. Hatherly,[2] the merchant, and about twenty passengers, all safe, and in health. They set sail, viz., the *William and Francis* from London, March the 9th, and the *Charles* from Barnstable, April 10th, and met near Cape Ann. Mr. Winslow[3] of Plymouth came in the *William and Francis*.

12.] The *James*, Mr. Grant master, arrived. Her passage was eight weeks from London. She brought sixty-one heifers and lost forty, and brought twelve passengers.

1641, with Hugh Peter, as agent of the colony. He was more in sympathy with the intolerance of the Presbyterians than with the free spirit of Independency. He bore himself with consistency, conforming neither to Independency when it was in power, nor later to the restored Church of England, being ejected at the Restoration from his living in Durham.

[1] Stephen Batchelor, who soon became minister at Lynn, was, like Dummer, one of the "Company of Husbandmen."

[2] Timothy Hatherley, frequently mentioned by Bradford as one of the merchants who aided the Pilgrims, was the founder of Scituate.

[3] Edward Winslow, a Worcestershire gentleman, born in 1595, was socially highest in station among the Plymouth men. He became later the most conspicuous in the band and was surpassed in usefulness only by Bradford and Brewster, if by them. He is the only one of the Plymouth men whose portrait has been transmitted to us. His marriage with the widow of William White, mother of Peregrine White, the first white child born in New England, was the earliest marriage in New England, May 12, 1621. He travelled over Europe before coming to America, and after coming was the trusted agent of his colony on various distant commissions, both in America and England. In 1633 he became governor of Plymouth for a year, but his tact and experience fitted him especially for work of a different kind. In 1635 he was again sent to England to represent not only Plymouth but Massachusetts Bay at the English court. Here he encountered the malcontents, who, smarting under Puritan discipline, were traducing New England. Through Thomas Morton of Merry Mount he suffered imprisonment. Returning to America, he was again chosen governor of Plymouth, but soon took the position of magistrate, becoming in 1643 a commissioner of the United Colonies. As he before pleaded and suffered in the presence of the King and Laud in behalf of the colonies, so now he confronted Gorton and others, who accused New England before the powers of the new régime. In 1646 we find him again in the old world, where he gained favor under the Commonwealth, and in 1655 was sent by Cromwell as one of the commissioners to direct an expedition to the West Indies. Here soon after the capture of Jamaica he died. He was humane as well as wise, his work with and for the Indians especially showing his kindly spirit.

13.] A day of thanksgiving in all the plantations, by public authority, for the good success of the king of Sweden, and Protestants in Germany, against the emperor, etc.,[1] and for the safe arrival of all the ships, they having not lost one person, nor one sick among them.

14.] The governor was invited to dinner aboard the *Whale*. The master fetched him in his boat, and gave him three pieces at his going off.

The French came in a pinnace to Penobscot, and rifled a trucking house belonging to Plymouth, carrying thence three hundred weight of beaver and other goods.[2] They took also one Dixy Bull and his shallop and goods.

One Abraham Shurd of Pemaquid, and one Capt. Wright, and others, coming to Pascataquack, being bound for this bay in a shallop with £200 worth of commodities, one of the seamen, going to light a pipe of tobacco, set fire on a barrel of powder, which tare the boat in pieces. That man was never seen: the rest were all saved, but the goods lost.

The man, that was blown away with the powder in the boat at Pascataquack, was after found with his hands and feet torn off. This fellow, being wished by another to forbear to take any tobacco, till they came to the shore, which was hard by, answered, that if the devil should carry him away quick, he would take one pipe. Some in the boat were so drunk and fast asleep, as they did not awake with the noise.

A shallop of one Henry Way of Dorchester, having been missing all the winter, it was found that the men in her, being five, were all killed treacherously by the eastern Indians.

Another shallop of his being sent out to seek out the other, was cast away at Aquamenticus, and two of the men drowned. A fishing shallop at Isle of Shoals was overset.

---

[1] The victory of Gustavus at Breitenfeld, followed by his occupation of Frankfort and Mainz, and the successes of the elector of Saxony in Bohemia.

[2] See Bradford, pp. 284, 285, in this series.

One Noddle, an honest man of Salem, carrying wood in a canoe, in the South River, was overturned and drowned.

July.] At a training at Watertown, a man of John Oldham's,[1] having a musket, which had been long charged with pistol bullets, not knowing of it, gave fire, and shot three men, two into their bodies, and one into his hands; but it was so far off, as the shot entered the skin and stayed there, and they all recovered.

The congregation at Boston wrote to the elders and brethren of the churches of Plymouth, Salem, etc., for their advice in three questions: 1. Whether one person might be a civil magistrate and a ruling elder at the same time? 2. If not, then which should be laid down? 3. Whether there might be divers pastors in the same church?—The 1st was agreed by all negatively; the 2d doubtfully; the 3d doubtful also.

The strife in Watertown congregation continued still; but at length they gave the separatists a day to come in, or else to be proceeded against.

5.] At the day, all came in and submitted, except John Masters, who, though he were advised by divers ministers and others, that he had offended in turning his back upon the sacrament, and departing out of the assembly, etc., because they had then admitted a member whom he judged unfit, etc.; yet he persisted. So the congregation (being loath to proceed against him) gave him a further day; 8, at which time, he continuing obstinate, they excommunicated him; but, about a fortnight after, he submitted himself, and was received in again.

At Watertown there was (in the view of divers witnesses) a great combat between a mouse and a snake; and, after a

[1] John Oldham came to Plymouth in 1623, and proving to be a disturber of the colony, became a rover. He had more courage and enterprise than piety, settling at Nantasket, then at Cape Ann, then at Watertown. In 1633, with three companions he made his way through the woods to the Connecticut, becoming the pioneer of the English occupation there. In 1636, as we shall see, his murder by the Indians, in his shallop, near Block Island, brought on the Pequot war.

long fight, the mouse prevailed and killed the snake. The pastor of Boston, Mr. Wilson, a very sincere, holy man, hearing of it, gave this interpretation: That the snake was the devil; the mouse was a poor contemptible people, which God had brought hither, which should overcome Satan here, and dispossess him of his kingdom. Upon the same occasion, he told the governor, that, before he was resolved to come into this country, he dreamed he was here, and that he saw a church arise out of the earth, which grew up and became a marvellous goodly church.

After many imparlances and days of humiliation, by those of Boston and Roxbury, to seek the Lord for Mr. Welde his disposing, and the advice of those of Plymouth being taken, etc., at length he resolved to sit down with them of Roxbury.

August 3.] The deputy, Mr. Thomas Dudley, being still discontented with the governor, partly for that the governor had removed the frame of his house, which he had set up at Newtown, and partly for that he took too much authority upon him, (as he conceived,) renewed his complaints to Mr. Wilson and Mr. Welde, who acquainting the governor therewith, a meeting was agreed upon at Charlestown, where were present the governor and deputy, Mr. Nowell, Mr. Wilson, Mr. Welde, Mr. Maverick, and Mr. Warham. The conference being begun with calling upon the Lord, the deputy began,—that howsoever he had some particular grievances, etc.; yet, seeing he was advised by those present, and divers of the assistants, to be silent in them, he would let them pass, and so come first to complain of the breach of promise, both in the governor and others, in not building at Newtown. The governor answered, that he had performed the words of the promise; for he had a house up, and seven or eight servants abiding in it, by the day appointed: and for the removing of his house, he alleged, that, seeing that the rest of the assistants went not about to build, and that his neighbors of Boston had been discouraged from removing thither by Mr. Deputy himself, and thereupon had (under all their hands) petitioned him, that (according to the promise he made to them when they first sate down with him at Boston, viz., that he would not remove, except they went with him) he would not leave them; —this was the occasion that he removed his house. Upon these and other speeches to this purpose, the ministers went apart for one hour; then returning, they delivered their opinions, that the governor was in fault for removing of his house so suddenly, without conferring with the deputy and the rest of the assistants; but if the deputy were the occasion of discouraging Boston men from removing, it would excuse the governor a tanto, but not a toto. The governor, professing himself willing to submit his own opinion to the judgment of so many wise and godly friends, acknowledged himself faulty.

After dinner, the deputy proceeded in his complaint, yet with this protestation, that what he should charge the governor with, was in love, and out of his care of the public, and that the things which he should produce were but for his own satisfaction, and not by way of accusation. Then demanded he of him the ground and limits of his authority, whether by the patent or otherwise. The governor answered, that he was willing to stand to that which he propounded, and would challenge no greater authority than he might by the patent. The deputy replied, that then he had no more authority than every assistant, (except power to call courts, and precedency, for honor and order). The governor answered, he had more; for the patent, making him a governor, gave him whatsoever power belonged to a governor by common law or the statutes, and desired him to show wherein he had exceeded, etc.; and speaking this somewhat apprehensively, the deputy began to be in passion, and told the governor, that if he were so round, he would be round too. The governor bad him be round, if he would. So the deputy rose up in great fury and passion, and the governor grew very hot also, so as they both fell into bitterness; but, by mediation of the mediators, they were soon pacified. Then the deputy proceeded to particulars, as followeth:

1st. By what authority the governor removed the ordnance and erected a fort at Boston.—The governor answered, that the ordnance lying upon the beach in danger of spoiling, and having often complained of it in the court, and nothing done, with the help of divers of the assistants, they were mounted upon their carriages, and removed where they might be of some use: and for the fort, it had been agreed, above a year before, that it should be erected there: and all this was done without any penny charge to the public.

2d. By what authority he lent twenty-eight pounds of powder to those of Plymouth.—Governor answered, it was of his own powder, and upon their urgent distress, their own powder proving naught, when they were to send to the rescue of their men at Sowamsett.

3d. By what authority he had licensed Edward Johnson[1] to sit down at Merrimack.—Governor answered, that he had licensed him only to go forth on trading, (as he had done divers others,) as belonging to his place.

4th. By what authority he had given them of Watertown leave to erect a wear upon Charles River, and had disposed of lands to divers, etc.—Governor answered, the people of Watertown, falling very short of corn the last year, for want of fish, did complain, etc., and desired leave to erect a wear; and upon this the governor told them, that he could not give them leave, but they must seek it of the court; but because it would be long before the courts began again, and, if they deferred till then, the season would be lost, he wished them to do it, and

---

[1] Edward Johnson probably came with Winthrop, a man from Kent. His service was both military and civil, and in 1642 he was one of the founders of Woburn. He lived long, his name occurring in various honorable connections. He is best known as author of a history of New England from 1628 to 1652, *The Wonder-Working Providence of Sion's Saviour in New England* (London, 1654), which is to be reprinted in this series.

there was no doubt but, being for so general a good, the court would allow of it; and, for his part, he would employ all his power in the court, so as he should sink under it, if it were not allowed; and besides, those of Roxbury had erected a wear without any license from the court. And for lands, he had disposed of none, otherwise than the deputy and other of the assistants had done,—he had only given his consent, but referred them to the court, etc. But the deputy had taken more upon him, in that, without order of court, he had empaled, at Newtown, above one thousand acres, and had assigned lands to some there.

5th. By what authority he had given license to Ratcliff and Grey (being banished men) to stay within our limits.—Governor answered, he did it by that authority, which was granted him in court, viz., that, upon any sentence in criminal causes, the governor might, upon cause, stay the execution till the next court. Now the cause was, that, being in the winter, they must otherwise have perished.

6th. Why the fines were not levied.—Governor answered, it belonged to the secretary and not to him: he never refused to sign any that were brought to him; nay, he had called upon the secretary for it; yet he confessed, that it was his judgment, that it were not fit, in the infancy of a commonwealth, to be too strict in levying fines, though severe in other punishments.

7th. That when a cause had been voted by the rest of the court, the governor would bring new reasons, and move them to alter the sentence:—which the governor justified, and all approved.

The deputy having made an end, the governor desired the mediators to consider, whether he had exceeded his authority or not, and how little cause the deputy had to charge him with it; for if he had made some slips, in two or three years' government, he ought rather to have covered them, seeing he could not be charged that he had taken advantage of his authority to oppress or wrong any man, or to benefit himself; but, for want of a public stock, had disbursed all common charges out of his own estate; whereas the deputy would never lay out one penny, etc.; and, besides, he could shew that under his hand, that would convince him of a greater exceeding his authority, than all that the deputy could charge him with, viz., that whereas Binks and Johnson were bound in open court to appear at next court to account to, etc., he had, out of court, discharged them of their appearance. The deputy answered, that the party, to whom they were to account, came to him and confessed that he was satisfied, and that the parties were to go to Virginia; so he thought he might discharge them.

Though the governor might justly have refused to answer these seven articles, wherewith the deputy had charged him, both for that he had no knowledge of them before, (the meeting being only for the deputy his personal grievances,) and also for that the governor was not to give account of his actions to any but to the court; yet, out of his desire of the public peace, and to clear his reputation with those to whom the deputy had accused him, he was willing to give him satisfaction, to the end, that he might free him of such jealousy as he had conceived, that the governor intended to make himself popular, that he might gain absolute power, and bring all the assistants under his subjection; which was very improbable, seeing the governor had propounded in court to have an order established for limiting the governor's authority, and had himself drawn articles for that end, which had been approved and established by the whole court; neither could he justly be charged to have transgressed any of them. So the meeting breaking up, without any other conclusion but the commending the success of it by prayer to the Lord, the governor brought the deputy onward of his way, and every man went to his own home.[1] See two pages after.

[1] Winthrop and Dudley were men differently constituted. While the former was mild, disposed to lenity, and always a seeker of peace, the latter was intol-

5.] The sachem, who was joined with Canonicus, the great sachem of Naragansett, called Mecumeh, after Miantonomoh, being at Boston, where [he] had lodged two nights with his squaw, and about twelve sanapps, being present at the sermon, three of his sanapps went, in the meantime, and brake into a neighbor's house, etc. Complaint being made thereof to the governor, after evening exercise, he told the sachem of it, and with some difficulty caused him to make one of his sanapps to beat them, and then sent them out of the town; but brought the sachem and the rest of [the] company to his house, and made much of them, (as he had done before,) which he seemed to be well pleased with; but that evening he departed.

At a court not long before, two of Chickatabott's men were convented and convicted for assaulting some English of Dorchester in their houses, etc. They were put in the bilboes, and Chickatabot required to beat them, which he did.

The congregation of Boston and Charlestown began the meeting-house at Boston, for which, and Mr. Wilson's house, they had made a voluntary contribution of about one hundred and twenty pounds.

14.] Fair weather and small wind, and N. E. at Boston, and, at the same time, such a tempest of wind N. E. a little without the bay, as no boat could bear sail, and one had her mast borne by the board. So again, when there hath [been] a very tempest at N. W. or W. in the bay, there hath been a stark calm one league or two off shore.

This summer was very wet and cold, (except now and then a hot day or two,) which caused great store of musketoes and rattle-snakes. The corn, in the dry, sandy grounds, was much better than other years, but in the fatter grounds much worse, and in Boston, etc., much shorn down close by the ground with worms.

erant, uncompromising, of quick temper, and disposed to ride roughshod. This is not the end of the discord between the two men. For full presentation of the matter see Winthrop, *Life and Letters of John Winthrop*, and Jones, *Thomas Dudley*. The concluding four words refer to p. 91 *post*.

The windmill was brought down to Boston, because, where it stood near Newtown, it would not grind but with a westerly wind.

Mr. Oldham had a small house near the wear at Watertown, made all of clapboards, burnt down by making a fire in it when it had no chimney.

This week they had in barley and oats, at Sagus, above twenty acres good corn, and sown with the plough.

Great store of eels and lobsters in the bay. Two or three boys have brought in a bushel of great eels at a time, and sixty great lobsters.

The Braintree company, (which had begun to sit down at Mount Wollaston,) by order of court, removed to Newtown. These were Mr. Hooker's company.[1]

The governor's wife was delivered of a son, who was baptized by the name of William. The governor himself held the child to baptism, as others in the congregation did use. William signifies a common man, etc.

30.] Notice being given of ten sagamores and many Indians assembled at Muddy River,[2] the governor sent Capt. Underhill, with twenty musketeers, to discover, etc.; but at Roxbury they heard they were broke up.

September 4.] One Hopkins, of Watertown, was convict for selling a piece and pistol, with powder and shot, to James Sagamore, for which he had sentence to be whipped and branded in the cheek. It was discovered by an Indian, one of James's men, upon promise of concealing him, (for otherwise he was sure to be killed).

[1] This is the first mention of a great figure in New England history. Thomas Hooker was born in Leicestershire in 1586. He was a scholar and fellow of Emmanuel College, Cambridge, and at this time, a man of mature years, was a "lecturer" at Braintree in Essex; the non-conforming ministers often continued their ministrations under this name. In due time we shall have mention of his arrival in New England, and of his emigration, with many followers, to Connecticut, perhaps a democratic secession from Massachusetts. Of Hooker's influence in establishing the institutions of Connecticut, and their subsequent importance as related to the Constitution of the United States, see Johnston, *Connecticut* (American Commonwealths Series), pp. 19, 69.

[2] Muddy River, now Brookline.

The ministers afterward, for an end of the difference between the governor and deputy, ordered, that the governor should procure them a minister at Newtown, and contribute somewhat towards his maintenance for a time; or, if he could not, by the spring, effect that, then to give the deputy, toward his charges in building there, twenty pounds. The governor accepted this order, and promised to perform it in one of the kinds. But the deputy, having received one part of the order, returned the same to the governor, with this reason to Mr. Wilson, that he was so well persuaded of the governor's love to him, and did prize it so much, as if they had given him one hundred pounds instead of twenty pounds, he would not have taken it.

Notwithstanding the heat of contention, which had been between the governor and deputy, yet they usually met about their affairs, and that without any appearance of any breach or discontent; and ever after kept peace and good correspondency together, in love and friendship.

One Jenkins, late an inhabitant of Dorchester, and now removed to Cape Porpus,[1] went with an Indian up into [the] country with store of goods to truck, and, being asleep in a wigwam of one of Passaconamy's men, was killed in the night by an Indian, dwelling near the Mohawks' country, who fled away with his goods, but was fetched back by Passaconamy. There was much suspicion, that the Indians had some plot against the English, both for that many Naragansett men, etc., gathered together, who, with those of these parts, pretended to make war upon the Neipnett men, and divers insolent speeches were used by some of them, and they did not frequent our houses as they were wont, and one of their pawawes told us, that there was a conspiracy to cut us off to get our victuals and other substance. Upon this there was a camp pitched at Boston in the night, to exercise the soldiers against need might be; and Capt. Underhill (to try how they would behave

[1] Cape Porpoise, near the mouth of Saco River, Maine.

themselves) caused an alarm to be given upon the quarters, which discovered the weakness of our people, who, like men amazed, knew not how to behave themselves, so as the officers could not draw them into any order. All the rest of the plantations took the alarm and answered it; but it caused much fear and distraction among the common sort, so as some, which knew of it before, yet through fear had forgotten, and believed the Indians had been upon us. We doubled our guards, and kept watch each day and night.

14.] The rumor still increasing, the three next sagamores were sent for, who came presently to the governor.

16, being the Lord's day.] In the evening Mr. Peirce, in the ship *Lyon*, arrived, and came to an anchor before Boston. He brought one hundred and twenty-three passengers, whereof fifty children, all in health; and lost not one person by the way, save his carpenter, who fell overboard as he was caulking a port. They had been twelve weeks aboard, and eight weeks from the Land's End. He had five days east wind and thick fog, so as he was forced to come, all that time, by the lead; and the first land he made was Cape Ann.

22.] The Barnstable ship went out at Pullen Point[1] to Marble Harbor.

27.] A day of thanksgiving at Boston for the good news of the prosperous success of the king of Sweden, etc.,[2] and for the safe arrival of the last ship and all the passengers, etc.

October 18.] Capt. Camock, and one Mr. Godfry, a merchant, came from Pascataquack in Captain Neal his pinnace, and brought sixteen hogsheads of corn to the mill. They went away November [*blank*].

25.] The governor, with Mr. Wilson, pastor of Boston, and the two captains, etc., went aboard the *Lyon*, and from

[1] Pullen's Point, in Boston harbor, still retains its name.
[2] The defeat and death of Tilly, and the entrance of Gustavus Adolphus into Munich.

thence Mr. Peirce carried them in his shallop to Wessaguscus.[1] The next morning Mr. Peirce returned to his ship, and the governor and his company went on foot to Plymouth, and came thither within the evening. The governor of Plymouth, Mr. William Bradford,[2] (a very discreet and grave man,) with Mr. Brewster,[3] the elder, and some others, came forth and met them without the town, and conducted them to the governor's house, where they were very kindly entertained, and feasted every day at several houses. On the Lord's day there was a sacrament, which they did partake in; and, in the afternoon, Mr. Roger Williams (according to their custom) propounded a question, to which the pastor, Mr. Smith,[4] spake briefly; then Mr. Williams prophesied; and after the governor of Plymouth spake to the question; after him the elder; then some two or three more of the congregation. Then the elder desired the governor of Massachusetts and Mr. Wilson to speak to it, which they did. When this was ended, the deacon, Mr.

[1] Now Weymouth.

[2] William Bradford, who died in 1657, after having been governor of Plymouth for thirty years, was born in 1588, at Austerfield, in southern Yorkshire, whence while still a youth he went to Holland. Here Bradford toiled as a silk worker, connecting himself with the Leyden company, and emigrating with them in the *Mayflower*. After the death of Carver, the first governor, he became the head and main-stay of the enterprise until his death; though for a few years, Edward Winslow and Thomas Prence relieved him in the chief place. He was widely accomplished, speaking Dutch and French and versed also in Latin, Greek, and Hebrew. The testimony as to his moderation and wisdom is uniform; and his *History of Plymouth Plantation*, recovered amid national rejoicings, after being long lost, is one of the most precious of American documents. It is reprinted in the present series.

[3] William Brewster was sixty years old at the time of the voyage of the *Mayflower*, and possessed a character which made his influence truly patriarchal. He had mingled in great affairs, having accompanied the envoy of Elizabeth to Holland on an important diplomatic errand, as secretary. Though never formally ordained, yet as ruling elder he exercised most of the functions of teacher and pastor of the congregation. Until his death in 1644 he stood by Bradford, a main pillar of the colony, and remains one of the most venerated figures of American history.

[4] Rev. Ralph Smith, after painful experiences at Salem and Nantasket, became minister at Plymouth, where, though not highly esteemed, he remained some years. Roger Williams, a veritable bird-of-passage, was for the moment in Plymouth.

Fuller,[1] put the congregation in mind of their duty of contribution; whereupon the governor and all the rest went down to the deacon's seat, and put into the box, and then returned.

27.] The wind N. W., Mr. Peirce set sail for Virginia.

31, being Wednesday.] About five in the morning the governor and his company came out of Plymouth; the governor of Plymouth, with the pastor and elder, etc., accompanying them near half a mile out of town in the dark. The Lieut. Holmes, with two others, and the governor's mare, came along with them to the great swamp, about ten miles. When they came to the great river, they were carried over by one Luddam, their guide, (as they had been when they came, the stream being very strong, and up to the crotch;) so the governor called that passage Luddam's Ford. Thence they came to a place called Hue's Cross. The governor, being displeased at the name, in respect that such things might hereafter give the Papists occasion to say, that their religion was first planted in these parts, changed the name, and called it Hue's Folly. So they came, that evening, to Wessaguscus, where they were bountifully entertained, as before, with store of turkeys, geese, ducks, etc., and the next day came safe to Boston.

About this time Mr. Dudley, his house, at Newtown, was preserved from burning down, and all his family from being destroyed by gunpowder, by a marvellous deliverance;—the hearth of the hall chimney burning all night upon a principal beam and store of powder being near, and not discovered till they arose in the morning, and then it began to flame out.

Mr. John Eliot, a member of Boston congregation, and one whom the congregation intended presently to call to the office of teacher, was called to be a teacher to the church at Roxbury; and though Boston labored all they could, both

---

[1] Samuel Fuller, associated with Governor John Carver as a deacon of the Pilgrim Church at the coming from Holland, a useful and respected man. He possessed some medical skill, and was even sent for from Boston and Salem.

with the congregation of Roxbury and with Mr. Eliot himself, alleging their want of him, and the covenant between them, etc., yet he could not be diverted from accepting the call of Roxbury, November 5. So he was dismissed.

About a fortnight before this, those of Charlestown, who had formerly been joined to Boston congregation, now, in regard of the difficulty of passage in the winter, and having opportunity of a pastor, one Mr. James,[1] who came over at this time, were dismissed from the congregation of Boston.

The congregation of Watertown discharged their elder, Richard Brown, of his office, for his unfitness in regard of his passion and distemper in speech, having been oft admonished and declared his repentance for it.

21.] The governor received a letter from Capt. Neal, that Dixy Bull and fifteen more of the English, who kept about the east, were turned pirates, and had taken divers boats, and rifled Pemaquid, etc.,—23. Hereupon the governor called a council, and it was agreed to send his bark with twenty men, to join with those of Pascataquack, for the taking of the said pirates.

22.] A fast was held by the congregation of Boston, and Mr. Wilson (formerly their teacher) was chosen pastor, and [blank] Oliver[2] a ruling elder, and both were ordained by imposition of hands, first by the teacher, and the two deacons, (in the name of the congregation,) upon the elder, and then by the elder and the deacons upon the pastor.

December 4.] At a meeting of all the assistants, it was agreed, in regard that the extremity of the snow and frost had hindered the making ready of the bark, and that they had certain intelligence, that those of Pascataquack had sent out two pinnaces and two shallops, above a fortnight before, to defer any further expedition against the pirates till they heard

[1] Thomas James, predecessor of John Harvard as minister of Charlestown, went soon to New Haven, whence probably he returned to England.

[2] Thomas Oliver, ancestor of an honorable line, prominent especially in the Revolution, during which his descendants were strongly opposed to independence.

what was done by those; and for that end it was agreed, to send presently a shallop to Pascataquack to learn more, etc.

5.] Accordingly, the governor despatched away John Gallopp[1] with his shallop. The wind being very great at S. W., he could reach no farther than Cape Ann harbor that night; and the winds blowing northerly, he was kept there so long, that it was January the 2d before he returned.

By letters from Capt. Neal and Mr. Hilton,[2] etc., it was certified, that they had sent out all the forces they could make against the pirates, viz., four pinnaces and shallops, and about forty men, who, coming to Pemaquid, were there windbound about three weeks.

It was further advertised, by some who came from Penobscott, that the pirates had lost one of their chief men by a musket shot from Pemaquid; and that there remained but fifteen, whereof four or five were detained against their wills; and that they had been at some English plantations, and taken nothing from them but what they paid for; and that they had given another pinnace in exchange for that of Mr. Maverick, and as much beaver and otter as it was worth more, etc.; and that they had made a law against excessive drinking; and that their order was, as such times as other ships use to have prayer, they would assemble upon the deck, and one sing a song, or speak a few senseless sentences, etc. They also sent a writing, directed to all the governors, signifying their intent not to do harm to any more of their countrymen, but to go to the southward, and to advise them not to send against them; for they were resolved to sink themselves rather than be taken: Signed underneath, Fortune le garde, and no name to it.

[1] John Gallop, a bold sailor who comes up hereafter in picturesque connections. Gallop's Island in Boston harbor perpetuates the name.

[2] Edward and William Hilton founded in 1623 the settlement at Dover, N. H.

1633

January 1.] Mr. Edward Winslow chosen governor of Plymouth, Mr. Bradford having been governor about ten years, and now by importunity gat off.[1]

9.] Mr. Oliver, a right godly man, and elder of the church of Boston, having three or four of his sons, all very young, cutting down wood upon the neck, one of them, being about fifteen years old, had his brains beaten out with the fall of a tree, which he had felled. The good old father (having the news of it in as fearful a manner as might be, by another boy, his brother) called his wife (being also a very godly woman) and went to prayer, and bare it with much patience and honor.

17.] The governor, having intelligence from the east, that the French had bought the Scottish plantation near Cape Sable, and that the fort and all the ammunition were delivered to them, and that the cardinal,[2] having the managing thereof, had sent some companies already, and preparation was made to send many more the next year, and divers priests and Jesuits among them,—called the assistants to Boston, and the ministers and captains, and some other chief men, to advise what was fit to be done for our safety, in regard the French were like to prove ill neighbors (being Papists;) at which meeting it was agreed, that a plantation and a fort should forthwith be begun at Natascott, partly to be some block in an

---

[1] High office was a burden rather than an honor, fines being sometimes exacted of those who refused to serve.

[2] Richelieu is here referred to, who was guiding the interests of France. The French were now at Port Royal. Of the friction among themselves and the anxieties with which they filled their English neighbors the *Journal* has much to say. See also *Transactions of the Royal Historical Society*, new series, XVI. 95, for details in the Admiralty Records.

enemy's way, (though it could not bar his entrance,) and especially to prevent an enemy from taking that passage from us; and also, that the fort begun at Boston should be finished —also, that a plantation should be begun at Agawam, (being the best place in the land for tillage and cattle,) least an enemy, finding it void, should possess and take it from us. The governor's son (being one of the assistants) was to undertake this, and to take no more out of the bay than twelve men; the rest to be supplied at the coming of the next ships.

A maid servant of Mr. Skelton of Salem, going towards Sagus, was lost seven days, and at length came home to Salem. All that time she was in the woods, having no kind of food, the snow being very deep, and as cold as at any time that winter. She was so frozen into the snow some mornings, as she was one hour before she could get up; yet she soon recovered and did well, through the Lord's wonderful providence.

About the beginning of this month of January the pinnaces, which went after the pirates, returned, the cold being so great as they could not pursue them; but, in their return, they hanged up at Richman's Isle an Indian, one Black Will, one of those who had there murdered Walter Bagnall. Three of the pirates' company ran from them and came home.

February 21.] The governor and four of the assistants, with three of the ministers, and others, about twenty-six in all, went, in three boats, to view Natascott, the wind W., fair weather; but the wind arose at N. W. so strong, and extreme cold, that they were kept there two nights, being forced to lodge upon the ground, in an open cottage, upon a little old straw, which they pulled from the thatch. Their victuals also grew short, so as they were forced to eat muscles, —yet they were very mean,—and came all safe home the third day after, through the Lord's special providence. Upon view of the place, it was agreed by all, that to build a fort there would be of too great charge, and of little use; whereupon the planting of that place was deferred.

22, or thereabouts.] The ship *William*, Mr. Trevore master, arrived at Plymouth with some passengers and goods for the Massachusetts Bay; but she came to set up a fishing at Scituate, and so to go to trade at Hudson's River.

By this ship we had intelligence from our friends in England, that Sir Ferdinando Gorges[1] and Capt. Mason (upon the instigation of Sir Christopher Gardiner, Morton, and Ratcliff) had preferred a petition to the lords of the privy council against us, charging us with many false accusations; but, through the Lord's good providence, and the care of our friends in England, (especially Mr. Emanuel Downing, who had married the governor's sister, and the good testimony given on our behalf by one Capt. Wiggin, who dwelt at Pascataquack, and had been divers times among us,) their malicious practice took not effect. The principal matter they had against us was, the letters of some indiscreet persons among us, who had written against the church government in England, etc., which had been intercepted by occasion of the death of Capt. Levett, who carried them, and died at sea.

26.] Two little girls of the governor's family were sitting under a great heap of logs, plucking of birds, and the wind driving the feathers into the house, the governor's wife caused them to remove away. They were no sooner gone, but the whole heap of logs fell down in the place, and had crushed them to death, if the Lord, in his special providence, had not delivered them.

March.] The governor's son, John Winthrop, went, with twelve more, to begin a plantation at Agawam, after called Ipswich.

One John Edye, a godly man of Watertown congregation, fell distracted, and, getting out one evening, could not be found; but, eight days after, he came again of himself. He had kept his strength and color, yet had eaten nothing (as must

---

[1] Sir Ferdinando Gorges, to do his rivals harm, here employs men driven out of Massachusetts.

needs be conceived) all that time. He recovered his understanding again in good measure, and lived very orderly, but would, now and then, be a little distempered.

April 10.] Here arrived Mr. Hodges, one of Mr. Peirce his mates. He came from Virginia in a shallop, and brought news that Mr. Peirce's ship was cast away upon a shoal four miles from Feake Isle, ten leagues to the N. of the mouth of Virginia Bay,[1] November 2d, about five in the morning, the wind S. W., through the negligence of one of his mates, who had the watch, and kept not his lead as he was exhorted. They had a shallop and their ship's boat aboard. All that went into the shallop came safe on shore, but the ship's boat was sunk by the ship's side, and [blank] men drowned in her, and ten of them were taken up alive into the shallop. There were in the ship twenty-eight seamen and ten passengers. Of these were drowned seven seamen and five passengers, and all the goods were lost, except one hogshead of beaver; and most of the letters were saved, and some other small things, which were driven on shore the next day, when the ship was broken in pieces. They were nine days in much distress, before they found any English. Plymouth men lost four hogsheads, 900 pounds of beaver, and 200 otter skins. The governor of Massachusetts lost, in beaver and fish, which he sent to Virginia, etc., near £100. Many others lost beaver, and Mr. Humfrey, fish.

May.] The *William and Jane*, Mr. Burdock master, arrived with thirty passengers and ten cows or more. She came in six weeks from London.

The *Mary and Jane* arrived, Mr. Rose master. She came from London in seven weeks, and brought one hundred and ninety-six passengers, (only two children died). Mr. Coddington, one of the assistants, and his wife, came in her. In her return she was cast away upon Isle Sable, but [blank] men were saved.

By these ships we understood, that Sir Christopher Gar-

[1] Chesapeake Bay.

diner, and Thomas Morton, and Philip Ratcliff, (who had been punished here for their misdemeanors,) had petitioned to the king and council against us, (being set on by Sir Ferdinando Gorges and Capt. Mason, who had begun a plantation at Pascataquack, and aimed at the general government of New England for their agent there, Capt. Neal). The petition was of many sheets of paper, and contained many false accusations, (and among some truths misrepeated,) accusing us to intend rebellion, to have cast off our allegiance, and to be wholly separate from the church and laws of England; that our ministers and people did continually rail against the state, church, and bishops there, etc. Upon which such of our company as were then in England, viz., Sir Richard Saltonstall, Mr. Humfrey, and Mr. Cradock, were called before a committee of the council, to whom they delivered in an answer in writing; upon reading wherof, it pleased the Lord, our gracious God and Protector, so to work with the lords, and after with the king's majesty, when the whole matter was reported to him by Sir Thomas Jermin, one of the council, (but not of the committee, who yet had been present at the three days of hearing, and spake much in the commendation of the governor, both to the lords and after to his majesty,) that he said, he would have them severely punished, who did abuse his governor and the plantation; that the defendants were dismissed with a favorable order for their encouragement, being assured from some of the council, that his majesty did not intend to impose the ceremonies of the church of England upon us; for that it was considered, that it was the freedom from such things that made people come over to us; and it was credibly informed to the council, that this country would, in time, be very beneficial to England for masts, cordage, etc., if the Sound should be debarred.[1]

We sent forth a pinnace after the pirate Bull, but, after

[1] *I. e.*, at times when the importation of naval stores from the Baltic was interrupted by the closing of the Sound, then a Danish strait.

she had been forth two months, she came home, having not found him. After, we heard he was gone to the French.

A Dutch pink arrived, which had been to the southward a trading.

June 2.] Capt. Stone arrived with a small ship with cows and some salt. The governor of Plymouth sent Capt. Standish to prosecute against him for piracy. The cause was, being at the Dutch plantation,[1] where a pinnace of Plymouth coming, and Capt. Stone and the Dutch governor having been drinking together, Capt. Stone, upon pretence that those of Plymouth had reproached them of Virginia, from whence he came, seized upon their pinnace, (with the governor's consent,) and offered to carry her away, but the Dutchmen rescued her; and the next day the governor and Capt. Stone entreated the master of the pinnace (being one of the council of Plymouth) to pass it by, which he promised by a solemn instrument under his hand; yet, upon their earnest prosecution at court, we bound over Capt. Stone (with two sureties) to appear in the admiralty court in England, etc. But, after, those of Plymouth, being persuaded that it would turn to their reproach, and that it could be no piracy, with their consent, we withdrew the recognizance.

15.] Mr. Graves, in the ship *Elizabeth Bonadventure*, from Yarmouth, arrived with ninety-five passengers, and thirty-four Dutch sheep, and two mares. They came from Yarmouth in six weeks; lost not one person, but above forty sheep.

19.] A day of thanksgiving was kept in all the congregations, for our delivery from the plots of our enemies, and for the safe arrival of our friends, etc.

July 2.] At a court it was agreed, that the governor, John Winthrop, should have, towards his charges this year, £150, and the money, which he had disbursed in public business, as officers' wages, etc., being between two and three hundred pounds, should be forthwith paid.

[1] Manhattan. See Bradford, in this series, pp. 310, 311.

12.] Mr. Edward Winslow, governor of Plymouth, and Mr. Bradford, came into the bay, and went away the 18th. They came partly to confer about joining in a trade to Connecticut, for beaver and hemp. There was a motion to set up a trading house there, to prevent the Dutch, who were about to build one; but, in regard the place was not fit for plantation, there being three or four thousand warlike Indians, and the river not to be gone into but by small pinnaces, having a bar affording but six feet at high water, and for that no vessels can get in for seven months in the year, partly by reason of the ice, and then the violent stream, etc., we thought not fit to meddle with it.[1]

24.] A ship arrived from Weymouth, with about eighty passengers, and twelve kine, who sate down at Dorchester. They were twelve weeks coming, being forced into the Western Islands by a leak, where they stayed three weeks, and were very courteously used by the Portugals; but the extremity of the heat there, and the continual rain brought sickness upon them, so as [blank] died.

Much sickness at Plymouth, and above twenty died of pestilent fevers.

Mr. Graves returned, and carried a freight of fish from hence and Plymouth.

By him the governor and assistants sent an answer to the petition of Sir Christopher Gardiner, and withal a certificate from the old planters concerning the carriage of affairs, etc.

August 6.] Two men servants to one Moodye, of Roxbury, returning in a boat from the windmill, struck upon the oyster bank. They went out to gather oysters, and, not making fast their boat, when the flood came, it floated away, and they were both drowned, although they might have waded out on either side; but it was an evident judgment of God upon them, for they were wicked persons. One of them, a little before, being reproved for his lewdness, and put in mind of hell, answered,

[1] But see Bradford, in this series, p. 300.

that if hell were ten times hotter, he had rather be there than he would serve his master, etc. The occasion was, because he had bound himself for divers years, and saw that, if he had been at liberty, he might have had greater wages, though otherwise his master used him very well.[1]

Mr. Graves returned. He carried between five and six thousand weight of beaver, and about thirty passengers. Capt. Walter Neal, of Pascataquack, and some eight of his company, went with him. He had been in the bay above ten days, and came not all that time to see the governor. Being persuaded by divers of his friends, his answer was, that he was not well entertained the first time he came hither, and, besides, he had some letters opened in the bay; ergo, except he were invited, he would not go see him. The 13th day he wrote to the governor, to excuse his not coming to see him, upon the same reasons. The governor returned him answer, that his entertainment was such as time and place could afford, (being at their first coming, before they were housed, etc.) and retorted the discourtesy upon him, in that he would thrust himself, with such a company, (he had five or six gentlemen with him,) upon a stranger's entertainment, at such an unseasonable time, and having no need so to do; and for his letters, he protested his innocency, (as he might well, for the letters were opened before they came into the bay); and so concluded courteously, yet with plain demonstration of his error. And, indeed, if the governor should have invited him, standing upon those terms, he had blemished his reputation.

There is mention made before of the answer, which was returned to Sir Christopher Gardiner his accusations, to which the governor and all the assistants subscribed, only the deputy refused. He made three exceptions: 1. For that we termed the bishops reverend bishops; which was only in repeating the accuser's words. 2. For that we professed to believe all

---

[1] The condition of indentured servants was often scarcely better than that of slaves. The man may well have had reason to be unhappy.

the articles of the Christian faith, according to the scriptures and the common received tenets of the churches of England. This he refused, because we differed from them in matter of discipline, and about the meaning of Christ's descension into hell; yet the faithful in England (whom we account the churches) expound it as we do, and not of a local descent, as some of the bishops do. 3. For that we gave the king the title of sacred majesty, which is the most proper title of princes, being the Lord's anointed, and the word a mere civil word, never applied in scripture to any divine thing, but sanctus used always, (Mr. Knox called the queen of Scotland by the same title). Yet by no reasons could he be drawn to yield to these things, although they were allowed by divers of the ministers and the chief of Plymouth.[1]

There was great scarcity of corn, by reason of the spoil our hogs had made at harvest, and the great quantity they had even in the winter, (there being no acorns;) yet people lived well with fish and the fruit of their gardens.

Sept. 4.] The *Griffin*, a ship of three hundred tons, arrived, (having been eight weeks from the Downs). This ship was brought in by John Gallop a new way by Lovell's Island, at low water, now called Griffin's Gap. She brought about two hundred passengers, having lost some four, whereof one was drowned two days before, as he was casting forth a line to take mackerel. In this ship came Mr. Cotton,[2] Mr. Hooker, and

[1] Dudley's ultra-Puritanism appears here.

[2] The arrival of John Cotton in New England almost marks an epoch. This man, perhaps the most influential of the non-conformist ministers in Old or New England, was born in Derby in 1584. At Cambridge, a brilliant scholar, he became fellow and dean of Emmanuel College, and soon after rector of St. Botolph's Church in Boston, Lincolnshire, a conspicuous post. Here for many years he so wrought that he quite transformed the town, moulded opinion throughout the shire, and became widely known through England. His non-conformity was marked and brought upon him displacement. In these days his spirit was liberal: like John Robinson he seems to have held that more light yet might be expected to break out from God's word, which believers must be ready to accept, and it may be surmised that had he remained in England he would have adopted the free spirit of the Independents. When Winthrop sailed in 1630, John Cotton

Mr. Stone, ministers, and Mr. Peirce, Mr. Haynes, (a gentleman of great estate,) Mr. Hoffe, and many other men of good estates. They gat out of England with much difficulty, all places being belaid to have taken Mr. Cotton and Mr. Hooker, who had been long sought for to have been brought into the high commission; but the master being bound to touch at the Wight, the pursuivants attended there, and, in the mean time, the said ministers were taken in at the Downs. Mr. Hooker

preached, at Southampton, a farewell sermon, as John Robinson did, ten years before, for the Pilgrims at Delfshaven. Cotton's decision to follow to America was momentous for the colony. (See his reasons for emigrating to New England in the *Hutchinson Papers*, ed. 1865, I. 60.) To his death in 1652 he was the dominant figure in church and state, the ultimate appeal in matters civil and religious, the shaper as much as Winthrop of the New England world, and the initiator of policies and institutions that have persisted to the present time. He was not always consistent: the straits of his New England environment, where tolerance, perhaps, would have brought destruction, forced him into a narrowness of spirit not in line with the breadth he earlier had shown; we shall come upon painful instances of his turning his back and worse, upon friends in distress. But his shortcomings of this sort admit of palliation.

Modern writers, chief among them Thornton, in *The Historical Relation of New England to the English Commonwealth* (1874), plausibly maintain that John Cotton was the source and spring from whom flowed Independency, both in Old and New England, therefore asserting for him a claim to a high place among the great names of the English Commonwealth. Independency, however, did not begin with Cotton, nor do we find in his profession of it some of its finer characteristics; nevertheless he had a great part in a most honorable development.

Though the prestige of Cotton was shaken by his vacillations and mistakes (it would have been more than human perhaps not to have swayed and bent in such a troubled sea), he recovered all he lost, and died at the height of influence. His death was accompanied by portents in the heavens, and from that day to this he has stood as one of the mightiest and worthiest of the earlier pillars. Cotton wrote much, and the modern reader is puzzled to understand how his writings, to our taste often tedious, produced such an effect. He must have possessed extraordinary magnetism, and a character in which Puritan strength was somewhat mitigated by traits of amiability.

Thomas Hooker now begins his American career, departing soon for Connecticut; and Samuel Stone, equally sturdy in character, if less in the foreground. He plays hereafter a picturesque part as chaplain of John Mason in the Pequot war.

John Haynes and Atherton Hough, men of repute and means, strengthened the plantation. The former soon became governor, but casting in his lot with the Connecticut pioneers, appears but for a moment upon the Massachusetts stage.

and Mr. Stone went presently to Newtown, where they were to be entertained, and Mr. Cotton stayed at Boston. On Saturday evening, the congregation met in their ordinary exercise, and Mr. Cotton, being desired to speak to the question, (which was of the church,) he showed, out of the Canticles, 6, that some churches were as queens, some as concubines, some as damsels, and some as doves, etc. He was then (with his wife) propounded to be admitted a member. The Lord's day following, he exercised in the afternoon, and being to be admitted, he signified his desire and readiness to make his confession according to order, which he said might be sufficient in declaring his faith about baptism, (which he then desired for his child, born in their passage, and therefore named Seaborn). He gave two reasons why he did not baptize it at sea, (not for want of fresh water, for he held, sea water would have served:) 1, because they had no settled congregation there; 2, because a minister hath no power to give the seals but in his own congregation. He desired his wife might also be admitted a member, and gave a modest testimony of her, but withal requested, that she might not be put to make open confession, etc., which he said was against the apostle's rule, and not fit for women's modesty; but that the elders might examine her in private. So she was asked, if she did consent in the confession of faith made by her husband, and if she did desire to be admitted, etc.; whereto she answered affirmatively; and so both were admitted, and their child baptized, the father presenting it, (the child's baptism being, as he did then affirm, in another case, the father's incentive for the help of his faith, etc.)

The said 4th of September, came in also the ship called the *Bird*, (Mr. Yates master). She brought [blank] passengers, having lost [blank]; and [blank] cows, having lost [blank]; and four mares. She had been twelve weeks at sea, being, at her first coming out, driven northerly to fifty-three.

About ten days before this time, a bark was set forth to Connecticut and those parts, to trade.

John Oldham, and three with him, went over land to Connecticut, to trade. The sachem used them kindly, and gave them some beaver. They brought of the hemp, which grows there in great abundance, and is much better than the English. He accounted it to be about one hundred and sixty miles. He brought some black lead, whereof the Indians told him there was a whole rock. He lodged at Indian towns all the way.

12.] Capt. John Stone (of whom mention is made before) carried himself very dissolutely in drawing company to drink, etc., and being found upon the bed in the night with one Barcroft's wife, he was brought before the governor, etc., and though it appeared he was in drink, and no act to be proved, yet it was thought fit he should abide his trial, for which end warrant was sent out to stay his pinnace, which was ready to set sail; whereupon he went to Mr. Ludlow, one of the assistants, and used braving and threatening speeches against him, for which he raised some company and apprehended him, and brought him to the governor, who put him in irons, and kept a guard upon him till the court, (but his irons were taken off the same day). At the court his indictment was framed for adultery, but found *ignoramus* by the great jury; but, for his other misdemeanors, he was fined £100, which yet was not levied of him; and ordered upon pain of death to come here no more, without license of the court; and the woman was bound to her good behavior.

17.] The governor and council met at Boston, and called the ministers and elders of all the churches, to consider about Mr. Cotton his sitting down. He was desired to divers places, and those who came with him desired he might sit down where they might keep store of cattle; but it was agreed, by full consent, that the fittest place for him was Boston, and in that respect those of Boston might take farms in any part of the bay not belonging to other towns; and that (keeping a lecture) he should have some maintenance out of the treasury. But divers of the council, upon their second thoughts, did after refuse this contribution.

October 2.] The bark *Blessing*, which was sent to the southward, returned. She had been at an island over against Connecticut, called Long Island, because it is near fifty leagues long, the east part about ten leagues from the main, but the west end not a mile. There they had store of the best wampampeak, both white and blue. The Indians there are a very treacherous people. They have many canoes so great as one will carry eighty men. They were also in the River of Connecticut, which is barred at the entrance, so as they could not find above one fathom of water. They were also at the Dutch plantation upon Hudson's River, (called New Netherlands,) where they were very kindly entertained, and had some beaver and other things, for such commodities as they put off. They showed the governor (called Gwalter Van Twilly)[1] their commission, which was to signify to them, that the king of England had granted the river and country of Connecticut to his own subjects; and therefore desired them to forbear to build there, etc. The Dutch governor wrote back to our governor, (his letter was very courteous and respectful, as it had been to a very honorable person,) whereby he signified, that the Lords the States had also granted the same parts to the West India Company, and therefore requested that we would forbear the same till the matter were decided between the king of England and the said lords.

The said bark did pass and repass over the shoals of Cape Cod, about three or four leagues from Nantucket Isle, where the breaches are very terrible, yet they had three fathom water all over.

The company of Plymouth sent a bark to Connecticut, at this time, to erect a trading house there. When they came, they found the Dutch had built there, and did forbid the Plymouth men to proceed; but they set up their house not-

[1] Wouter van Twiller.

withstanding, about a mile above the Dutch. This river runs so far northward, that it comes within a day's journey of a part of Merrimack called [blank] and so runs thence N. W. so near the Great Lake, as [allows] the Indians to pass their canoes into it over land. From this lake, and the hideous swamps about it, come most of the beaver which is traded between Virginia and Canada, which runs forth of this lake; and Patomack River in Virginia comes likewise out of it, or very near, so as from this lake there comes yearly to the Dutch about ten thousand skins, which might easily be diverted by Merrimack, if a course of trade were settled above in that river.[1]

10.] A fast was kept at Boston, and Mr. Leverett,[2] an ancient, sincere professor, of Mr. Cotton's congregation in England, was chosen a ruling elder, and Mr. Firmin, a godly man, an apothecary of Sudbury in England, was chosen deacon, by imposition of hands; and Mr. Cotton was then chosen teacher of the congregation of Boston, and ordained by imposition of the hands of the presbytery, in this manner: First, he was chosen by all the congregation testifying their consent by erection of hands. Then Mr. Wilson, the pastor, demanded of him, if he did accept of that call. He paused, and then spake to this effect: that howsoever he knew himself unworthy and unsufficient for that place; yet, having observed all the passages of God's providence, (which he reckoned up in particular) in calling him to it, he could not but accept it. Then the pastor and the two elders laid their hands upon his head, and the pastor prayed, and then, taking off their hands, laid them on again, and, speaking to him by his name, they did thenceforth design him to the said office, in the name of the Holy Ghost, and did give him the charge of the congregation, and did thereby (as by a sign from God) indue him with the gifts fit for his office; and lastly did bless him. Then the neighboring

---

[1] Winthrop's geography, based on Indian reports imperfectly understood, is naturally confused.

[2] Thomas Leverett, father of John Leverett, eminent in the next generation.

ministers, which were present, did (at the pastor's motion) give him the right hands of fellowship, and the pastor made a stipulation between him and the congregation. When Mr. Cotton accepted of the office, he commended to the congregation such as were to come over, who were of his charge in England, that they might be comfortably provided for.

The same day, Mr. Grant, in the ship *James*, arrived at Salem, having been but eight weeks between Gravesend and Salem. He brought Capt. Wiggin and about thirty, with one Mr. Leveridge, a godly minister, to Pascataquack, (which the Lord Say and the Lord Brook had purchased of the Bristol men,) and about thirty for Virginia, and about twenty for this place, and some sixty cattle. He brought news, that the *Richard*, a bark of fifty tons, which came forth with the *Griffin*, being come above three hundred leagues, sprang such a leak, as she was forced to bear up, and was put in at Weymouth.

11.] A fast at Newtown, where Mr. Hooker was chosen pastor, and Mr. Stone teacher, in such a manner as before at Boston.

The wolves continued to do much hurt among our cattle; and this month, by Mr. Grant, there came over four Irish greyhounds, which were sent to the governor by Mr. Downing, his brother-in-law.

November.] A great mortality among the Indians. Chickatabot, the sagamore of Naponsett, died, and many of his people. The disease was the small pox. Some of them were cured by such means as they had from us; many of their children escaped, and were kept by the English.

Capt. Wiggin of Pascataquack wrote to the governor, that one of his people had stabbed another, and desired he might be tried in the bay, if the party died. The governor answered, that if Pascataquack lay within their limits, (as it was supposed,) they would try him.

A small ship of about sixty tons was built at Medford, and called the *Rebecca*.

This year a watermill was built at Roxbury, by Mr. Dummer.

The scarcity of workmen had caused them to raise their wages to an excessive rate, so as a carpenter would have three shillings the day, a laborer two shillings and sixpence, etc.; and accordingly those who had commodities to sell advanced their prices sometime double to that they cost in England, so as it grew to a general complaint, which the court, taking knowledge of, as also of some further evils, which were springing out of the excessive rates of wages, they made an order, that carpenters, masons, etc., should take but two shillings the day, and laborers but eighteen pence, and that no commodity should be sold at above four pence in the shilling more than it cost for ready money in England; oil, wine, etc., and cheese, in regard of the hazard of bringing, etc., [excepted]. The evils which were springing, etc., were: 1. Many spent much time idly, etc., because they could get as much in four days as would keep them a week. 2. They spent much in tobacco and strong waters, etc., which was a great waste to the commonwealth, which, by reason of so many foreign commodities expended, could not have subsisted to this time, but that it was supplied by the cattle and corn, which were sold to new comers at very dear rates, viz., corn at six shillings the bushel, a cow at £20,—yea, some at £24, some £26,—a mare at £35, an ewe goat at 3 or £4; and yet many cattle were every year brought out of England, and some from Virginia. Soon after order was taken for prices of commodities, viz., not to exceed the rate of four pence in the shilling above the price in England, except cheese and liquors, etc.

The ministers in the bay and Sagus did meet, once a fortnight, at one of their houses by course, where some question of moment was debated. Mr. Skelton, the pastor of Salem, and Mr. Williams,[1] who was removed from Plymouth thither, (but not in any office, though he exercised by way of prophecy,)

---

[1] Roger Williams here enters upon his career of criticism and dissent.

took some exception against it, as fearing it might grow in time to a presbytery or superintendency, to the prejudice of the churches' liberties. But this fear was without cause; for they were all clear in that point, that no church or person can have power over another church; neither did they in their meetings exercise any such jurisdiction, etc.

News of the taking of Machias by the French. Mr. Allerton of Plymouth, and some others, had set up a trading wigwam there, and left in it five men and store of commodities. La Tour, governor of the French in those parts, making claim to the place, came to displant them, and, finding resistance, killed two of the men, and carried away the other three, and the goods.

Some differences fell out still, now and then, between the governor and the deputy, which yet were soon healed. It had been ordered in court, that all hands should help to the finishing of the fort at Boston, and all the towns in the bay had gone once over, and most the second time; but those of Newtown being warned, the deputy would not suffer them to come, neither did acquaint the governor with the cause, which was, for that Salem and Sagus had not brought in money for their parts. The governor, hearing of it, wrote friendly to him, showing him that the intent of the court was, that the work should be done by those in the bay, and that, after, the others should pay a proportionable sum for the house, etc., which must be done by money; and therefore desired him that he would send in his neighbors. Upon this, Mr. Haynes and Mr. Hooker came to the governor to treat with him about it, and brought a letter from the deputy full of bitterness and resolution not to send till Salem, etc. The governor told them it should rest till the court, and withal gave the letter to Mr. Hooker with this speech: I am not willing to keep such an occasion of provocation by me. And soon after he wrote to the deputy (who had before desired to buy a fat hog or two of him, being somewhat short of provisions) to desire him to send for one, (which he would have sent him, if he had known when his occasion had been to have made use of it,) and to accept it as a testimony of his good will; and, lest he should make any scruple of it, he made Mr. Haynes and Mr. Hooker (who both sojourned in his house) partakers with him. Upon this the deputy returned this answer: "Your overcoming yourself hath overcome me. Mr. Haynes, Mr. Hooker, and myself, do most kindly accept your good will; but we desire, without offence, to refuse your offer, and that I may only trade with you for two hogs;" and so very lovingly concluded. —The court being two days after, ordered, that Newtown should do their work as others had done, and then Salem, etc., should pay for three days at eighteen pence a man.

11.] The congregation of Boston met to take order for Mr. Cotton's passage and house, and his and Mr. Wilson's maintenance. Mr. Cotton had disbursed eighty pounds for his passage, and towards his house, which he would not have again; so there was about £60 raised (by voluntary contribution) towards the finishing of his house, and about £100 towards their maintenance. At this meeting there arose some difference between the governor and Mr. Cottington, who charged the governor, that he took away the liberty of the rest, because (at the request of the rest) he had named some men to set out men's lands, etc., which grew to some heat of words; but the next Lord's day they both acknowledged openly their failing, and declared that they had been reconciled the next day.

26.] Mr. Wilson (by leave of the congregation of Boston, whereof he was pastor) went to Agawam to teach the people of that plantation, because they had yet no minister. Whiles he was there, December 4, there fell such a snow (knee deep) as he could not come back for [blank] days, and a boat, which went thither, was frozen up in the river.

December 5.] John Sagamore died of the small pox, and almost all his people; (above thirty buried by Mr. Maverick of Winesemett in one day). The towns in the bay took away many of the children; but most of them died soon after.

James Sagamore of Sagus died also, and most of his folks. John Sagamore desired to be brought among the English, (so he was;) and promised (if he recovered) to live with the English and serve their God. He left one son, which he disposed to Mr. Wilson, the pastor of Boston, to be brought up by him. He gave to the governor a good quantity of wampompeague, and to divers others of the English he gave gifts, and took order for the payment of his own debts and his men's. He died in a persuasion that he should go to the Englishmen's God. Divers of them, in their sickness, confessed that the Englishmen's God was a good God; and that, if they recovered, they would serve him.

It wrought much with them, that when their own people forsook them, yet the English came daily and ministered to them; and yet few, only two families, took any infection by it. Among others, Mr. Maverick[1] of Winesemett is worthy of a perpetual remembrance. Himself, his wife, and servants, went daily to them, ministered to their necessities, and buried their dead, and took home many of their children. So did other of the neighbors.

This infectious disease spread to Pascataquack, where all the Indians (except one or two) died.

One Cowper of Pascataquack, going to an island, upon the Lord's day, to fetch some sack to be drank at the great house, he and a boy, coming back in a canoe, (being both drunk,) were driven to sea and never heard of after.

At the same plantation, a company having made a fire at a tree, one of them said, Here this tree will fall, and here will I lie; and accordingly it fell upon him and killed him.

[1] This estimable man was on account of his Episcopal leanings looked upon askance in the community, where, though recognized as a man of substance and worth, he was given no public place. An evidence of the Puritan bitterness exists in the fact that Winthrop, or some successor, has in the manuscript drawn a pen through the word "perpetual" in the tribute to his humanity.

It pleased the Lord to give special testimony of his presence in the church of Boston, after Mr. Cotton was called to office there. More were converted and added to that church, than to all the other churches in the bay, (or rather the lake, for so it were more properly termed, the bay being that part of sea without between the two capes, Cape Cod and Cape Ann). Divers profane and notorious evil persons came and confessed their sins, and were comfortably received into the bosom of the church. Yea, the Lord gave witness to the exercise of prophecy, so as thereby some were converted, and others much edified. Also, the Lord pleased greatly to bless the practice of discipline, wherin he gave the pastor, Mr. Wilson, a singular gift, to the great benefit of the church.

After much deliberation and serious advice, the Lord directed the teacher, Mr. Cotton, to make it clear by the scripture, that the minister's maintenance, as well as all other charges of the church, should be defrayed out of a stock, or treasury, which was to be raised out of the weekly contribution; which accordingly was agreed upon.

27.] The governor and assistants met at Boston, and took into consideration a treatise, which Mr. Williams (then of Salem) had sent to them, and which he had formerly written to the governor and council of Plymouth, wherein, among other things, he disputes their right to the lands they possessed here, and concluded that, claiming by the king's grant, they could have no title, nor otherwise, except they compounded with the natives.[1] For this, taking advice with some of the most judicious ministers, (who much condemned Mr. Williams's error and presumption,) they gave order, that he should be convented at the next court, to be censured, etc. There were three passages chiefly whereat they were much offended: 1, for that he chargeth King James to have told a solemn public lie, because in his patent he blessed God that he was the first Christian prince that had discovered this land;

---

[1] A just and generous assertion of Indian rights.

2, for that he chargeth him and others with blasphemy for calling Europe Christendom, or the Christian world; 3, for that he did personally apply to our present king, Charles, these three places in the Revelations, viz., [*blank*].

Mr. Endecott being absent, the governor wrote to him to let him know what was done, and withal added divers arguments to confute the said errors, wishing him to deal with Mr. Williams to retract the same, etc. Whereto he returned a very modest and discreet answer. Mr. Williams also wrote to the governor, and also to him and the rest of the council, very submissively, professing his intent to have been only to have written for the private satisfaction of the governor, etc., of Plymouth, without any purpose to have stirred any further in it, if the governor here had not required a copy of him; withal offering his book, or any part of it, to be burnt.

At the next court he appeared penitently, and gave satisfaction of his intention and loyalty. So it was left, and nothing done in it.[1]

---

[1] Neither the character of Roger Williams nor the circumstances of the case, as far as we know them, allow us to believe that he abandoned his position.

1634

January 21.] News came from Plymouth, that Capt. Stone, who this last summer went out of the bay or lake, and so to Aquamenticus, where he took in Capt. Norton, putting in at the mouth of Connecticut, in his way to Virginia, where the Pequins inhabit, was there cut off by them, with all his company, being eight. The manner was thus: Three of his men, being gone ashore to kill fowl, were cut off. Then the sachem, with some of his men, came aboard, and staid with Capt. Stone in his cabin, till Capt. Stone (being alone with him) fell on sleep. Then he knocked him on the head, and all the rest of the English being in the cook's room, the Indians took such pieces as they found there ready charged, and bent them at the English; whereupon one took a piece, and by accident gave fire to the powder, which blew up the deck; but most of the Indians, perceiving what they went about, shifted overboard, and after they returned, and killed such as remained, and burned the pinnace. We agreed to write to the governor of Virginia, (because Stone was one of that colony,) to move him to revenge it, and upon his answer to take further counsel.

20.] Hall and the two others, who went to Connecticut November 3, came now home, having lost themselves and endured much misery. They informed us, that the small pox was gone as far as any Indian plantation was known to the west, and much people dead of it, by reason whereof they could have no trade.

At Naragansett, by the Indians' report, there died seven hundred; but, beyond Pascataquack, none to the eastward.

24.] The governor and council met again at Boston, to

consider of Mr. Williams's letter, etc., when, with the advice of Mr. Cotton and Mr. Wilson, and weighing his letter, and further considering of the aforesaid offensive passages in his book, (which, being written in very obscure and implicative phrases, might well admit of doubtful interpretation,) they found the matters not to be so evil as at first they seemed. Whereupon they agreed, that, upon his retractation, etc., or taking an oath of allegiance to the king, etc., it should be passed over.

An Englishman of Sacoe, travelling into the country to trade, was killed by the Indians.

30.] John Seales, who ran from his master to the Indians, came home again. He was at a place twelve miles off, where were seven Indians, whereof four died of the pox while he was there.

February 1.] Mr. Cradock's house at Marblehead was burnt down about midnight before, there being then in it Mr. Allerton, and many fishermen, whom he employed that season, who all were preserved by a special providence of God, with most of his goods therein, by a tailor, who sate up that night at work in the house, and, hearing a noise, looked out and saw the house on fire above the oven in the thatch.

This winter was very mild, little wind, and most S. and S. W. but oft snows, and great. One snow, the 15th of this month, was near two feet deep all over.

Such of the Indians' children as were left were taken by the English, most whereof did die of the pox soon after, three only remaining, whereof one, which the governor kept, was called Know-God, (the Indians' usual answer being, when they were put in mind of God, Me no know God).

22.] The grampus[1] came up towards Charlestown against the tide of ebb.

This season Mr. Allerton fished with eight boats at Marble Harbor.

[1] It is doubtful whether "grampus" means a ship, or the fish of that name.

By this time seventeen fishing ships were come to Richman's Isle and the Isles of Shoals.

March 4.] By order of court a mercate[1] was erected at Boston, to be kept upon Thursday, the fifth day of the week, being the lecture day. Samuel Cole set up the first house for common entertainment, and John Cogan, merchant, the first shop.

Upon offer of some new comers to give liberally towards the building of a galley for defence of the bay, and upon consultation with divers experienced seamen and others, it was thought fitter for our condition to build a vessel forty feet in length, and twenty-one in breadth, to be minion[2] proof, and the upper deck musket proof, to have one sail, and to carry whole culverin and other small pieces, eight in all. This was found to be so chargeable, and so long time ere it could be finished, that it was given over.

At this court all swamps, above one hundred acres, were made common, etc. Also Robert Cole, having been oft punished for drunkenness, was now ordered to wear a red D about his neck for a year.

7.] At the lecture at Boston a question was propounded about veils. Mr. Cotton concluded, that where (by the custom of the place) they were not a sign of the women's subjection, they were not commanded by the apostle. Mr. Endecott opposed, and did maintain it by the general arguments brought by the apostle. After some debate, the governor, perceiving it to grow to some earnestness, interposed, and so it brake off.

Among other testimonies of the Lord's gracious presence with his own ordinances, there was a youth of fourteen years of age (being the son of one of the magistrates) so wrought upon by the ministry of the word, as, for divers months, he was held under such affliction of mind, as he could not be brought to apprehend any comfort in God, being much hum-

---

[1] Market. [2] A small piece of ordnance.

bled and broken for his sins, (though he had been a dutiful child, and not given up to the lusts of youth,) and especially for his blasphemous and wicked thoughts, whereby Satan buffeted him, so as he went mourning and languishing daily; yet, attending to the means, and not giving over prayer, and seeking counsel, etc., he came at length to be freed from his temptations, and to find comfort in God's promises, and so, being received into the congregation, upon good proof of his understanding in the things of God, he went on cheerfully in a Christian course, falling daily to labor, as a servant, and as a younger brother of his did, who was no whit short of him in the knowledge of God's will, though his youth kept him from daring to offer himself to the congregation.[1]—Upon this occasion it is not impertinent (though no credit nor regard be to be had of dreams in these days) to report a dream, which the father of these children had at the same time, viz., that, coming into his chamber, he found his wife (she was a very gracious woman) in bed, and three or four of their children lying by her, with most sweet and smiling countenances, with crowns upon their heads, and blue ribbons about their leaves. When he awaked, he told his wife his dream, and made this interpretation of it, that God would take of her children to make them fellow heirs with Christ in his kingdom.

Satan bestirred himself to hinder the progress of the gospel, as, among other practices, appeared by this: He stirred up a spirit of jealousy between Mr. James, the pastor of Charlton, and many of his people, so as Mr. Nowell, and some others, who had been dismissed from Boston, began to question their fact of breaking from Boston, and it grew to such a principle of conscience among them, as the advice of the other ministers was taken in it, who, after two meetings, could not agree about their continuance or return.

One Mr. Morris, ensign to Capt. Underhill, taking some dis-

[1] Conjectured by Savage to have been the governor's son Deane.

taste in his office, requested the magistrates, that he might be discharged of it, and so was, whereby he gave offence to the congregation of Boston, so as, being questioned and convinced of sin in forsaking his calling, he did acknowledge his fault, and, at the request of the people, was by the magistrates chosen lieutenant to the same company, for he was a very stout man and an experienced soldier.

April 1.] Order was taken for ministering an oath to all house keepers and sojourners, being twenty years of age and not freemen, and for making a survey of the houses and lands of all freemen.

Notice being sent out of the general court to be held the 14th day of the third month, called May, the freemen deputed two of each town to meet and consider of such matters as they were to take order in at the same general court; who, having met, desired a sight of the patent, and, conceiving thereby that all their laws should be made at the general court, repaired to the governor to advise with him about it, and about the abrogating of some orders formerly made, as for killing of swine in corn, etc. He told them, that, when the patent was granted, the number of freemen was supposed to be (as in like corporations) so few, as they might well join in making laws; but now they were grown to so great a body, as it was not possible for them to make or execute laws, but they must choose others for that purpose: and that howsoever it would be necessary hereafter to have a select company to intend that work, yet for the present they were not furnished with a sufficient number of men qualified for such a business, neither could the commonwealth bear the loss of time of so many as must intend it. Yet this they might do at present, viz., they might, at the general court, make an order, that, once in the year, a certain number should be appointed (upon summons from the governor) to revise all laws, etc., and to reform what they found amiss therein; but not to make any new laws, but prefer their grievances to the court of assistants; and that no assessment should be laid upon the country without the consent of such a committee, nor any lands disposed of.[1]

3.] The governor went on foot to Agawam, and because the people there wanted a minister, spent the Sabbath with them, and exercised by way of prophecy, and returned home the 10th.

20.] John Coggeshall,[2] gentleman, being dismissed from the church of Roxbury to Boston, though he were well known and approved of the church, yet was not received but by confession of his faith, etc.

May 3.] News came of the death of Hockin and the Plymouth man at Kenebeck,[3] (and of the arrival of the ship at Pemaquid, which brought thirty passengers for this place).

The occasion of the death of those men at Kenebeck was this: The Plymouth men had a grant, from the grand patentees of New England, of Kenebeck, with liberty of sole trade, etc.

---

[1] On this beginning of representative government in Massachusetts, it is pertinent to quote Savage. "No country on earth can afford the perfect history of any event more interesting to its own inhabitants than that which is here related. Winthrop seems to have spoken like an absolute sovereign, designing to grant a favor to his subjects, by admitting them to a representation at court. Such was the origin of most of the assemblies, in other nations, of delegates of the people, by whom some influence of the majority is imparted to the government. . . . The very humble powers, he proposed that the representative should receive from his constituent, it is hardly necessary to add, were immediately transcended; and the assembly, as it ought, was ever afterwards by itself thought competent to the enaction of any regulation for the public welfare." He quotes from the *Records*, I. 115, the following action of the representatives: "It was further ordered, that it shall be lawful for the freemen of every plantation to choose two or three of each town, before every general court, to confer of and prepare such public business as by them shall be thought fit to consider of at the next general court; and that such persons as shall be hereafter so deputed by the freemen of [the] several plantations, to deal in their behalf in the public affairs of the commonwealth, shall have the full power and voice of all the said freemen derived to them for the making and establishing of laws, granting of lands, etc., and to deal in all other affairs of the commonwealth, wherein the freemen have to do, the matter of election of magistrates and other officers only excepted, wherein every freeman is to give his own voice."

[2] John Coggeshall, a man much trusted and esteemed, forfeited later the good-will of Massachusetts by his heterodoxy, and proceeding to Rhode Island, took a leading part in its affairs.

[3] See the account of the episode in Bradford, pp. 304-306.

The said Hockin came in a pinnace, belonging to the Lord Say and Lord Brook at Pascataquack, to trade at Kenebeck. Two of the magistrates of Plymouth, being there, forbad him; yet he went up the river; and, because he would not come down again, they sent three men in a canoe to cut his cables. Having cut one, Hockin presented a piece, and sware he would kill him that went to cut the other. They bad him do if he durst, and went on to cut it. Thereupon he killed one of them, and instantly one in the Plymouth pinnace (which rode by them, and wherein five or six men stood with their pieces ready charged) shot and killed Hockin.

15.] At the general court at Boston, upon the complaint of a kinsman of the said Hockin, John Alden, one of the said magistrates of Plymouth, who was present when Hockin was slain, being then at Boston, was called and bound with sureties not to depart out of our jurisdiction without leave had; and withal we wrote to Plymouth to certify them what we had done, and to know whether they would do justice in the cause, (as belonging to their jurisdiction,) and to have a speedy answer, etc. This we did, that notice might be taken, that we did disavow the said action, which was much condemned of all men, and which was feared would give occasion to the king to send a general governor over; and besides had brought us all and the gospel under a common reproach of cutting one another's throats for beaver.

By this time the fort at Boston was in defence, and divers pieces of ordnance mounted in it.

Those of Newtown complained of straitness for want of land, especially meadow, and desired leave of the court to look out either for enlargement or removal, which was granted; whereupon they sent men to see Agawam and Merimack, and gave out they would remove, etc.

14.] At the general court, Mr. Cotton preached, and delivered this doctrine, that a magistrate ought not to be turned into the condition of a private man without just cause, and to be publicly convict, no more than the magistrates may not turn a private man out of his freehold, etc., without like public trial, etc. This falling in question in the court, and the opinion of the rest of the ministers being asked, it was referred to further consideration.

The court chose a new governor, viz., Thomas Dudley, Esq., the former deputy; and Mr. Ludlow was chosen deputy; and John Haines, Esq., an assistant, and all the rest of the assistants chosen again.

At this court it was ordered, that four general courts should be kept every year, and that the whole body of the freemen should be present only at the court of election of magistrates, etc., and that, at the other three, every town should send their deputies, who should assist in making laws, disposing lands, etc.[1] Many good orders were made this court. It held three days, and all things were carried very peaceably, notwithstanding that some of the assistants were questioned by the freemen for some errors in their government, and some fines imposed, but remitted again before the court brake up. The court was kept in the meeting-house at Boston, and the new governor and the assistants were together entertained at the house of the old governor, as before.

The week the court was, there came in six ships, with store of passengers and cattle.

Mr. Parker, a minister, and a company with him, being

[1] The changes here mentioned were for the little colony quite revolutionary. The election of Dudley to the chief place, and the coming into power of the popular deputies, were acquiesced in by Winthrop, whose ideas were not democratic, with much moderation of spirit. He writes at a later time: "The best part of a community is always the least, and of that best part the wiser is always the lesser." (Savage's *Winthrop*, II. 428.) Cotton, too, condemned democracy. In 1636 he wrote Lord Say: "Democracy, I do not conceive that ever God did ordain as a fit government either for church or commonwealth. If the people be governor who shall be governed? As for monarchy and aristocracy, they are both of them clearly approved and directed in scripture, yet so as referreth the sovereignty to himself and setteth up theocracy in both, as the best form of government in the commonwealth as in the church." Hutchinson, *History of Massachusetts*, I. 497, Appendix III.

about one hundred, went to sit down at Agawam, and divers others of the new comers.

One [blank,] a godly minister, upon conscience of his oath and care of the commonwealth, discovered to the magistrates some seditious speeches of his own son, delivered in private to himself; but the court thought not fit to call the party in question then, being loath to have the father come in as a public accuser of his own son, but rather desired to find other matter, or other witness against him.

24.] Mr. Fleming, master of a ship of Barnstable, went hence to the eastward to cut masts there, and so to return to England. There returned with him Ensign Motham and another.

These ships, by reason of their short passage, had store of provisions left, which they put off at easy rates, viz. biscuit at 20s. the hundred; beef at £6 the hogshead, etc.

Newtown men, being straitened for ground, sent some to Merimack to find a fit place to transplant themselves

June 1.] The *Thunder*, which went to Bermuda the 17th October, now returned, bringing corn and goats from Virginia, (for the weavils had taken the corn at Bermuda before they came there). Ensign Jenyson went in her for pilot, and related, at his return, that there was a very great change in Bermuda since he dwelt there, divers lewd persons being become good Christians. They have three ministers, (one a Scotchman,) who take great pains among them, and had lately (by prayer and fasting) dispossessed one possessed with a devil. They obtained his recovery while the congregation were assembled.

He brought news, also, of a great ship arrived in Patomack River in Virginia, with a governor and colony sent by the Lord Bartimore, who was expected there shortly himself, and that they resisted those of Virginia, who came to trade in that river.

It appeared after, that the king had written to Sir John Harvey, knight, governor of Virginia, to give all assistance to that new plantation, which was called Maryland by the queen of England; and those who came over were, many of them, Papists, and did set up mass openly.

July.] The *Hercules* of Dover returned by St. George's to cut masts to carry to England.

The last month arrived here fourteen great ships, and one at Salem.

Mr. Humfrey[1] and the lady Susan, his wife, one of the Earl of Lincoln's sisters, arrived here. He brought more ordnance, muskets, and powder, bought for the public by moneys given to that end; for godly people in England began now to apprehend a special hand of God in raising this plantation, and their hearts were generally stirred to come over. Among others, we received letters from a godly preacher, Mr. Levinston a Scotchman in the north of Ireland, whereby he signified, that there were many good Christians in those parts resolved to come hither, if they might receive satisfaction concerning some questions and propositions which they sent over. Likewise, Mr. Humfrey brought certain propositions from some persons of great quality and estate, (and of special note for piety,) whereby they discovered their intentions to join with us, if they might receive satisfaction therein. It appeared further, by many private letters, that the departure of so many of the best, both ministers and Christians, had bred sad thoughts in those behind of the Lord's intentions in this work, and an apprehension of some evil days to come upon England. Then it began now to be apprehended by the archbishops, and others of the council, as a matter of state, so as they sent out warrant to stay the ships, and to call in our patent; but, upon petition of the shipmasters, (attending how beneficial

---

[1] John Humfrey or Humphrey, who was interested in New England from the beginning, and had been long expected, now arrived with his wife, sister of the Lady Arbella Johnson. Much was expected from his wealth and influence, and he was immediately made assistant. Lacking resolution and experiencing ill-luck, he played no great part. Settling in Lynn, he lost his home by fire and at length, disheartened, abandoned the country.

this plantation was to England) in regard of the Newfoundland fishing, which they took in their way homeward, the ships were at that time released. But Mr. Cradock (who had been governor in England before the government was sent over) had strict charge to deliver in the patent; whereupon he wrote to us to send it home. Upon receipt of his letter, the governor and council consulted about it, and resolved to answer Mr. Cradock's letter, but not to return any answer or excuse to the council at that time.

For the success of the passengers and cattle in the ships: Divers of the ships lost many cattle; but the two which came from Ipswich, of more than one hundred and twenty, lost but seven. None of the ships lost any passengers, but the *Elizabeth Dorcas*, which, having a long passage, and being hurt upon a rock at Scilly, and very ill victualled, she lost sixty passengers at sea, and divers came sick on shore, who all recovered, (through the mercy of God,) except [*blank*].

Mr. Humfrey brought sixteen heifers given by a private friend, viz. Mr. Richard Andrews,[1] to the plantation, viz. to every of the ministers one, and the rest to the poor, and one half of the increase of the ministers' to be reserved for other ministers. Mr. Wilson, so soon as he had his, gave it to Mr. Cotton. By Mr. Humfrey's means much money was procured, and divers promised yearly pensions.

Six of Newtown went in the *Blessing*, (being bound to the Dutch plantation,) to discover Connecticut River, intending to remove their town thither.

9.] Mr. Bradford and Mr. Winslow, two of the magistrates of Plymouth, with Mr. Smith, their pastor, came to Boston by water, to confer with some of our magistrates and ministers about their case of Kenebeck. There met hereabout Mr. Winthrop, Mr. Cotton, and Mr. Wilson, and after they had

[1] "Of the liberality of this distinguished friend of Massachusetts and Plymouth colonies, further notice will occur in our progress. He was an alderman of the city; and Thomas, probably his brother, became mayor of London." (Savage.)

sought the Lord, they fell first upon some passages which they had taken some offence at, but those were soon cleared. Then for the matter itself, it fell into these two points: 1, whether their right of trade there were such, as they might lawfully hinder others from coming there; 2, admitting that, whether in point of conscience, they might so far stand upon their right as to take away or hazard any man's life in defence of it.

For the first, their right appeared to be good; for that, besides the king's grant, they had taken up that place as vacuum domicilium, and so had continued, without interruption or claim of any of the natives, for divers years; and also had, by their charge and providence, drawn down thither the greatest part of the trade, by carrying wampampeage thither, which none of the English had known the use of before. For the second, they alleged, that their servant did kill Hockin to save other of their men, whom he was ready to have shot. Yet they acknowledged, that they did hold themselves under guilt of the breach of the sixth commandment, in that they did hazard man's life for such a cause, and did not rather wait to preserve their right by other means, which they rather acknowledged, because they wished it were not done; and hereafter they would be careful to prevent the like.

The governor and Mr. Winthrop wrote their letters into England to mediate their peace, and sent them by Mr. Winslow.

Sir Ferdinando Gorges and Capt. Mason sent [blank] to Pascataquack and Aquamenticus, with two sawmills, to be erected, in each place one.

Mr. Cradock wrote to the governor and assistants, and sent a copy of the council's order, whereby we were required to send over our patent. Upon long consultation whether we should return answer or not, we agreed, and returned answer to Mr. Cradock, excusing that it could not be done but by a general court, which was to be holden in September next.[1]

[1] Cradock's letter was of a character to awaken grave apprehensions.

Mr. Winthrop, the late governor, received a letter from the Earl of Warwick, wherein he congratulated the prosperity of our plantation, and encouraged our proceedings, and offered his help to further us in it.

29.] The governor and council, and divers of the ministers, and others, met at Castle Island,[1] and there agreed upon erecting two platforms and one small fortification to secure them both, and, for the present furtherance of it, they agreed to lay out £5 a man till a rate might be made at the next general court. The deputy, Roger Ludlow, was chosen overseer of this work.

August 2.] Mr. Samuel Skelton, pastor of Salem, died.

4.] At the court, the new town at Agawam was named Ipswich, in acknowledgment of the great honor and kindness done to our people which took shipping there, etc.; and a day of thanksgiving appointed, a fortnight after, for the prosperous arrival of the others, etc.

A letter was delivered to Mr. Winthrop by Mr. Jeffery, an old planter, written to him from Morton, wherein he related, how he had obtained his long suit, and that a commission was granted for a general governor to be sent over, with many railing speeches and threats against this plantation, and Mr. Winthrop in particular. Mr. Winthrop acquainted the governor and council with it, and some of the ministers.

This summer was hotter than many before.

12.] About midnight, one Craford, (who came this summer,) with his brother and servant, having put much goods in a small boat in Charles River, over against Richard Brown his house, overset the boat with the weight of some hogsheads, (as was supposed,) so as they were all three drowned; yet one of them could swim well, and though the neighbors came running forth, instantly, upon their cry, yet none could be saved.

Our neighbors of Plymouth and we had oft trade with the Dutch at Hudson's River, called by them New Netherlands.

[1] Still so called, in Boston harbor.

We had from them about forty sheep, and beaver, and brass pieces, and sugar, etc., for sack, strong waters, linen cloth, and other commodities. They have a great trade of beaver,—about nine or ten thousand skins in a year. Our neighbors of Plymouth had great trade also this year at Kenebeck, so as Mr. Winslow carried with him into England, this year, about twenty hogsheads of beaver, the greatest part whereof was traded for wampampeage.

One pleasant passage happened, which was acted by the Indians. Mr. Winslow, coming in his bark from Connecticut to Narigansett—and he left her there,—and intending to return by land, he went to Osamekin[1] the sagamore, his old ally, who offered to conduct him home to Plymouth. But, before they took their journey, Osamekin sent one of his men to Plymouth to tell them that Mr. Winslow was dead; and directed him to show how and where he was killed. Whereupon there was much fear and sorrow at Plymouth. The next day, when Osamekin brought him home, they asked him why he sent such word, etc. He answered, that it was their manner to do so, that they might be more welcome when they came home.

19.] Mr. Bradford and Mr. Collier of Plymouth came to Boston, having appointed a meeting here the week before, but by reason of foul weather were driven back. They had written to Capt. Wiggin of Pascataquack about the meeting for hearing the cause of Hockin's death.

Corn was this year at four shillings the bushel, and some at three shillings, and some cheaper.

29.] The *Dove*, a pinnace of about fifty tons,[2] came from Maryland upon Patomack River, with corn, to exchange for fish and other commodities. The governor, Leonard Calvert, and two of the commissioners, wrote to the governor here,

---

[1] Osamekin, thus naïvely mendacious, was Massasoit, it will be remembered.

[2] The *Ark* and *Dove*, ship and pinnace, had in the preceding spring brought to Maryland its first colonists.

to make offer of trade of corn, etc., and the governor of Virginia wrote also on their behalf, and one Capt. Young wrote to make offer to deliver cattle here. Near all their company came sick hither, and the merchant died within one week after.

September 4.] The general court began at Newtown, and continued a week, and then was adjourned fourteen days. Many things were there agitated and concluded, as fortifying in Castle Island, Dorchester, and Charlestown; also against tobacco, and costly apparel, and immodest fashions; and committees appointed for setting out the bounds of towns; with divers other matters, which do appear upon record. But the main business, which spent the most time, and caused the adjourning of the court, was about the removal of Newtown. They had leave, the last general court, to look out some place for enlargement or removal, with promise of having it confirmed to them, if it were not prejudicial to any other plantation; and now they moved, that they might have leave to remove to Connecticut.[1] This matter was debated divers days, and many reasons alleged pro and con. The principal reasons for their removal were, 1. Their want of accommodation for their cattle, so as they were not able to maintain their ministers, nor could receive any more of their friends to help them; and here it was alleged by Mr. Hooker, as a fundamental error, that towns were set so near each to other.

2. The fruitfulness and commodiousness of Connecticut, and the danger of having it possessed by others, Dutch or English.

3. The strong bent of their spirits to remove thither.

Against these it was said, 1. That, in point of conscience, they ought not to depart from us, being knit to us in one body, and bound by oath to seek the welfare of this commonwealth.

---

[1] This record of the discussion preceding a most important undertaking is of great interest. For an intelligent "reading between the lines" as to the settlement of Connecticut, see Johnston, *Connecticut*, ch. III. Hooker may have felt that he and John Cotton could hardly dwell together in the same community in peace. The more democratic spirit also of the outgoing man was plainly evident in what presently followed.

2. That, in point of state and civil policy, we ought not to give them leave to depart. 1. Being we were now weak and in danger to be assailed. 2. The departure of Mr. Hooker would not only draw many from us, but also divert other friends that would come to us. 3. We should expose them to evident peril, both from the Dutch (who made claim to the same river, and had already built a fort there) and from the Indians, and also from our own state at home, who would not endure they should sit down without a patent in any place which our king lays claim unto.

3. They might be accommodated at home by some enlargement which other towns offered.

4. They might remove to Merimack, or any other place within our patent.

5. The removing of a candlestick is a great judgment, which is to be avoided.

Upon these and other arguments the court being divided, it was put to vote; and, of the deputies, fifteen were for their departure, and ten against it. The governor and two assistants were for it, and the deputy and all the rest of the assistants were against it, (except the secretary, who gave no vote;) whereupon no record was entered, because there were not six assistants in the vote, as the patent requires. Upon this grew a great difference between the governor and assistants, and the deputies. They would not yield the assistants a negative voice, and the others (considering how dangerous it might be to the commonwealth, if they should not keep that strength to balance the greater number of the deputies) thought it safe to stand upon it. So, when they could proceed no farther, the whole court agreed to keep a day of humiliation to seek the Lord, which accordingly was done, in all the congregations, the 18th day of this month; and the 24th the court met again. Before they began, Mr. Cotton preached, (being desired by all the court, upon Mr. Hooker's instant excuse of his unfitness for that occasion). He took his text out of Hag. ii. 4, etc., out of which he laid down the nature or strength (as he termed it) of the magistracy, ministry, and people, viz.,—the strength of the magistracy to be their authority; of the people, their liberty; and of the ministry, their purity; and showed how all of these had a negative voice, etc., and that yet the ultimate resolution, etc., ought to be in the whole body of the people, etc., with answer to all objections, and a declaration of the people's duty and right to maintain their true liberties against any unjust violence, etc., which gave great satisfaction to the company. And it pleased the Lord so to assist him, and to bless his own ordinance, that the affairs of the court went on cheerfully; and although all were not satisfied about the negative voice to be left to the magistrates, yet no man moved aught about it, and the congregation of Newtown came and accepted of such enlargement as had formerly been offered them by Boston and Watertown; and so the fear of their removal to Connecticut was removed.

At this court Mr. Goodwin, a very reverend and godly man, being the elder of the congregation of Newtown, having, in heat of argument, used some unreverend speech to one of the assistants, and being reproved for the same in the open court, did gravely and humbly acknowledge his fault, etc.

18.] At this court were many laws made against tobacco, and immodest fashions, and costly apparel, etc., as appears by the Records; and £600[1] raised towards fortifications and other charges, which were the more hastened, because the *Griffin* and another ship now arriving with about two hundred passengers and one hundred cattle, (Mr. Lothrop and Mr. Simmes, two godly ministers, coming in the same ship,)[2] there

---

[1] "The apportionment," says Savage, "is worth transcribing from the *Records*, I. 128, as, we may be confident, it represents the relative wealth of the settlements: 'Boston, Dorchester, and Newtown, each, £80; Roxbury, £70; Watertown, £60; Saugus and Ipswich, each, £50; Salem and Charlestown, each, £45; Medford, £26; Wessaguscus, £10; Barecove, £4.'"

[2] Most celebrated among the passengers, though not mentioned here, was Anne Hutchinson, now soon to declare herself.

came over a copy of the commission granted to the two archbishops and ten others of the council, to regulate all plantations, and power given them, or any five of them, to call in all patents, to make laws, to raise tythes and portions for ministers, to remove and punish governors, and to hear and determine all causes, and inflict all punishments, even death itself, etc.[1] This being advised from our friends to be intended specially for us, and that there were ships and soldiers provided, given out as for the carrying the new governor, Capt. Woodhouse, to Virginia, but suspected to be against us, to compel us, by force, to receive a new governor, and the discipline of the church of England, and the laws of the commissioners,—occasioned the magistrates and deputies to hasten our fortifications, and to discover our minds each to other; which grew to this conclusion, viz.[2]

At this court, as before, the assistants had their diet at the governor's at Newtown, and the first day all the deputies. He had £100 allowed him for his charges, and £500 more was raised towards fortifications, etc.

30.] About this time one Alderman, of Bear Cove, being about fifty years old, lost his way between Dorchester and Wessaguscus, and wandered in the woods and swamps three days and two nights, without taking any food, and, being near spent, God brought him to Scituate; but he had torn his legs much, etc. Other harm he had none.

October 5.] It being found, that the four lectures did spend too much time, and proved over burdensome to the ministers and people, the ministers, with the advice of the magistrates, and with consent of their congregations, did agree to reduce them to two days, viz., Mr. Cotton at Boston one

---

[1] This commission may be seen in Bradford, this series, pp. 415-419.
[2] How far the colony had abandoned the temper shown in the *Farewell to the Church of England*, of three years before, Winthrop's entry makes plain, though the "conclusion" is not stated. It would have gone hard with Puritanism in New England, had not King and bishops now begun to feel the heat of a back-fire at home.

Thursday, or the 5th day of the week, and Mr. Hooker at Newtown the next 5th day, and Mr. Warham at Dorchester one 4th day of the week, and Mr. Welde at Roxbury the next 4th day.

Mr. Lathrop, who had been pastor of a private congregation in London, and for the same kept long time in prison, (upon refusal of the oath ex-officio,)[1] being at Boston upon a sacrament day, after the sermon, etc., desired leave of the congregation to be present at the administration, etc., but said that he durst not desire to partake in it, because he was not then in order, (being dismissed from his former congregation,) and he thought it not fit to be suddenly admitted into any other, for example sake, and because of the deceitfulness of man's heart. He went to Scituate, being desired to be their pastor.

14.] It was informed the governor, that some of our people, being aboard the bark of Maryland, the sailors did revile them, calling them holy brethren, the members, etc., and withal did curse and swear most horribly, and use threatening speeches against us. The governor wrote to some of the assistants about it, and, upon advice with the ministers, it was agreed to call them in question; and to this end (because we knew not how to get them out of their bark) we apprehended the merchant of the ship, being on shore, and committed him to the marshal, till Mr. Maverick came and undertook that the offenders should be forthcoming. The next day (the governor not being well) we examined the witnesses, and found them fall short of the matter of threatening, and not to agree about the reviling speeches, and, beside, not able to design certainly the men that had so offended. Whereupon (the bark staying only upon this) the bail was discharged, and a letter written to the master, that, in regard such disorders were com-

---

[1] The oath ex-officio, a part of the procedure of the court of high commission, was used to elicit confession from clergymen suspected of tendencies toward nonconformity.

mitted aboard his ship, it was his duty to inquire out the offenders and punish them; and withal to desire him to bring no more such disordered persons among us.

Mr. Wilson's hay, being stacked up not well dried, fell on fire, to his great prejudice at this season; fired by his own servants, etc., as they intended to prevent firing.

The weather was very fine and hot, without rain, near six weeks.

The Lords Say and Brook wrote to the governor and Mr. Bellingham,[1] that howsoever they might have sent a man of war to beat down the house at Kenebeck, for the death of Hockin, etc., yet they thought better to take another course; and therefore desired that some of ours might be joined with Capt. Wiggin, their agent at Pascataquack, to see justice done, etc.

20.] Six men of Salem, going on fowling in a canoe, were overset near Kettle Island, and five of them drowned.

November 5.] At the court of assistants complaint was made by some of the country, (viz., Richard Brown of Watertown, in the name of the rest,) that the ensign at Salem was defaced, viz. one part of the red cross taken out. Upon this, an attachment was awarded against Richard Davenport, ensign-bearer, to appear at the next court to answer. Much matter was made of this, as fearing it would be taken as an act of rebellion, or of like high nature, in defacing the king's colors; though the truth were, it was done upon this opinion, that the red cross was given to the king of England by the pope, as an ensign of victory, and so a superstitious thing, and a relique of antichrist.[2] What proceeding was hereupon, will

---

[1] Richard Bellingham, afterward governor, a man contentious and more democratic than many, survived to a great age—his life being, as Hubbard says, "a long thread of above eighty years." His talents were adapted less for eloquence than advice, "like a vessel whose vent holds no good proportion with its capacity." Hubbard, *General History of New England*, quoted by Savage.

[2] The picturesque incident here referred to, than which scarcely any other incident of early New English history is better known, was a bold defiance of King and Church, who at this time were threatening heavily.

appear after, at next court, in the first month; (for, by reason of the great snows and frosts, we used not to keep courts in the three winter months).

The *Rebecka* came from Narigansett with five hundred bushels of corn given to Mr. John Oldham. The Indians had promised him one thousand bushels, but their store fell out less than they expected. They gave him also an island in the Narigansett Bay, called Chippacursett, containing about one thousand acres, six miles long, and two miles broad. This is a very fair bay, being above twelve leagues square, with divers great islands in it, a deep channel close to the shore, being rocky. Mr. Peirce took the height there, and found it forty-one degrees, forty-one minutes, being not above half a degree to the southward of us. In his voyage to and fro, he went over the shoals, having, most part, five or six fathom, within half a mile and less of the shore from the north part of Cape Cod to Natuckett[1] Island, which is about twenty leagues—and, in the shallowest place, two and an half fathom. The country on the west of the Bay of Naragansett is all champaign for many miles, but very stony, and full of Indians. He saw there above one thousand men, women, and children, yet the men were many abroad on hunting. Natuckett is an island full of Indians, about ten leagues in length east and west.

6.] There came to the deputy governor, about fourteen days since, a messenger from the Pekod sachem, to desire our friendship.[2] He brought two bundles of sticks, whereby he signified how many beaver and otter skins he would give us for that end, and great store of wampompeage, (about two bushels, by his description). He brought a small present with him, which the deputy received, and returned a moose coat of as good value, and withal told him, that he must send persons

[1] Nantucket.

[2] The contact with the Pequots thus described marks a critical time. These savages were of a fiercer character than the New England tribes in general, a recent intrusion into Connecticut from west of the Hudson of a sept probably allied with the Mohawks. Johnston, *Connecticut*, p. 28.

of greater quality, and then our governor would treat with them. And now there came two men, who brought another present of wampompeage. The deputy brought them to Boston, where most of the assistants were assembled, by occasion of the lecture, who, calling to them some of the ministers, grew to this treaty with them: That we were willing to have friendship etc.; but because they had killed some Englishmen, viz. Capt. Stone, etc., they must first deliver up those who were guilty of his death, etc. They answered, that the sachem, who then lived, was slain by the Dutch, and all the men, who were guilty, etc., were dead of the pox, except two, and that if they were worthy of death, they would move their sachem to have them delivered, (for they had no commission to do it;) but they excused the fact, saying that Capt. Stone, coming into their river, took two of their men and bound them, and made them show him the way up the river, which when they had done, he with two others and the two Indians, (their hands still bound,) went on shore, and nine of their men watched them, and when they were on sleep in the night, they killed them; then going towards the pinnace to have taken that, it suddenly blew up into the air. This was related with such confidence and gravity, as, having no means to contradict it, we inclined to believe it. But, the governor not being present, we concluded nothing; but some of us went with them the next day to the governor.

The reason why they desired so much our friendship was, because they were now in war with the Naragansetts, whom, till this year, they had kept under, and likewise with the Dutch, who had killed their old sachem and some other of their men, for that the Pekods had killed some Indians, who came to trade with the Dutch at Connecticut; and, by these occasions, they could not trade safely any where. Therefore they desired us to send a pinnace with cloth, and we should have all their trade.

They offered us also all their right at Connecticut, and to

further us what they could, if we would settle a plantation there.

When they came to the governor, they agreed, according to the former treaty, viz. to deliver us the two men, who were guilty of Capt. Stone's death, when we would send for them; to yield up Connecticut; to give us four hundred fathom of wampompeage, and forty beaver, and thirty otter skins; and that we should presently send a pinnace with cloth to trade with them, and so should be at peace with them, and as friends to trade with them, but not to defend them, etc.

The next morning news came, that two or three hundred of the Naragansetts were come to Cohann, viz. Neponsett, to kill the Pekod ambassadors, etc. Presently we met at Roxbury, and raised some few men in arms, and sent to the Naragansett men to come to us. When they came there were no more but two of their sachems, and about twenty more, who had been on hunting thereabouts, and came to lodge with the Indians at Cohann, as their manner is. So we treated with them about the Pekods, and, at our request, they promised they should go and come to and from us in peace, and they were also content to enter further treaty of peace with them; and in all things showed themselves very ready to gratify us. So the Pekods returned home, and the Naragansetts departed well satisfied; only they were told in private, that if they did make peace with the Pekods, we would give them part of that wampompeage, which they should give us; (for the Pekods held it dishonorable to offer them any thing as of themselves, yet were willing we should give it them, and indeed did offer us so much for that end).

The agreement they made with us was put in writing, and the two ambassadors set to their marks—one a bow with an arrow in it, and the other a hand.

13.] The *Regard*, a ship of Barnstable, of about two hundred tons, arrived with twenty passengers and about fifty cattle.

One thing I think fit to observe, as a witness of God's providence for this plantation. There came in this ship one Mansfield, a poor godly man of Exeter, being very desirous to come to us, but not able to transport his family. There was in the city a rich merchant, one Marshall, who being troubled in his dreams about the said poor man, could not be quiet till he had sent for him, and given him £50, and lent him £100, willing him withal, that, if he wanted, he should send to him for more. This Mansfield grew suddenly rich, and then lost his godliness, and his wealth soon after.

18.] About this time an open pinnace of one Mr. Sewall[1] of Ipswich, going deep laden from Boston, was cast away upon the rocks at the head of Cape Ann, in a N. E. storm; but all the men were saved.

21.] One Willys, a godly man, and member of Boston church, and one Dorety, an honest man, and two boys, going over to Noddle's Island to fetch wood, in a small boat, and none of them having any skill or experience, were cast away in a N. E. tempest, as they came home in the night laden, being then ebbing water. We sent two boats on the Lord's day, (so soon as they were missing, being the 23d,) but they could not find men, or boat, or wood, in any part of the bay. Three days after, the boat was found at Muddy River, overturned.

27.] The assistants met at the governor's, to advise about the defacing of the cross in the ensign at Salem, where (taking advice with some of the ministers) we agreed to write to Mr. Downing in England, of the truth of the matter, under all our hands, that, if occasion were, he might show it in our excuse; for therein we expressed our dislike of the thing, and our purpose to punish the offenders, yet with as much wariness as we might, being doubtful of the lawful use of the cross in an

---

[1] The ancestor of a distinguished and widely distributed American family, of which the famous chief-justice, in the next generation, was the most interesting Massachusetts member.

ensign, though we were clear that fact,[1] as concerning the matter, was very unlawful.

It was then informed us, how Mr. Eliot, the teacher of the church of Roxbury, had taken occasion, in a sermon, to speak of the peace made with the Pekods, and to lay some blame upon the ministry for proceeding therein, without consent of the people, and for other failings, (as he conceived). We took order, that he should be dealt with by Mr. Cotton, Mr. Hooker, and Mr. Welde, to be brought to see his error, and to heal it by some public explanation of his meaning; for the people began to take occasion to murmur against us for it.[2]

It was likewise informed, that Mr. Williams of Salem had broken his promise to us, in teaching publickly against the king's patent, and our great sin in claiming right thereby to this country, etc., and for usual terming the churches of England antichristian. We granted summons to him for his appearance at the next court.[3]

The aforesaid three ministers, upon conference with the said Mr. Eliot, brought him to acknowledge his error in that he had mistaken the ground of his doctrine, and that he did acknowledge, that, for a peace only, (whereby the people were not to be engaged in a war,) the magistrates might conclude, *plebe inconsulto,* and so promised to express himself in public next Lord's day.

24.] One Scott and Eliot of Ipswich were lost in their way homewards, and wandered up and down six days, and eat nothing. At length they were found by an Indian, being almost senseless for want of rest, etc.

About the same time one [blank] was twenty-one days

---

[1] Fact in the sense of action, Lat. *factum.*

[2] Eliot probably knew well the character of the Pequots, and remonstrated as a friend of the Massachusetts Indians, with whom his relations were becoming close, and whose welfare was seriously threatened. Evidently his disposition was more democratic than that of some of his contemporaries.

[3] An evidence that Roger Williams meant to be just, though sometimes his judgments were strained.

upon Plumb Island, and found by chance frozen in the snow, yet alive, and did well. He had been missing twenty days, and himself said he had no food all that time.

December 4.] Was an extraordinary tempest of wind and snow, at N. N. E. which continued twenty-four hours, and after that such frost as, within two days, the whole bay was frozen over, but free again before night.

11.] The lectures at Boston and Newtown returned again to their former course, because the weather was many times so tedious as people could not travel, etc.

This day, after the lecture, the inhabitants of Boston met to choose seven men who should divide the town lands among them. They chose by papers,[1] and in their choice left out Mr. Winthrop, Coddington, and other of the chief men; only they chose one of the elders and a deacon, and the rest of the inferior sort, and Mr. Winthrop had the greater number before one of them by a voice or two. This they did, as fearing that the richer men would give the poorer sort no great proportions of land, but would rather leave a great part at liberty for new comers and for common, which Mr. Winthrop had oft persuaded them unto, as best for the town, etc. Mr. Cotton and divers others were offended at this choice, because they declined the magistrates; and Mr. Winthrop refused to be one upon such an election as was carried by a voice or two, telling them, that though, for his part, he did not apprehend any personal injury, nor did doubt of their good affection towards him, yet he was much grieved that Boston should be the first who should shake off their magistrates, especially Mr. Coddington,[2] who had been always so forward for their en-

[1] *I. e.*, by secret ballot.
[2] William Coddington, already mentioned, served as colonial treasurer and as assistant. Winthrop and Cotton here strongly disapproved the public action which left out of the commission for the distribution of the lands, a worthy magistrate. Coddington before long departed as an exile to Aquidneck, where he lived until nearly fourscore, the most eminent citizen of Rhode Island, a fellow-spirit of Roger Williams at Providence. But he grew weary at last of his radical environment.

largement; adding further reason of declining this choice, to blot out so bad a precedent. Whereupon, at the motion of Mr. Cotton, who showed them, that it was the Lord's order among the Israelites to have all such businesses committed to the elders, and that it had been nearer the rule to have chosen some of each sort, etc., they all agreed to go to a new election, which was referred to the next lecture day.

The reason why some were not willing that the people should have more land in the bay than they might be likely to use in some reasonable time, was partly to prevent the neglect of trades, and other more necessary employments, and partly that there might be place to receive such as should come after; seeing it would be very prejudicial to the commonwealth, if men should be forced to go far off for land, while others had much, and could make no use of it, more than to please their eye with it.

One Abigail Gifford, widow, being kept at the charge of the parish of Wilsden in Middlesex, near London, was sent by Mr. Ball's ship into this country, and being found to be sometimes distracted, and a very burdensome woman, the governor and assistants returned her back by warrant, 18, to the same parish, in the ship *Rebecca*.

22.] A fast was kept by the church of Charlton, and Mr. Symmes chosen their teacher.

By a letter from Plymouth it was certified, that the Dutch of Hudson's River had been at Connecticut, and came in warlike manner to put the Plymouth men out of their house there; but when they stood upon their defence, they departed, without offering any violence.

1635

11 mo. 13.[1] The church of Boston kept a day of humiliation for the absence of their pastor and other brethren, gone to England, and like to be troubled and detained there, and for that the Lord had made a breach upon them by those four which were drowned, as is before set down; at which fast Mr. Cotton preached out of Numbers xxxv. 13, and one of the members taught out of that in Lamentations iii. 39: Wherefore doth a living man complain?

19.] All the ministers, except Mr. Ward[2] of Ipswich, met at Boston, being requested by the governor and assistants, to consider of these two cases: 1. What we ought to do, if a general governor should be sent out of England? 2. Whether it be lawful for us to carry the cross in our banners?—In the first case, they all agreed, that, if a general governor were sent, we ought not to accept him, but defend our lawful possessions, (if we were able;) otherwise to avoid or protract. For the matter of the cross, they were divided, and so deferred it to another meeting.

About the middle of this month, Mr. Allerton's pinnace came from the French about Port Royal. They went to fetch

---

[1] Here for the first time the author abandons the Roman names of the months, substituting in accordance with Puritan sentiment a system of numbering, beginning with March as the first month. In this edition the more familiar names of the months are inserted in italics. The date above is for January 13, 1634/5.

[2] Nathaniel Ward, minister of Ipswich, author of the *Body of Liberties*, presently to be mentioned, was a most curious and racy personality. He was bred a lawyer, but taking orders, was deprived for non-conformity, and came to New England in 1634. Though quite in accord with his contemporaries in orthodoxy, and the special spokesman of the prevailing intolerance, he stands in refreshing contrast with the exaggerated gravity and dulness of so many of his brethren. See Tyler, *American Literature*, I. 271. His *Simple Cobler of Aggawam* Savage calls "very attractive for its humor, and curious for its execrable spirit."

the two men, which had been carried by the French from Machias, and to demand the goods taken, etc. But Mr. La Tout made them answer, that he took them as lawful prize, and that he had authority from the king of France, who challenged all from Cape Sable to Cape Cod, wishing them to take notice, and to certify the rest of the English, that, if they traded to the east of Pemaquid, he would make prize of them. Being desired to show his commission, he answered, that his sword was commission sufficient, where he had strength to overcome; where that wanted, he would show his commission.[1]

In the end of this month, three men had their boat frozen up at Bird Island, as they were coming from Deer Island, so as they were compelled to lodge there all night; and in the morning they came over the ice to Noddle's Isle, and thence to Molten's Point in Charlestown, and thence over the ice, by Mr. Hoffe's, to Boston. At the same time six others were kept a week at the Governor's Garden; and in the end gate with their boat to Mattapan Point; for, near all that time, there was no open place between the Garden and Boston, neither was there any passing at Charlestown for two or three days, the wind about the N. W. three weeks, with much snow and extreme frost.[2]

Mo. 12. (*February.*)] About the middle of this month, a proper young man, servant to Mr. Bellingham, passing over

---

[1] Massachusetts, in particular Boston, stood from this time forward in the fore-front of the English settlements as they faced the French. The latter came at last to call English colonists in general "Bostonnais"; and so late as our Revolution, George Rogers Clark in the far West found that the French and savages confronting him had been incited "to fight Boston." At the present moment, two Frenchmen, La Tour and d'Aulnay, had been appointed to govern the French claim, the jurisdiction of the former extending east of the St. Croix River; of the latter, to the west. As the western limits of "Acadie" were quite undetermined, disputes early arose with the English on the Maine coast. La Tour and d'Aulnay presently also fell out between themselves. The relations of Massachusetts with these two men were very trying, and occasion some of Winthrop's liveliest pages. Winsor, *Memorial History of Boston*, I. 282.

[2] Bird Island has disappeared. The Governor's Garden was no doubt the present Governor's Island. To a large extent the localities of the harbor retain their ancient names.

the ice to Winnesemett, fell in, and was drowned. Divers others fell in, in that and other places, but, by God's providence, were saved.

14.] Capt. Wiggin, governor at Pascataquack, under the Lords Say and Brook, wrote to our governor, desiring to have two men tried here, who had committed sodomy with each other, and that on the Lord's day, in time of public exercise. The governor and divers of the assistants met and conferred about it, but did not think fit to try them here.

Mo. 1. (*March*) 4.] A general court at Newtown. Mr. Hooker preached, and showed the three great evils.

At this court, one of the deputies[1] was questioned for denying the magistracy among us, affirming that the power of the governor was but ministerial, etc. He had also much opposed the magistrates, and slighted them, and used many weak arguments against the negative voice, as himself acknowledged upon record. He was adjudged by all the court to be disabled for three years from bearing any public office.

One of the assistants was called to the lower end of the table to answer for refusing to pay towards a rate made by the court, and was fined £5, which was after released.

Mr. Endecott was called to answer for defacing the cross in the ensign; but, because the court could not agree about the thing, whether the ensigns should be laid by, in regard that many refused to follow them, the whole cause was deferred till the next general court; and the commissioners for military affairs gave order, in the mean time, that all the ensigns should be laid aside, etc.

---

[1] This deputy, so democratic in his ideas, was Israel Stoughton, who later returning to England, rose to a lieutenant-colonelcy among the Ironsides. His son William was the first lieutenant-governor under the charter of William and Mary, and chief-justice during the witch-trials, where he shared in the delusion to which few of his contemporaries were superior. He is more honorably remembered for his gift to Harvard College, where Stoughton Hall perpetuates his name.

At this court brass farthings were forbidden, and musket bullets made to pass for farthings.

A commission for military affairs was established, which had power of life and limb, etc.[1]

15.] Two of the elders of every church met at Sagus, and spent there three days. The occasion was, that divers of the brethren of that church, not liking the proceedings of the pastor, and withal making question, whether they were a church or not, did separate from church communion. The pastor and other brethren desired the advice and help of the rest of the churches, who, not thinking fit to judge of the cause, without hearing the other side, offered to meet at Sagus about it. Upon this the pastor, etc., required the separate members to deliver their grievances in writing, which they refusing to do, the pastor, etc., wrote to all the churches, that, for this cause, they were purposed to proceed against them as persons excommunicated; and therefore desired them to stay their journey, etc. This letter being read at a lecture at Boston, (where some of the elders of every church were present,) they all agreed (with consent of their churches) to go presently to Sagus, to stay this hasty proceeding, etc. Accordingly, being met, and both parties (after much debate) being heard, it was agreed, that they were a true church, though not constituted, at first, in due order, yet after consent and practice of a church estate had supplied that defect; and so all were reconciled.

Mo. 2. (*April.*)] Some of our people went to Cape Cod, and made some oil of a whale, which was cast on shore. There were three or four cast up, as it seems there is almost every year.

26.] An alarm was raised in all our towns, and the governor and assistants met at Boston, and sent forth a shallop to Cape Ann, to discover what ships were there. For the fishermen had brought in word to Marblehead, that two ships had been hovering upon the coast all the day; one of about four

---

[1] For a full account of the great power granted this commission, see *Massachusetts Colonial Records*, I. 139.

hundred tons, and the other three hundred and fifty, and were gone in to Cape Ann. But it proved to be only one ship of eighty tons, bound for Richman's Isle, and the other a small pinnace of ten tons.

30.] The governor and assistants sent for Mr. Williams. The occasion was, for that he had taught publicly, that a magistrate ought not to tender an oath to an unregenerate man, for that we thereby have communion with a wicked man in the worship of God, and cause him to take the name of God in vain. He was heard before all the ministers, and very clearly confuted. Mr. Endecott was at first of the same opinion, but he gave place to the truth.

Mo. 3. (*May*) 6.] A general court was held at Newtown, where John Haynes, Esq., was chosen governor, Richard Bellingham, Esq., deputy governor, and Mr. Hough and Mr. Dummer chosen assistants to the former; and Mr. Ludlow, the late deputy, left out of the magistracy. The reason was, partly, because the people would exercise their absolute power, etc., and partly upon some speeches of the deputy, who protested against the election of the governor as void, for that the deputies of the several towns had agreed upon the election before they came, etc. But this was generally discussed, and the election adjudged good.

Mr. Endecott was also left out, and called into question about the defacing the cross in the ensign; and a committee was chosen, viz., every town chose one, (which yet were voted by all the people,) and the magistrates chose four, who, taking the charge to consider of the offence, and the censure due to it, and to certify the court, after one or two hours time, made report to the court, that they found his offence to be great, viz., rash and without discretion, taking upon him more authority than he had, and not seeking advice of the court, etc.; uncharitable, in that he, judging the cross, etc., to be a sin, did content himself to have reformed it at Salem, not taking care that others might be brought out of it also; laying a blemish also upon the rest of the magistrates, as if they would suffer idolatry, etc., and giving occasion to the state of England to think ill of us;—for which they adjudged him worthy admonition, and to be disabled for one year from bearing any public office; declining any heavier sentence, because they were persuaded he did it out of tenderness of conscience, and not of any evil intent.[1]

Some petitions of grievances were tendered to the court in the beginning of it, but the court refused to hear any, or to meddle in any courses but making freemen, until the elections were passed. The governor and deputy were elected by papers, wherein their names were written; but the assistants were chosen by papers, without names, viz. the governor propounded one to the people; then they all went out, and came in at one door, and every man delivered a paper into a hat. Such as gave their vote for the party named, gave in a paper with some figures or scroll in it; others gave in a blank.

The new governor, in his speech to the people, declared his purpose to spare their charge towards his allowance this year, partly in respect of their love showed towards him, and partly for that he observed how much the people had been pressed lately with public charges, which the poorer sort did much groan under.[2]

A petition was preferred by many of Dorchester, etc., for releasing the sentence against Mr. Stoughton the last general court; but it was rejected, and the sentence affirmed by the country to be just.

Divers jealousies, that had been between the magistrates and deputies, were now cleared, with full satisfaction to all parties.

The matter of altering the cross in the ensign was referred to the next meeting, (the court being adjourned for three

[1] That spirits like Williams and Endicott, extremists in different directions, caused constant anxiety to the wary and tactful leaders is in these years often evidenced.

[2] The well-to-do Haynes could no doubt afford to perform this gracious act.

weeks,) it being propounded to turn it to the red and white rose, etc., and every man was to deal with his neighbors, to still their minds, who stood so stiff for the cross, until we should fully agree about it, which was expected, because the ministers had promised to take pains about it, and to write into England, to have the judgments of the most wise and godly there.

The deputies having conceived great danger to our state, in regard that our magistrates, for want of positive laws, in many cases, might proceed according to their discretions, it was agreed that some men should be appointed to frame a body of grounds of laws, in resemblance to a Magna Charta, which, being allowed by some of the ministers, and the general court, should be received for fundamental laws.

At this general court, some of the chief of Ipswich desired leave to remove to Quascacunquen, to begin a town there, which was granted them, and it was named Newberry.

Also, Watertown and Roxbury had leave to remove whither they pleased, so as they continued under this government. The occasion of their desire to remove was, for that all towns in the bay began to be much straitened by their own nearness to one another, and their cattle being so much increased.

21.] A Dutch ship of one hundred and sixty tons arrived at Marblehead. Capt. Hurlston came merchant. She came from Christopher Island. She brought one hundred and forty tons of salt, and ten thousand weight of tobacco.

This island lies in eighteen degrees, and is about thirty miles in compass, inhabited by two colonies, one English and another French. There is in it about four thousand persons. They have three English churches, but the people are very wicked, as the merchant (who dwelt there five years) complained. The salt is made with the sun in a natural pan, half a mile from the sea. Their rain begins in September, and continues till February.

Mo. 4. (*June*) 3.] Here arrived two Dutch ships, who brought twenty-seven Flanders mares, at £34 a mare, and three horses; sixty-three heifers, at £12 the beast; and eighty-eight sheep, at 50s. the sheep. They came from the Tessell[1] in five weeks three days, and lost not one beast or sheep. Here arrived also, the same day, the *James*, a ship of three hundred tons, with cattle and passengers, which came all safe from Southampton within the same time. Mr. Graves was master, who had come every year for these seven years. 7. The Lord's day there came in seven other ships, and one to Salem, and four more to the mouth of the bay, with store of passengers and cattle. They came all within six weeks.

For preventing the loss of time, and drunkenness, which sometimes happened, by people's running to the ships, and the excessive prices of commodities, it was ordered, that one in each town should buy for all, etc., and should retail the same within twenty days at five per hundred, if any came to buy in that time. But this took no good effect; for most of the people would not buy, except they might buy for themselves; and the merchants appointed could not disburse so much money, etc.; and the seamen were much discontented, yet some of them brought their goods on shore and sold them there.

16.] A bark of forty tons arrived, set forth with twenty servants, by Sir Richard Saltonstall, to go plant at Connecticut.

By a letter from the Lord Say, and report of divers passengers, it was certified to us, that Capt. Mason and others, the adversaries of this colony, had built a great ship to send over the general governor, etc., which, being launched, fell in sunder in the midst.

It appeared likewise, by a copy of a petition sent over to us, that they had divided all this country of New England, viz. between St. Croix in the east, and that of Lord Bartimore, called Maryland, into twelve provinces, disposed to twelve in

---

[1] Texel, North Holland.

England, who should send each ten men to attend the general governor coming over; but the project [took] not effect. The Lord frustrated their design.[1]

Two carpenters, going to wash themselves in the river between Mount Woollaston and Wessaguscus, were carried away with the tide, and drowned.

24.] Mr. Graves, in the *James*, and Mr. Hodges, in the *Rebecka*, set sail for the Isle of Sable for sea-horse (which are there in great number) and wild cows. Mr. John Rose, being cast ashore there in the [*Mary and Jane*] two years since, and making a small pinnace of the wreck of his ship, sailed thence to the French upon the main, being thirty leagues off, by whom he was detained prisoner, and forced to pilot them to the island, where they had great store of sea-horse teeth, and cattle, and store [of] black foxes; and they left seventeen men upon the island to inhabit it. The island is thirty miles long, two miles broad in most places, a mere sand, yet full of fresh water in ponds, etc. He saw about eight hundred cattle, small and great, all red, and the largest he ever saw, and many foxes, whereof some perfect black. There is no wood upon it, but store of wild peas and flags by the ponds, and grass. In the middle of it is a pond of salt water, ten miles long, full of plaice, soles, etc. The company, which went now, carried twelve landmen, two mastiffs, a house, and a shallop.

August 26.] They returned from their voyage. They found there upon the island sixteen Frenchmen, who had wintered there, and built a little fort, and had killed some black foxes. They had killed also many of the cattle, so as they found not above one hundred and forty, and but two or three calves. They could kill but few sea-horse, by reason they were forced to travel so far in the sand as they were too weak to stick them, and they came away at such time as they used to go up

[1] The friends of Sir Ferdinando Gorges were too much engrossed at home to aid in this sweeping obliteration of what had been established. For the *quo warranto* writ issued against Massachusetts, see *Hutchinson Papers*, ed. 1865, I. 114.

highest to eat green peas. The winter there is very cold, and the snow above knee deep.

Mo. 5. (*July*) 8.] At the general court, Mr. Williams of Salem was summoned, and did appear. It was laid to his charge, that, being under question before the magistracy and churches for divers dangerous opinions, viz. 1, that the magistrate ought not to punish the breach of the first table, otherwise than in such cases as did disturb the civil peace; 2, that he ought not to tender an oath to an unregenerate man; 3, that a man ought not to pray with such, though wife, child, etc.; 4, that a man ought not to give thanks after the sacrament nor after meat, etc.; and that the other churches were about to write to the church of Salem to admonish him of these errors; notwithstanding the church had since called him to [the] office of a teacher. Much debate was about these things. The said opinions were adjudged by all, magistrates and ministers, (who were desired to be present,) to be erroneous, and very dangerous, and the calling of him to office, at that time, was judged a great contempt of authority. So, in fine, time was given to him and the church of Salem to consider of these things till the next general court, and then either to give satisfaction to the court, or else to expect the sentence; it being professedly declared by the ministers, (at the request of the court to give their advice,) that he who should obstinately maintain such opinions, (whereby a church might run into heresy, apostacy, or tyranny, and yet the civil magistrate could not intermeddle,) were to be removed, and that the other churches ought to request the magistrates so to do.

At this court Wessaguscus was made a plantation, and Mr. Hull, a minister in England, and twenty-one families with him, allowed to sit down there—after called Weymouth.

A plantation was likewise erected at Bear's Cove, after called Hingham.

12.] Mr. Luxon arrived here in a small pinnace. He fished at the Isle of Shoals, as he had done many years, and, returning to sell his fish at market, was taken in foggy weather, and carried into the bay of Port Royal, and there wrecked upon a small island about [blank] leagues from the main. So he built a pinnace, and came hither in her.[1]

Salem men had preferred a petition, at the last general court, for some land in Marblehead Neck, which they did challenge as belonging to their town; but, because they had chosen Mr. Williams their teacher, while he stood under question of authority, and so offered contempt to the magistrates, etc., their petition was refused till, etc. Upon this the church of Salem write to other churches, to admonish the magistrates of this as a heinous sin, and likewise the deputies; for which, at the next general court, their deputies were not received until they should give satisfaction about the letter.

Mo. 6. Aug. 16.] The wind having blown hard at S. and S. W. a week before, about midnight it came up at N. E. and blew with such violence, with abundance of rain, that it blew down many hundreds of trees, near the towns, overthrew some houses, [and] drave the ships from their anchors. The *Great Hope*, of Ipswich, being about four hundred tons, was driven on ground at Mr. Hoff's Point, and brought back again presently by a N. W. wind, and ran on shore at Charlestown. About eight of the clock the wind came about to N. W. very strong, and, it being then about high water, by nine the tide was fallen about three feet. Then it began to flow again about one hour, and rose about two or three feet, which was conceived to be, that the sea was grown so high abroad with the N. E. wind, that, meeting with the ebb, it forced it back again.

This tempest was not so far as Cape Sable, but to the south more violent, and made a double tide all that coast.

[1] The ship-captains, messengers back and forth across the sea, and guides and protectors of those who came over, were naturally held in great respect, no doubt with good reason, for only bold and skilful men were adequate to the navigation. They were accorded the title of "Mr.," which in those days meant something. Luxon appears as master of the *Fellowship*, of 170 tons.

In this tempest, the *James* of Bristol, having one hundred passengers,[1] honest people of Yorkshire, being put into the Isle of Shoals, lost there three anchors; and, setting sail, no canvas nor ropes would hold, but she was driven within a cable's length of the rocks at Pascataquack, when suddenly the wind, coming to N. W., put them back to the Isle of Shoals, and, being there ready to strike upon the rocks, they let out a piece of their mainsail, and weathered the rocks. In the same tempest a bark of Mr. Allerton's was cast away upon Cape Ann, and twenty-one persons drowned; among the rest one Mr. Avery, a minister in Wiltshire, a godly man, with his wife and six small children, were drowned. None were saved but one Mr. Thacher and his wife, who were cast on shore, and preserved by a powder horn and a bag with a flint, and a goat and a cheese, cast on shore after them, and a truss of bedding, and some other necessaries: and the third day after a shallop came thither to look for another shallop, which was missing in the storm, and so they were preserved. So as there did appear a miraculous providence in their preservation. The general court gave Mr. Thacher £26.13.4, towards his losses, and divers good people gave him besides. The man was cast on shore, when he had been (as he thought) a quarter of an hour beaten up and down by the waves, not being able to swim one stroke; and his wife sitting in the scuttle of the bark, the deck was broke off, and brought on shore, as she stuck in it. One of the children was then cast dead on shore, and the rest never found.[2]

Gabriel lost at Pemaquid; and Mr. Witheridge and the

[1] Among these storm-tost people was Rev. Richard Mather, from Lancashire, ancestor of the famous Mather family. Of the voyage in which he so nearly perished, he kept an interesting diary, preserved in Young, *Chronicles of Massachusetts*, XXII.

[2] The sufferings of Parsons Avery and Thacher are described by Cotton Mather in an interesting and characteristic passage (*Magnalia*, book I., ch. II.). Here we are told that these outer ledges were named from the event *Avery's Fall* and *Thacher's Woe*, names not yet forgotten. Parson Avery of Newbury and his "swan-song" find noble commemoration in the ballad of Whittier.

Dartmouth ships cut all their masts at St. George. The tide rose at Naragansett fourteen feet higher than ordinary, and drowned eight Indians flying from their wigwams.

At this time a French ship came with commission from the king of France, (as they pretended,) and took Penobscott, a Plymouth trading house, and sent away the men which were in it, but kept their goods and gave them bills for them, and bad them tell all the plantations, as far as forty degrees, that they would come with eight ships, next year, and displant them all. But, by a letter which the captain wrote to the governor of Plymouth, it appeared they had commission from Mons. Roselly,[1] commander at the fort near Cape Breton, called La Havre, to displant the English as far as Pemaquid, and by it they professed all courtesy to us here.

Mr. Williams, pastor of Salem, being sick and not able to speak, wrote to his church a protestation, that he could not communicate with the churches in the bay; neither would he communicate with them, except they would refuse communion with the rest; but the whole church was grieved herewith.

The Dorchester men being set down at Connecticut, near the Plymouth trading house, the governor, Mr. Bradford, wrote to them, complaining of it as an injury, in regard of their possession and purchase of the Indians, whose right it was, and the Dutch sent home into Holland for commission to deal with our people at Connecticut.[2]

September 1.] At this general court was the first grand jury, who presented above one hundred offences, and, among others, some of the magistrates.

At this court Mr. Endecott made a protestation in justification of the letter formerly sent from Salem to the other churches against the magistrates and deputies, for which he was committed; but, the same day, he came and acknowledged his fault, and was discharged.

[1] Claude Razilly, governor of Acadia and Canada.
[2] See Bradford, in this series, p. 325.

Divers lewd servants (viz., six) ran away, and stole a skiff and other things. A commission was granted, at the general court, to Capt. Trask to fetch them and other such from the eastward. He pursued them to the Isle of Shoals, and so to Pascataquack, where, in the night, he surprised them in a house, and brought them to Boston. At next court they were severely whipped, and ordered to pay all charges, etc.

At this court there was granted to Mr. Buckly and [*blank*]¹ merchant, and about twelve more families, to begin a town at Musketaquid, for which they were allowed six miles upon the river, and to be free from public charges three years; and it was named Concord. A town was also begun above the falls of Charles River.

At the Dutch plantation, this summer, a ship's long boat was overset with a gust, and five men in her, who gat upon her keel, and were driven to sea four days, in which time three of them dropt off and were drowned; and the fifth day the fourth, being sore beaten, and pained with hunger and thirst, wilfully fell off and was drowned. Soon after the wind came up at S. E. and carried the boat, with the fifth man, to the Long Island, and, being only able to creep on shore, he was found by the Indians, and preserved. He was grown very poor, and almost senseless, with hunger and watching, and

---

¹ This was the Rev. Peter Bulkeley, who with Major Simon Willard now founded the first town beyond tide-water, Concord. Bulkeley came from Bedfordshire, a youth of good family, a fellow of St. John's College, Cambridge, and later married to a gentlewoman whose nephew was Thomas Allen, lord mayor of London. Late in life, a second wife was daughter of Sir Richard Chitwood. In the well-placed Puritan families, alliance with the ministers was held desirable and honorable. Bulkeley, though of quick temper, was greatly respected, and from his ample estate was liberal to Harvard College and to his indentured servants. The founders of Concord were twelve families who seem to have followed Simon Willard from Kent. It was an excellent stock, the names of the settlers appearing and reappearing in historical and literary connections down to the present moment. Cotton Mather, *Magnalia*, part II., ch. x., compares Bulkeley to Farel, the Genevan divine, *quo nemo tonuit fortius*, than whom no one thundered louder.

would say, that he saw such and such come to give him meat, etc.[1]

The Plymouth men had hired the *Great Hope,* to go to displant the French, and regain their possession at Penobscott. The master, Mr. Girling, was to have for it £200. They sent their bark with him and about twenty men; but when they came, they found the French had notice, and had so strongly intrenched themselves, (being eighteen,) as, having spent near all their powder and shot, the bark left the ship there, and came here to advise with us what further to do; for they had lately lost another bark laden with corn, and could not spare this to send back again. The general court, being assembled, agreed to aid them with men and munition, and therefore wrote to them to send one with commission to treat with us about it, resolving to drive them out, whatsoever it should cost, (yet first to put them to bear the charge, if it might be;) for we saw that their neighborhood would be very dangerous to us.[2]

The next week they sent Mr. Prence and Capt. Standish to us, with commission to treat. Four of the commissioners gave them a meeting, which grew to this issue,—that they refused to deal further in it, otherwise than as a common cause of the whole country, and so to contribute their part. We refused to deal in it, otherwise than as in their aid, and so at their charge; for indeed we had then no money in the treasury, neither could we get provision of victuals, on the sudden, for one hundred men, which were to be employed. So we deferred all to further counsel.[3]

Mo. 8. (*October*) 6.] Two shallops, going laden with goods

---

[1] The episode is graphically described in the "Voyages of David Pieterszoon de Vries"; see *Collections of the New York Historical Society,* second series, III. 75. The boat's crew belonged to de Vries's ship.

[2] See Bradford, pp. 319–321.

[3] The pressure from the French had a certain good effect in causing the English colonies to stand closely together. The Dutch, though looked on with jealousy, were, as Protestants, less objectionable than the Catholic neighbors.

to Connecticut, were taken in the night with an easterly storm, and cast away upon Brown's Island, near the Gurnett's Nose, and the men all drowned.[1]

Here arrived two great ships, the *Defence* and the *Abigail*, with Mr. Wilson, pastor of Boston, Mr. Shepard, Mr. Jones, and other ministers; amongst others, Mr. Peter, pastor of the English church in Rotterdam, who, being persecuted by the English ambassador,—who would have brought his and other churches to the English discipline,—and not having had his health these many years, intended to advise with the ministers here about his removal.[2]

[1] The island has nearly disappeared, a dangerous shoal remaining, on which from Burial Hill in Plymouth, one to-day may see the surf beating.

[2] These were important arrivals, the freight of the two ships counting for much, and several of the personages on board surpassing in consequence all but two or three of their predecessors. Thomas Shepard, of Emmanuel College, Cambridge, soon took the place of Hooker at Newtown, and was a light of especial brilliancy. Though but thirty years old he soon made a great name, dying, however, in his prime before his usefulness was fully rounded. Wilson always affected powerfully his environment, and the younger John Winthrop was only inferior to his father as a state-founder. No man was more profoundly involved in the currents of this troubled time, as well in Europe as in America, than the Rev. Hugh Peter, or Peters. He landed in Boston, a man of thirty-seven, already widely experienced and distinguished. A boy from Cornwall he came to Trinity College, Cambridge, and at once after attaining maturity became a famous preacher, drawing great crowds at St. Sepulchre's, in London. He went to Germany in the Thirty Years' War to see Gustavus Adolphus and afterward settled at Rotterdam as friend and successor of Dr. William Ames, a Puritan worthy of the first rank. Adopting the principles of the Independents, he at last sought New England, his steps thitherward being hastened perhaps by the fact that through his wife he was allied with the Winthrops. From the first he played a leading part, helping the colony more through an energetic pushing of practical schemes—fisheries, ship-building, trade enterprises—than by his professional ministrations. In the church his spirit was less liberal than it afterward became among different surroundings. Particular acts of his may be disapproved, but on the whole the colony was much the better from his being in it. After his return to England in 1641, his life became in the highest degree eventful. He threw himself as an Independent into the Civil War, showing surpassing power as a preacher, but using his practical ability and narrative skill in the most varied ways. Fairfax and Cromwell valued his counsel and used his executive ability. He was the especial *bête noire* of the cavaliers and Presbyterians, who regarded him as a character almost infernal. Yet to individual opponents he often showed great kindness, and did much to ameliorate the horrors of war. Through clouds of unmeasured abuse, we at this distance

The special goodness of the Lord appeared in this, that the passengers came safe and hale in all [the] ships, though some of them long passages,—the *Abigail* ten weeks from Plymouth, with two hundred and twenty persons, and many cattle, infected also with the small pox; yet, etc. There came also John Winthrop, the younger, with commission from the Lord Say, Lord Brook, and divers other great persons in England, to begin a plantation at Connecticut, and to be governor there. They sent also men and ammunition, and £2000 in money, to begin a fortification at the mouth of the river.

Here came also one Mr. Henry Vane,[1] son and heir to Sir

can make out a figure beset with limitations, but endowed with large ability, intense zeal and sincerity, who strove to good purpose for worthy ends. At the Restoration he was a particular mark for vengeance, it being alleged that he and Cornet Joyce were the masked headsmen who did duty on the scaffold at the execution of Charles I. This he denied, and also many other accusations; the prosecution was pitiless, and he perished in 1660 through unspeakable humiliation and torture. Firth, in the *Dictionary of National Biography, s. v.*

[1] Henry Vane, for his abilities, his heroic life and death, his services to Anglo-Saxon freedom, which make him a significant figure even to the present moment, may well be regarded as the most illustrious character who touches early New England history. While his personal contact with America was only for a brief space, his life became a strenuous upholding of American ideas: if government of, by, and for the people is the principle which English-speaking men feel especially bound to maintain, the life and death of Vane contributed powerfully to cause this idea to prevail. He was born in 1612, of an ancient lineage, his father being famed as a diplomatist and statesman, a courtier favored by both king and queen. Though Vane was scarcely beyond boyhood, he had travelled widely in Europe, seen much of great men and events, and shown independence of character by embracing austere Puritanism, thus sacrificing his prospects and incurring the displeasure of friends. His course in New England, which Winthrop will describe, though showing boyish indiscretion and shortcoming, is prophetic of great things both as to his force and high purpose. Returning to England after less than two years' stay, he becomes the friend of Pym, Hampden, Milton and Cromwell, and in due time, as his adversary Baxter puts it, became "within the Long Parliament that which Cromwell was without," the recognized leader. Republican ideas sprang up first among the rank and file of the victorious Ironsides, but Vane embraced them in due time, striving in the forefront for popular government during the era of the Commonwealth. Long the warm friend of Cromwell, he parted from Cromwell when the latter at last despaired of popular government. He sought for England not freedom alone but order as well, maintaining in *The Healing Question* that by a people's

Henry Vane, comptroller of the king's house, who, being a young gentleman of excellent parts, and had been employed by his father (when he was ambassador) in foreign affairs; yet, being called to the obedience of the gospel, forsook the honors and preferments of the court, to enjoy the ordinances of Christ in their purity here. His father, being very averse to this way, (as no way savoring the power of religion,) would hardly have consented to his coming hither, but that, acquainting the king with his son's disposition and desire, he commanded him to send him hither, and gave him license for three years' stay here.

This noble gentleman, having order from the said lords and others, treated with the magistrates here, and those who were to go to Connecticut, about the said design of the lords, to this issue,—that either the three towns gone thither should give place, upon full satisfaction, or else sufficient room must be found there for the lords and their companions, etc., or else they would divert their thoughts and preparations some other ways.

November 1.] Mr. Vane was admitted a member of the church of Boston.

October.] At this general court, Mr. Williams, the teacher at Salem, was again convented, and all the ministers in the bay being desired to be present, he was charged with the said two letters,—that to the churches, complaining of the magistrates for injustice, extreme oppression, etc., and the other to his own church, to persuade them to renounce communion with all the churches in the bay, as full of antichristian pollution, etc. He justified both these letters, and maintained all his opinions; and, being offered further conference or disputation, and a month's respite, he chose to dispute presently.

---

convention "fundamentals" should be laid down for the guidance and restraint of the law-makers—a written constitution therefore framed according to the American idea. He went down fighting to the last in a struggle that was premature, sealing his faith by martyrdom in 1662. See Firth, in the *Dictionary of National Biography*, and lives of Vane by Sikes, Upham, Forster, Ireland, and Hosmer.

So Mr. Hooker was appointed to dispute with him, but could not reduce him from any of his errors. So, the next morning, the court sentenced him to depart out of our jurisdiction within six weeks, all the ministers, save one, approving the sentence; and his own church had him under question also for the same cause; and he, at his return home, refused communion with his own church, who openly disclaimed his errors, and wrote an humble submission to the magistrates, acknowledging their fault in joining with Mr. Williams in that letter to the churches against them, etc.

15.] About sixty men, women, and little children, went by land toward Connecticut with their cows, horses, and swine, and, after a tedious and difficult journey, arrived safe there.

The pinnace, which Sir Richard Saltonstall sent to take possession of a great quantity of land at Connecticut, was, in her return into England, cast away upon the Isle Sable. The men were kindly entertained by the French there, and had passage to Le Havre, some twenty leagues east of Cape Sable, where Monsieur commander of Roselle[1] was governor, who entertained them very courteously, and furnished them with a shallop to return to us, and gave four of their company passage into France, but made them pay dear for their shallop; and in their return, they put into Penobscot, at such time as Girling's ship lay there; so that they were kept prisoners there till the ship was gone, and then sent to us with a courteous letter to our governor. A little before, our governor had written to him, (viz. Mons. D'Aulnay,) to send them home to us; but they were come before.

It is useful to observe, as we go along, such especial providences of God as were manifested for the good of these plantations.

Mr. Winslow, the late governor of Plymouth, being this

[1] The Chevalier Rasilly was chief governor of Acadia, La Tour and d'Aulnay, already mentioned, being his subordinates. Winsor, *Memorial History of Boston*, I. 283.

year in England, petitioned the council there for a commission to withstand the intrusions of the French and Dutch, which was likely to take effect, (though undertaken by ill advice, for such precedents might endanger our liberty, that we should do nothing hereafter but by commission out of England;) but the archbishops, being incensed against him, as against all these plantations, informed the rest, that he was a separatist, etc., and that he did marry, etc., and thereupon gate him committed; but, after some few months, he petitioned the board, and was discharged.

Another providence was in the voyage of Mr. Winthrop, the younger, and Mr. Wilson into England, who, returning in the winter time, in a small and weak ship, bound for Barnstaple, were driven by foul weather upon the coast of Ireland, not known by any in the ship, and were brought, through many desperate dangers, into Galloway, where they parted, Mr. Winthrop taking his journey over land to Dublin, and Mr. Wilson by sea, and being come within sight of Lundy, in the mouth of Severn, they were forced back by tempest to Kinsale, where some ships perished in their view. Mr. Wilson, being in Ireland, gave much satisfaction to the Christians there about New England.

Mr. Winthrop went to Dublin, and from thence to Antrim in the north, and came to the house of one Sir John Clotworthy,[1] the evening before the day when divers godly persons were appointed to meet at his house, to confer about their voyage to New England, by whom they were thoroughly informed of all things, and received great encouragement to proceed on in their intended course. From thence he passed over into Scotland, and so through the north of England; and all the way he met with persons of quality, whose thoughts were towards New England, who observed his coming among them as a special providence of God.

---

[1] Sir John Clotworthy became eminent later as a member of the Long Parliament.

November 3.] At the court of assistants, John Pratt of Newtown was questioned about the letter he wrote into England, wherein he affirmed divers things, which were untrue and of ill report, for the state of the country, as that here was nothing but rocks, and sands, and salt marshes, etc. He desired respite for his answer to the next morning; then he gave it in writing, in which, by making his own interpretation of some passages, and acknowledging his error in others, he gave satisfaction. This was delivered in under his own hand, and the hands of Mr. Hooker and some of the ministers, and satisfaction acknowledged under the hands of the magistrates.

Mr. Winthrop, jun., the governor appointed by the lords for Connecticut, sent a bark of thirty tons, and about twenty men, with all needful provisions, to take possession of the mouth of Connecticut, and to begin some building.

9.] About this time an open pinnace, returning from Connecticut, was cast away in Manemett Bay; but all the men (being six) were saved, and came to Plymouth, after they had wandered ten days in extreme cold and deep snow, not meeting with any Indian or other person.

26.] There came twelve men from Connecticut. They had been ten days upon their journey, and had lost one of their company, drowned in the ice by the way; and had been all starved, but that, by God's providence, they lighted upon an Indian wigwam. Connecticut River was frozen up the 15th of this month.

Mr. Hugh Peter, preaching at Boston and Salem, moved the country to raise a stock for fishing, as the only probable means to free us from that oppression, which the seamen and others held us under.

28.] Here arrived a small Norsey bark, of twenty-five tons, sent by the Lords Say, etc., with one Gardiner,[1] an

---

[1] This was Lyon Gardiner, builder and commander of the fort at Saybrook at the mouth of the Connecticut, during the Pequot war. He was brave and intelligent. Work base is the Dutch *werkbaas*, engineer (work-boss).

expert engineer or work base, and provisions of all sorts, to begin a fort at the mouth of Connecticut. She came through many great tempests; yet, through the Lord's great providence, her passengers, twelve men, two women and goods, all safe. Mr. Winthrop had sent, four days before, a bark, with carpenters and other workmen, to take possession of the place, (for the Dutch intended to take it,) and to raise some buildings.

A great shallop, coming from Pascataquack in a N. E. wind with snow, lost her way, and was forced into Anasquam; and going out with a N. W. wind, through the unskilfulness of the men, was cast upon the rocks, and lost £100 worth of goods.

A shallop of William Lovell, laden with goods to Salem, worth £100, was, by foul weather, put into Plymouth, and, coming out, the men went aboard a small bark by the way, and their shallop brake loose and was lost, and, about two months after, was found about Nawset,[1] not much hurt, and the goods were, most of them, saved by some Plymouth men, who had notice of it by the Indians.

10ber, (*December*) 10.] The ship *Rebecka*, about sixty tons, came from Connecticut, and brought in her about seventy men and women, which came down to the river's mouth to meet the barks which should have brought their provisions; but, not meeting them, they went aboard the *Rebecka*, which, two days before, was frozen twenty miles up the river, but a small rain falling set her free; but coming out, she ran on ground at the mouth of the river, and was forced to unlade. They came to Massachusetts in five days, which was a great mercy of God, for otherwise they had all perished with famine, as some did.

While the *Rebecka* lay there, the Dutch sent a sloop to take possession of the mouth of the river; but our men gate two pieces on shore, and would not suffer them to land.

[1] Eastham.

The 2d and 3d of this month fell a snow about knee deep, with much wind from the N. and N. E.

Mr. Norton,[1] a godly man, and a preacher in England, coming with his family to the Massachusetts, the ship, wherein he was, was by contrary winds put into Plymouth, where he continued preaching to them all the winter; and although Mr. Smith, their pastor, gave over his place, that he might have it, and the church used him with all respect, and large offers, etc., yet he left them and came to Massachusetts, alleging that his spirit could not close with them, etc.

[1] John Norton, from Hertfordshire, after the usual shaping at Cambridge, emerged into non-conformity, and now at twenty-nine, with a reputation for good parts, appeared in America. He became teacher at Ipswich, and during Winthrop's life makes no great figure in affairs. On Cotton's death he became his successor, which some hold to have been unfortunate on account of the fierce fanaticism with which he prosecuted Quakers and Baptists. (Brooks Adams, *Emancipation of Massachusetts*, pp. 102 *et seqq.*) At the Restoration, the colony sent him with Simon Bradstreet to England to make peace with Charles II. Naturally the representatives of a colony so well known for its sympathy with the lost cause underwent hardship and contumely, which perhaps contributed to Norton's death in 1663.

1636

11 mo. January.] The governor and assistants met at Boston to consider about Mr. Williams, for that they were credibly informed, that, notwithstanding the injunction laid upon him (upon the liberty granted him to stay till the spring) not to go about to draw others to his opinions, he did use to entertain company in his house, and to preach to them, even of such points as he had been censured for; and it was agreed to send him into England by a ship then ready to depart. The reason was, because he had drawn above twenty persons to his opinion, and they were intended to erect a plantation about the Naragansett Bay, from whence the infection would easily spread into these churches, (the people being, many of them, much taken with the apprehension of his godliness). Whereupon a warrant was sent to him to come presently to Boston, to be shipped, etc. He returned answer, (and divers of Salem came with it,) that he could not come without hazard of his life, etc. Whereupon a pinnace was sent with commission to Capt. Underhill, etc., to apprehend him, and carry him aboard the ship, (which then rode at Natascutt;) but, when they came at his house, they found he had been gone three days before; but whither they could not learn.

He had so far prevailed at Salem, as many there (especially of devout women) did embrace his opinions, and separated from the churches, for this cause, that some of their members, going into England, did hear the ministers there, and when they came home the churches here held communion with them.

This month one went by land to Connecticut, and returned safe.

Mr. Hugh Peter went from place to place laboring, both publicly and privately, to raise up men to a public frame of spirit, and so prevailed, as he procured a good sum of money to be raised to set on foot the fishing business, to the value of [blank,] and wrote into England to raise as much more. The intent was to set up a magazine of all provisions and other necessaries for fishing, that men might have things at hand, and for reasonable prices; whereas now the merchants and seamen took advantage to sell at most excessive rates, (in many things two for one, etc.)

Mr. Batchellor of Sagus was convented before the magistrates. The cause was, for that, coming out of England with a small body of six or seven persons, and having since received in many more at Sagus, and contention growing between him and the greatest part of his church, (who had, with the rest, received him for their pastor,) he desired dismission for himself and his first members, which being granted, upon supposition that he would leave the town, (as he had given out,) he with the said six or seven persons presently renewed their old covenant, intending to raise another church in Sagus; whereat the most and chief of the town being offended, for that it would cross their intentions of calling Mr. Peter or some other minister, they complained to the magistrates, who, foreseeing the distraction which was like to come by this course, had forbidden him to proceed in any such church way, until the cause were considered by the other ministers, etc. But he refused to desist. Whereupon they sent for him, and upon his delay, day after day, the marshal was sent to fetch him. Upon his appearance and submission, and promise to remove out of the town within three months, he was discharged.

18.] Mr. Vane[1] and Mr. Peter, finding some distraction in the commonwealth, arising from some difference in judgment, and withal some alienation of affection among the magistrates

---

[1] The deference shown Vane at his coming partook almost of infatuation, and was due no doubt to his wealth and high connections, and in some measure, too, to the remarkable character which he manifested even as a youth. It was certainly presumptuous that, young and inexperienced as he was, he should have set himself up to be an arbiter in the disputes of the fathers and founders.

and some other persons of quality, and that hereby factions began to grow among the people, some adhering more to the old governor, Mr. Winthrop, and others to the late governor, Mr. Dudley,—the former carrying matters with more lenity, and the latter with more severity,—they procured a meeting, at Boston, of the governor, deputy, Mr. Cotton, Mr. Hooker, Mr. Wilson, and there was present Mr. Winthrop, Mr. Dudley, and themselves; where, after the Lord had been sought, Mr. Vane declared the occasion of this meeting, (as is before noted,) and the fruit aimed at, viz. a more firm and friendly uniting of minds, etc., especially of the said Mr. Dudley and Mr. Winthrop, as those upon whom the weight of the affairs did lie, etc., and therefore desired all present to take up a resolution to deal freely and openly with the parties, and they each with other, that nothing might be left in their breasts, which might break out to any jar or difference hereafter, (which they promised to do). Then Mr. Winthrop spake to this effect: that when it pleased Mr. Vane to acquaint him with what he had observed, of the dispositions of men's minds inclining to the said faction, etc., it was very strange to him, professing solemnly that he knew not of any breach between his brother Dudley and himself, since they were reconciled long since, neither did he suspect any alienation of affection in him or others from himself, save that, of late, he had observed, that some new comers had estranged themselves from him, since they went to dwell at Newtown; and so desired all the company, that, if they had seen any thing amiss in his government or otherwise, they would deal freely and faithfully with him, and for his part he promised to take it in good part, and would endeavor, by God's grace, to amend it. Then Mr. Dudley spake to this effect: that for his part he came thither a mere patient, not with any intent to charge his brother Winthrop with any thing; for though there had been formerly some differences and breaches between them, yet they had been healed, and, for his part, he was not willing to renew them again; and so left it to others to utter their own complaints. Whereupon the governor, Mr. Haynes, spake to this effect: that Mr. Winthrop and himself had been always in good terms, etc.; therefore he was loath to give any offence to him, and he hoped that, considering what the end of this meeting was, he would take it in good part, if he did deal openly and freely, as his manner ever was. Then he spake of one or two passages, wherein he conceived, that [he] dealt too remissly in point of justice; to which Mr. Winthrop answered, that his speeches and carriage had been in part mistaken; but withal professed, that it was his judgment, that in the infancy of plantation, justice should be administered with more lenity than in a settled state, because people were then more apt to transgress, partly of ignorance of new laws and orders, partly through oppression of business and other straits; but, if it might be made clear to him, that it was an error, he would be ready to take up a stricter course. Then the ministers were desired to consider of the question by the next morning, and to set down a rule in the case. The next morning, they delivered their several reasons, which all sorted to this conclusion, that strict discipline, both in criminal offences and in martial affairs, was more needful in plantations than in a settled state, as tending to the honor and safety of the gospel. Whereupon Mr. Winthrop acknowledged that he was convinced, that he had failed in over much lenity and remissness, and would endeavor (by God's assistance) to take a more strict course hereafter. Whereupon there was a renewal of love amongst them, and articles drawn to this effect:—

1. That there should be more strictness used in civil government and military discipline.

2. That the magistrates should (as far as might be) ripen their consultations beforehand, that their vote in public might bear (as the voice of God).

3. That, in meetings out of court, the magistrates should not discuss the business of parties in their presence, nor deliver their opinions, etc.

4. That trivial things, etc., should be ended in towns, etc.

5. If differences fall out among them in public meetings, they shall observe these rules:—

1. Not to touch any person differing, but speak to the cause.

2. To express their difference in all modesty and due respect to the court and such as differ, etc.

3. Or to propound their difference by way of question.

4. Or to desire a deferring of the cause to further time.

5. After sentence, (if all have agreed,) none shall intimate his dislike privately; or, if one dissent, he shall sit down, without showing any further distaste, publicly or privately.

6. The magistrates shall be more familiar and open each to other, and more frequent in visitations, and shall, in tenderness and love, admonish one another, (without reserving any secret grudge,) and shall avoid all jealousies and suspicions, each seeking the honor of another, and all, of the court, not opening the nakedness of one another to private persons; in all things seeking the safety and credit of the gospel.

7. To honor the governor in submitting to him the main direction and ordering the business of the court.

8. One assistant shall not seem to gratify any man in undoing or crossing another's proceedings, without due advice with him.

9. They shall grace and strengthen their under officers in their places, etc.

10. All contempts against the court, or any of the magistrates, shall be specially noted and punished; and the magistrates shall appear more solemnly in public, with attendance, apparel, and open notice of their entrance into the court.[1]

---

[1] "Though several principles of sound policy were established, the general result of this conference must, I think, be regretted. When the administration of Winthrop was impeached by Gov. Haynes for too great lenity, it seems natural that such severe tempers as Dudley, and Vane, and Peter, should unite in the attack; and as the rest of the clergy probably agreed with their ardent brother Peter, the maxims of the first governor of the colony would be overruled; but

Mo. 12. (*February*) 1.] Mr. Shepherd, a godly minister, come lately out of England, and divers other good Christians, intending to raise a church body, came and acquainted the magistrates therewith, who gave their approbation. They also sent to all the neighboring churches for their elders to give their assistance, at a certain day, at Newtown, when they should constitute their body. Accordingly, at this day, there met a great assembly, where the proceeding was as followeth:

Mr. Shepherd and two others (who were after to be chosen to office) sate together in the elder's seat. Then the elder of them began with prayer. After this, Mr. Shepherd prayed with deep confession of sin, etc., and exercised out of Eph. v.—that he might make it to himself a holy, etc.; and also opened the cause of their meeting, etc. Then the elder desired to know of the churches assembled, what number were needful to make a church, and how they ought to proceed in this action. Whereupon some of the ancient ministers, conferring shortly together, gave answer: That the scripture did not set down any certain rule for the number. Three (they thought) were too few, because by Matt. xviii. an appeal was allowed from three; but that seven might be a fit number. And, for their proceeding, they advised, that such as were to join should make confession of their faith, and declare what work of grace the Lord had wrought in them; which accordingly they did, Mr. Shepherd first, then four others, then the elder, and one who was to be deacon, (who had also prayed,) and another member. Then the covenant was read, and they all gave a solemn assent to it. Then the elder desired of the churches, that, if they did approve them to be a church, they would give

when their united influence was strong enough to compel him to acknowledge his remissness in discipline, we are bound, as in our early history we often are, to lament the undue dictation of the church. It should be remembered, that Haynes and Hooker were, at this very time, preparing to establish themselves as the Moses and Aaron of a new plantation; and they might *decently* have left Massachusetts to be governed by rules, which, though not always observed, had been found beneficial by the earlier inhabitants." (Savage.)

them the right hand of fellowship. Whereupon Mr. Cotton, (upon short speech with some others near him,) in the name of their churches, gave his hand to the elder, with a short speech of their assent, and desired the peace of the Lord Jesus to be with them. Then Mr. Shepherd made an exhortation to the rest of his body, about the nature of their covenant, and to stand firm to it, and commended them to the Lord in a most heavenly prayer. Then the elder told the assembly, that they were intended to choose Mr. Shepherd for their pastor, (by the name of the brother who had exercised,) and desired the churches, that, if they had any thing to except against him, they would impart it to them before the day of ordination. Then he gave the churches thanks for their assistance, and so left them to the Lord.[1]

At the last general court, it was referred to the military commissioners to appoint colors for every company; who did accordingly, and left out the cross in all of them, appointing the king's arms to be put into that of Castle Island,[2] and Boston to be the first company.

3.] Mr. John Maverick, teacher of the church of Dorchester, died, being near sixty years of age. He was a [blank] man of a very humble spirit, and faithful in furthering the work of the Lord here, both in the churches and civil state.

24.] Mr. Winslow of Plymouth came to treat with those of Dorchester about their land at Connecticut, which they had taken from them. It being doubtful whether that place were within our patent or not, the Plymouth men, about three years since, had treaty with us about joining in erecting a planta-

---

[1] Since the former church in Newtown was now removing in its corporate capacity to Connecticut, a new one must be formed. The elaborate detail shows that Congregationalism was completely developed, the usages of the Church of England, in which the elders were bred, being entirely cast off.

[2] The spirit of Endicott prevailed as regards the idolatrous emblem; though a few years later, when it was found the Parliamentary army in England retained the cross, it was restored in the colony.

tion and trade there. We thought not fit to do any thing then, but gave them leave to go on. Whereupon they bought a portion of land of the Indians, and built a house there, and the Dorchester men (without their leave) were now setting down their town in the same place; but, after, they desired to agree with them; for which end Mr. Winslow came to treat with them, and demanded one sixteenth part of their lands, and £100, which those of Dorchester not consenting unto, they brake off, those of Plymouth expecting to have due recompense after, by course of justice, if they went on. But divers resolved to quit the place, if they could not agree with those of Plymouth.[1]

25.] The distractions about the churches of Salem and Sagus, and the removal of other churches, and the great scarcity of corn, etc., occasioned a general fast to [be] proclaimed, which, because the court was not at hand, was moved by the elders of the churches, and assented unto by the ministers. The church of Boston renewed their covenant this day, and made a large explanation of that which they had first entered into, and acknowledged such failings as had fallen out, etc.

Mo. 1. (*March*) 8.] A man's servant in Boston, having stolen from his master, and being threatened to be brought before the magistrates, went and hanged himself. Herein three things were observable: 1. That he was a very profane fellow, given to cursing, etc., and did use to [go] out of the assembly, upon the Lord's day, to rob his master. 2. The manner of his death, being with a small codline, and his knees touching the floor of the chamber, and one coming in when he was scarce dead, (who was a maid, and while she went to call out, etc., he was past recovery). 3. His discontent, arising from the long time he was to serve his master, (though he were well used). The same day came a letter from his father, out of the Bermuda, with money to buy out his time, etc.

[1] See Bradford, in this series, p. 327.

The *Rebecka* came from Bermuda with thirty thousand weight of potatoes, and store of oranges and limes, which were a great relief to our people; but their corn was sold to the West Indies three months before. Potatoes were bought there for two shillings and eight pence the bushel, and sold here for two pence the pound.

11.] Some occasions of difference had fallen out between the church of Charlton and Mr. James, their pastor. The teacher, Mr. Simmes, and the most of the brethren, had taken offence at divers speeches of his, (he being a very melancholick man, and full of causeless jealousies, etc.,) for which they had dealt with him, both privately and publicly; but, receiving no satisfaction, they wrote to all the neighboring churches for their advice and help in the case, who, sending chosen men, (most elders,) they met there this day, and finding the pastor very faulty, yet because they had not proceeded with him in a due order,—for of the two witnesses produced, one was the accuser,—they advised, that, if they could not comfortably close, himself and such as stood on his part, (if they would,) should desire dismission, which should be granted them, for avoiding extremities; but if he persisted, etc., the church should cast him out.

30.] Mr. Allerton returned in his pinnace from the French at Penobscott. His bark was cast upon an island, and beat out her keel, and so lay ten days; yet he gate help from Pemaquid, and mended her, and brought her home.

Mr. Wither, in a vessel of fifty tons, going to Virginia, was cast away upon Long Island with a W. N. W. wind. The company (being about thirty) were, most of them, very profane persons, and in their voyage did much reproach our colony, vowing they would hang, drown, or, etc., before they would come hither again. Seven were drowned in landing; some gate in a small boat to the Dutch plantation; two were killed by the Indians, who took all such goods as they left on shore. Those who escaped, went towards Virginia in a Dutch bark;

and were never heard of after; but were thought to be wrecked, by some Dutch pails, etc., which were found by the Indians thereabout.

Mo. 2. (*April*) 1.] Mr. Mather[1] and others, of Dorchester, intending to begin a new church there, (a great part of the old one being gone to Connecticut,) desired the approbation of the other churches and of the magistrates; and, accordingly, they assembled this day, and, after some of them had given proof of their gifts, they made confession of their faith, which was approved of; but proceeding to manifest the work of God's grace in themselves, the churches, by their elders, and the magistrates, etc., thought them not meet, at present, to be the foundation of a church; and thereupon they were content to forbear to join till further consideration. The reason was, for that most of them (Mr. Mather and one more excepted) had builded their comfort of salvation upon unsound grounds, viz., some upon dreams and ravishes of spirit by fits; others upon the reformation of their lives; others upon duties and performances, etc.; wherein they discovered three special errors: 1. That they had not come to hate sin, because it was filthy, but only left it, because it was hurtful. 2. That, by reason of this, they had never truly closed with Christ, (or rather Christ with them,) but had made use of him only to help the imperfection of their sanctification and duties, and not made him their sanctification, wisdom, etc. 3. They expected

---

[1] Though in general the reader finds Savage's genealogies quite too particular, the Mather family in Massachusetts was so famous that space may properly be taken to describe it. He says: "This was the father of Increase Mather, president of Harvard College, who was father of the more celebrated Cotton Mather, a name that will forever be perpetuated, while the strange contents of the *Magnalia*, in which are equally striking his voracious appetite and ill digestion of learning, excite the curiosity of antiquaries. Three other sons of Richard, the gentleman named in our text, were clergymen, as also a great grandson, who was a minister in Boston. Richard and his wife, Katharine, were received into Boston church 25 October preceding. He married, in his old age, the widow of the *great* Cotton, and his son, Increase, married a daughter, whence the author of the *Magnalia* obtained his name of baptism."

to believe by some power of their own, and not only and wholly from Christ.

Those of Dorchester, who had removed their cattle to Connecticut before winter, lost the greatest part of them this winter; yet some, which came late, and could not be put over the river, lived very well all the winter without any hay. The people also were put to great straits for want of provisions. They eat acorns, and malt, and grains. They lost near £2000 worth of cattle.

7.] At a general court it was ordered, that a certain number of the magistrates should be chosen for life; (the reason was, for that it was showed from the word of God, etc., that the principal magistrates ought to be for life). Accordingly, the 25th of the 3d mo. John Winthrop and Thomas Dudley were chosen to this place, and Henry Vane, by his place of governor, was president of this council for his year.[1] It was likewise ordered, that quarter courts should be kept in several places for ease of the people, and, in regard of the scarcity of victuals, the remote towns should send their votes by proxy to the court of elections; and that no church, etc., should be allowed, etc., that was gathered without consent of the churches and the magistrates.

Mr. Benjamin's house burnt, and £100 in goods lost.

12.] The *Charity*, of Dartmouth, of one hundred and twenty tons, arrived here, laden with provisions. She came in with a strong N. W. wind, and was in great danger to have been lost between Allerton Point and Natascott; but the Lord, in mercy to his people, delivered her, after she had struck twice, and upon the ebb. Mr. Peter bought all the provisions at fifty in the hundred, (which saved the country £200,) and distributed them to all the towns, as each town needed.[2]

---

[1] This council for life lasted for three years only, it being found to excite popular jealousy against the magistrates. It seems to have been constituted in the hope of tempting over some of the peers, or gentry likely to become peers. The members of such a council were assured a place of dignity.

[2] An instance of Hugh Peter's fine spirit of practical benevolence.

The church of Salem was still infected with Mr. Williams his opinions, so as most of them held it unlawful to hear in the ordinary assemblies in England, because their foundation was antichristian, and we should, by hearing, hold communion with them; and some went so far as they were ready to separate from the church upon it. Whereupon the church sent two brethren, and a letter, to the elders of the other churches, for their advice in three points: 1. Whether (for satisfying the weak) they might promise not to hear in England any false church. This was not thought safe, because then they would draw them to the like towards the other churches here, who were all of opinion, that it was lawful, and that hearing was not church communion. 2. If they were not better, to grant them dismission to be a church by themselves. This was also opposed, for that it was not a remedy of God's ordering; neither would the magistrates allow them to be a church, being but three men and eight women; and besides, it were dangerous to raise churches on such grounds. 3. Whether they ought then to excommunicate them, if they did withdraw, etc. This was granted, yet, withal, that if they did not withdraw or run into contempt, they ought, in these matters of difference of opinion in things not fundamental nor scandalous, etc., to bear each with other.

Mo. 3. (*May*) 15.] Mr. Peter, preaching at Boston, made an earnest request to the church for [*blank*] things: 1. That they would spare their teacher, Mr. Cotton, for a time, that he might go through the Bible, and raise marginal notes upon all the knotty places of the scriptures. 2. That a new book of martyrs might be made, to begin where the other had left.[1] 3. That a form of church government might be drawn according to the scriptures. 4. That they would take order for employment of people, (especially women and children, in the

---

[1] The suggestion of a continuation of Fox's *Book of Martyrs* is pathetic as coming from one whose own martyrdom twenty-four years later was so noteworthy.

winter time;) for he feared that idleness would be the ruin both of church and commonwealth.

Here arrived a ship, called the *St. Patrick*, belonging to Sir Thomas Wentworth,[1] deputy of Ireland, one Palmer master. When she came near Castle Island, the lieutenant of the fort went aboard her, and made her strike her flag, which the master took as a great injury, and complained of it to the magistrates, who, calling the lieutenant before them, heard the cause, and declared to the master that he had no commission so to do. And because he had made them strike to the fort, (which had then no colors abroad,) they tendered the master such satisfaction as he desired, which was only this, that the lieutenant, aboard their ship, should acknowledge his error, that so all the ship's company might receive satisfaction, lest the lord deputy should have been informed, that we had offered that discourtesy to his ship, which we had never offered to any before.

25.] Henry Vane, Esq., before mentioned, was chosen governor; and, because he was son and heir to a privy counsellor in England, the ships congratulated his election with a volley of great shot. The next week he invited all the masters (there were then fifteen great ships, etc.,) to dinner. After they had dined, he propounded three things to them: 1. That all ships, which should come after this year, should come to an anchor before they came at the fort, except they did send their boat before, and did satisfy the commander that they were friends. 2. That, before they offered any goods to sale, they would deliver an invoice, etc., and give the governor, etc., twenty-four hours' liberty to refuse, etc. 3. That their men might not stay on shore (except upon necessary business) after sunset. These things they all willingly condescended unto.

31.] Mr. Hooker, pastor of the church of Newtown, and the most of his congregation, went to Connecticut. His wife

[1] Sir Thomas Wentworth was later the great Earl of Strafford.

was carried in a horse litter; and they drove one hundred and sixty cattle, and fed of their milk by the way.[1]

The last winter Capt. Mason died. He was the chief mover in all the attempts against us, and was to have sent the general governor, and for this end was providing shipping; but the Lord, in mercy, taking him away, all the business fell on sleep, so as ships came and brought what and whom they would, without any question or control.[2]

Divers of the ships this spring, both out of the Downs and from Holland, came in five weeks; and Mr. Ball his ship went from hence to England the 16th of January, and saw land there in eighteen days.

One Miller, master's mate in the *Hector*, spake to some of our people aboard his ship, that, because we had not the king's colors at our fort, we were all traitors and rebels, etc. The governor sent for the master, Mr. Ferne, and acquainted him with it, who promised to deliver him to us. Whereupon we sent the marshal and four sergeants to the ship for him, but the master not being aboard, they would not deliver him; whereupon the master went himself and brought him to the court, and the words being proved against him by two witnesses, he was committed. The next day the master, to pacify his men, who were in a great tumult, requested he might be delivered to him, and did undertake to bring him before us again the day after, which was granted him, and he brought him to us at the time appointed. Then, in the presence of all the rest of the masters, he acknowledged his offence, and set his hand to a submission,[3] and was discharged. Then the governor desired the masters, that they would deal freely, and tell us, if they did take any offence, and what they required of

---

[1] Hooker's departure with the Newtown church was an epoch-making event. For a good account of its significance see Johnston, *Connecticut*, ch. III.

[2] John Mason, patentee, under the Council for New England, of "Mariana" (1622), of New Hampshire and Maine jointly with Gorges (1622), of New Hamphire separately (1629), and of "Laconia" jointly with Gorges (1629).

[3] For the language of Miller's submission, see *Colonial Records*, I. 179.

us. They answered, that, in regard they should be examined upon their return, what colors they saw here, they did desire that the king's colors might be spread at our fort. It was answered, that we had not the king's colors. Thereupon two of them did offer them freely to us. We replied, that for our part we were fully persuaded, that the cross in the ensign was idolatrous, and therefore might not set it in our ensign; but, because the fort was the king's, and maintained in his name, we thought that his own colors might be spread there. So the governor accepted the colors of Capt. Palmer, and promised they should be set up at Castle Island. We had conferred over night with Mr. Cotton, etc., about the point. The governor, and Mr. Dudley, and Mr. Cotton, were of opinion, that they might be set up at the fort upon this distinction, that it was maintained in the king's name. Others, not being so persuaded, answered, that the governor and Mr. Dudley, being two of the council, and being persuaded of the lawfulness, etc., might use their power to set them up. Some others, being not so persuaded, could not join in the act, yet would not oppose, as being doubtful, etc.

[June 28, 1636. The governor and John Winthrop returned a letter of thanks to Mr. Robert Houghton of Southwark, brewer, and Mr. Wm. Hiccock, etc., for ten barrels of gunpowder, which they sent to this colony the last year upon the motion of Captain Underhill.][1]

Mo. 5. (*July*) 9.] The governor, etc., went to Salem.

Many ships lying ready at Natascott to set sail, Mr. Peter went down and preached aboard the *Hector*, and the ships going forth met with an east wind, which put them in again; whereupon he stayed and kept the sabbath with them.

5.] Mr. Buckly and Mr. Jones, two English ministers, appointed this day to gather a church at Newtown, to settle at Concord. They sent word, three days before, to the governor

[1] This passage was written by Winthrop in another part of the manuscript volume, but we are apparently warranted in treating it as a portion of the *Journal*.

and deputy, to desire their presence; but they took it in ill part, and thought not fit to go, because they had not come to them before, (as they ought to have done, and as others had done before,) to acquaint them with their purpose.

Mr. Winthrop, jun., gave £5 towards the building of the meeting-house at Charlton. I sent it by James Brown.

20.] John Gallop, with one man more, and two little boys, coming from Connecticut in a bark of twenty tons, intending to put in at Long Island to trade, and being at the mouth of the harbor, were forced, by a sudden change of the wind, to bear up for Block Island or Fisher's Island, lying before Naragansett, where they espied a small pinnace, which, drawing near unto, they found to be Mr. Oldham's (an old planter,[1] and a member of Watertown congregation, who had been long out a trading, having with him only two English boys, and two Indians of Naragansett). So they hailed him, but had no answer; and the deck was full of Indians, (fourteen in all,) and a canoe was gone from her full of Indians and goods. Whereupon they suspected they had killed John Oldham, and the rather, because the Indians let slip and set up sail, being two miles from shore, and the wind and tide being off the shore of the island, whereby they drove towards the main at Naragansett. Whereupon they went ahead of them, and having but two pieces and two pistols, and nothing but duck shot, they bear up near the Indians, (who stood ready armed with guns, pikes, and swords,) and let fly among them, and so galled them as they all gate under hatches. Then they stood off again, and returning with a good gale, they stemmed her upon the quarter and almost overset her, which so frightened the Indians, as six of them leaped overboard and were drowned. Yet they durst not board her, but stood off again, and fitted their anchor, so as, stemming her the second time, they bored

[1] John Gallopp and John Oldham, heretofore described as adventurous sailors and traders along the coast, stand now as the prominent figures at the outset of the Pequot war.

her bow through with their anchor, and so sticking fast to her, they made divers shot through her, (being but inch board,) and so raked her fore and aft, as they must needs kill or hurt some of the Indians; but, seeing none of them come forth, they gate loose from her and stood off again. Then four or five more of the Indians leaped into the sea, and were likewise drowned. So there being now but four left in her, they boarded her; whereupon one Indian came up and yielded; him they bound and put into hold. Then another yielded, whom they bound. But John Gallop, being well acquainted with their skill to untie themselves, if two of them be together, and having no place to keep them asunder, he threw him bound into [the] sea; and, looking about, they found John Oldham under an old seine, stark naked, his head cleft to the brains, and his hand and legs cut as if they had been cutting them off, and yet warm. So they put him into the sea; but could not get to the other two Indians, who were in a little room underneath, with their swords. So they took the goods which were left, and the sails, etc., and towed the boat away; but night coming on, and the wind rising, they were forced to turn her off, and the wind carried her to the Naragansett shore.

26.] The two Indians, which were with Mr. Oldham, and one other, came from Canonicus, the chief sachem of Naragansett, with a letter from Mr. Williams to the governor, to certify him what had befallen Mr. Oldham, and how grievously they were afflicted, and that Miantunnomoh was gone, with seventeen canoes and two hundred men, to take revenge, etc. But, upon examination of the Indian who was brought prisoner to us, we found that all the sachems of the Naragansett, except Canonicus and Miantunnomoh, were the contrivers of Mr. Oldham's death; and the occasion was, because he went to make peace, and trade with the Pekods last year, as is before related. The prisoner said also, that Mr. Oldham's two Indians were acquainted with it; but, because they were sent as messengers from Canonicus, we would not imprison them. But the governor wrote back to Mr. Williams to let the Naragansetts know, that we expected they should send us the two boys, and take revenge upon the islanders; and withal gave Mr. Williams a caution to look to himself, if we should have occasion to make war upon the Naragansetts, for Block Island was under them. And the next day, 27, he wrote to Canonicus by one of those two Indians, and that he had suspicion of him, etc., yet he had sent him back, because he was a messenger, but did expect that, if he should send for the said two Indians, he should send them to us to clear themselves.

30.] Mr. Oldham's two boys were sent home by one of Miantunnomoh his men, with a letter from Mr. Williams, signifying that Miantunnomoh had caused the sachem of Niantick to send to Block Island for them; and that he had near one hundred fathom of wampom and other goods of Mr. Oldham's, which should be reserved for us; and that three of the seven, which were drowned, were sachems; and one of the two, which were hired by the sachem of Niantick, was dead also. So we wrote back to have the rest of those, which were accessory, to be sent to us, and the rest of the goods, and that he should tell Canonicus and Miantunnomoh, that we held them innocent; but that six other under-sachems were guilty, etc.

Mo. 6. (*August*) 3.] Samuel Maverick, who had been in Virginia near twelve months, now returned with two pinnaces, and brought some fourteen heifers, and about eighty goats, (having lost above twenty goats by the way). One of his pinnaces was about forty tons, of cedar, built at Barbathes,[1] and brought to Virginia by Capt. Powell, who there dying, she was sold for a small matter. There died in Virginia, (by his relation,) this last year, above eighteen hundred, and corn was there at twenty shillings the bushel, the most of the people having lived a great time of nothing but purslain, etc. It is very strange, what was related by him and many others,

[1] Barbadoes.

that, above sixty miles up James River, they dig nowhere but they find the ground full of oyster shells, and fishes' bones, etc.; yea, he affirmed that he saw the bone of a whale taken out of the earth (where they digged for a well) eighteen feet deep.

8.] Lieutenant Edward Gibbons,[1] and John Higginson, with Cutshamekin, the sagamore of Massachusetts, were sent to Canonicus to treat with him about the murder of John Oldham. 13. They returned, being very well accepted, and good success in their business. They observed in the sachem much state, great command over his men, and marvellous wisdom in his answers and the carriage of the whole treaty, clearing himself and his neighbors of the murder, and offering assistance for revenge of it, yet upon very safe and wary conditions.

25.] The governor and council, having lately assembled the rest of the magistrates and ministers, to advise with them about doing justice upon the Indians for the death of Mr. Oldham, and all agreeing that it should be attempted with expedition, did this day send forth ninety men, distributed to four commanders,—Capt. John Underhill, Capt. Nathaniel Turner, Ensign Jenyson, and Ensign Davenport; and over them all, as general, John Endecott, Esq., one of the assistants, was sent. They were embarked in three pinnaces, and carried two shallops and two Indians with them. They had commission to put to death the men of Block Island, but to spare the women and children, and to bring them away, and to take possession of the island; and from thence to go to the Pequods to demand the murderers of Capt. Stone and other English, and one thousand fathom of wampom for damages, etc., and some of their children as hostages, which if they should refuse, they were to obtain it by force. No man was impressed for this service, but all went voluntaries.

26.] Miantunnomoh, sachem of Naragansett, sent a mes-

[1] Gibbons rose to the rank of assistant and major-general of the forces.

senger to us, with a letter from Mr. Williams, to signify to us, that they had taken one of the Indians, who had broken prison and was escaped away, and had him safe for us, when we would send for him, (we had before sent to him to that end;) and the other (being also of Block Island) he had sent away, (not knowing, as it seemed, that he had been our prisoner,) according to their promise, that they would not entertain any of that island, which should come to them. But we conceived it was rather in love to him; for he had been his servant formerly.

We sent for the two Indians. One was sent us; the other was dead before the messengers came.

A ship of one hundred and twenty tons was built at Marblehead, and called the *Desire*.

7ber, (*September*) 8.] At a general court, a levy was made of £1200 to pay the country's debts.

The trade of beaver and wampom was to be farmed, and all others restrained from trading.

23.] A new church was gathered at Dorchester, with approbation of the magistrates and elders, etc.

August 24.][1] John Endecott, Esq., and four captains under him, with twenty men a-piece, set sail. They arrived at Block Island the last of the same. The wind blowing hard at N. E. there went so great a surf, as they had much to do to land; and about forty Indians were ready upon the shore to entertain them with their arrows, which they shot oft at our men; but, being armed with corslets, they had no hurt, only one was lightly hurt upon his neck, and another near his foot. So soon as one man leaped on shore, they all fled. The island is about ten miles long, and four broad, full of small hills, and all overgrown with brush-wood of oak,—no good timber in it,—so as they could not march but in one file and in the

[1] This entry is put in by Winthrop out of course, a September entry having preceded: he no doubt desired to have in one narrative his account of Endicott's expedition, and goes back here to the outset of the undertaking.

narrow paths. There were two plantations, three miles in sunder, and about sixty wigwams,—some very large and fair,—and above two hundred acres of corn, some gathered and laid on heaps, and the rest standing. When they had spent two days in searching the island, and could not find the Indians, they burnt their wigwams, and all their matts, and some corn, and staved seven canoes, and departed. They could not tell what men they killed, but some were wounded and carried away by their fellows.

Thence they went to the mouth of the Connecticut, where they lay wind-bound four days, and taking thence twenty men and two shallops, they sailed to the Pequot harbor, where an Indian came to them in a canoe, and demanded what they were, and what they would have. The general told him, he came from the governor of Massachusetts to speak with their sachems. He told him, Sassacus was gone to Long Island. Then he bade him go tell the other sachem, etc. So he departed; and in the mean time our men landed, but with much danger, if the Indians had made use of their advantage, for all the shore was high, rugged rocks, etc. Then the messenger returned, and the Indians began to gather about our men till there were about three hundred of them; and some four hours past while the messenger went to and fro, bringing still excuses for the sachem's not coming. At last the general told the messenger, and the rest of the Indians near, the particulars of his commission, and sent him to tell the sachem, that if he would not come to him, nor yield to those demands, he would fight with them. The messenger told him, that the sachem would meet him, if our men would lay down their arms, as his men should do their bows, etc. When the general saw they did but dally, to gain time, he bad them be gone, and shift for themselves; for they had dared the English to come fight with them, and now they were come for that purpose. Thereupon they all withdrew. Some of our men would have made a shot at them, but the general would not suffer them;

but when they were gone out of musket shot, he marched after them, supposing they would have stood to it awhile, as they did to the Dutch. But they all fled, and shot at our men from the thickets and rocks, but did us no harm. Two of them our men killed, and hurt others. So they marched up to their town, and burnt all their wigwams and matts, but their corn being standing, they could not spoil it. At night they returned to their vessels, and the next day they went ashore on the west side of the river, and burnt all their wigwams, and spoiled their canoes; and so set sail, and came to the Naragansett, where they landed their men, and, the 14th of 7ber, they came all safe to Boston, which was a marvellous providence of God, that not a hair fell from the head of any of them, nor any sick or feeble person among them. As they came by Naragansett, Cutshamakin, an Indian, who went with them for an interpreter, who, being armed with a corslet and a piece, had crept into a swamp and killed a Pequot, and having flayed off the skin of his head,[1] he sent it to Canonicus, who presently sent it to all the sachems about him, and returned many thanks to the English, and sent four fathom of wampom to Cutshamakin.

The soldiers who went were all voluntaries, and had only their victuals provided, but demanded no pay. The whole charge of the voyage came to about £200. The seamen had all wages.[2]

The Naragansett men told us after, that thirteen of the

---

[1] Scalping, though usual in Canada, was not at this time customary among the Indians of southern New England.

[2] The reprisals of Endicott, as to ruthlessness, appear to be of a piece with the harsh warfare against Indians of later times. Palliation may be found in the fact that the Pequots were interlopers, a body perhaps of Iroquois extraction, which had thrust itself in between the Mohegans and Narragansetts, and preyed like wolves upon its neighbors right and left. The condition of the colonies was indeed very critical: had the Pequots succeeded (as but for Roger Williams they probably would have done) in forming a union with the Narragansetts, the English could hardly have maintained themselves. See Ellis, *John Mason*, in Sparks's *American Biography*, second series, vol. III., p. 360.

Pequods were killed, and forty wounded; and but one of Block Island killed.

At the last general court, order was taken to restrain the trade with the Indians, and the governor and council appointed to let it to farm, for a rent to be paid to the treasury.

The inhabitants of Boston, who had taken their farms and lots at Mount Woollaston, finding it very burdensome to have their business, etc. so far off, desired to gather a church there. Many meetings were about it. The great let was, in regard it was given to Boston for upholding the town and church there, which end would be frustrate by the removal of so many chief men as would go thither. For helping of this, it was propounded, that such as dwelt there should pay six-pence the acre, yearly, for such lands as lay within a mile of the water, and three-pence for that which lay further off.

A ship of Barnstaple arrived here with eighty heifers.

Another from Bristol arrived, a fortnight after, with some cattle and passengers; but she had delivered most of her cattle and passengers at Pascataquack for Sir Ferdinando Gorge his plantation at Aquamenticus.

Canonicus sent word of some English, whom the Pequods had killed at Saybrook; and Mr. Williams wrote, that the Pequods and Naragansetts were at truce, and that Miantunnomoh told him, that the Pequods had labored to persuade them, that the English were minded to destroy all Indians. Whereupon we sent for Miantunnomoh to come to us.

Another windmill was erected at Boston, and one at Charlestown; and a watermill at Salem, and another at Ipswich, and another at Newbury.

A CONTINUATION OF THE HISTORY OF NEW ENGLAND[1]

1636

8ber (*October*).] AFTER Mr. Endecott and our men were departed from the Pequod,[2] the twenty men of Saybrook lay wind-bound there, and went to fetch some of the Indians' corn; and having fetched every man one sackful to their boat, they returned for more, and having loaded themselves, the Indians set upon them. So they laid down their corn and gave fire upon them, and the Indians shot arrows at them. The place was open for the distance of musket shot, and the Indians kept the covert, save when they came forth, about ten at a time, and discharged their arrows. The English put themselves into a single file, and some ten only (who had pieces which could reach them) shot; the others stood ready to keep them from breaking in upon our men. So they continued the most part of the afternoon. Our men killed some of them, as they supposed, and hurt others; and they shot only one of ours, and he was armed, all the rest being without arms.[3] He was shot through the leg. Their arrows were all shot compass,[4]

---

[1] The manuscript of this, the second, part of the *Journal*, after having been copied by Savage, while still in his possession was destroyed by fire in 1825. Though his transcript, as he tells us, had not undergone "perfect verification" beyond 1639, there is no reason to think that his usual faithfulness is lacking; while therefore the loss is greatly to be regretted, we can be confident of having an accurate story.   [2] Now the Thames River.

[3] "Armed," that is, provided with defensive armor.

[4] "'To keep compass" is in archery, according to the *Century Dictionary*, "to preserve a due elevation." To reach the distant foe the arrows, of necessity, described a high arc within view of the soldiers, who had time to dodge. The helplessness of the savages before fire-arms is very apparent.

so as our men, standing single, could easily see and avoid them; and one was employed to gather up their arrows. At last they emptied their sacks, and retired safe to their boat.

About two days after, five men of Saybrook went up the river about four miles, to fetch hay in a meadow on Pequot side. The grass was so high as some Pequots, being hid in it, set upon our men, and one, that had hay on his back, they took; the others fled to their boat, one of them having five arrows in him, (but yet recovered). He who was taken was a godly young man, called [blank] Butterfield; (whereupon the meadow was named Butterfield Meadow). About fourteen days after, six of Saybrook, being sent to keep the house in their corn-field, about two miles from the fort, three of them went forth on fowling, (which the lieutenant had strictly forbidden them). Two had pieces, and the third only a sword. Suddenly about one hundred Indians came out of the covert, and set upon them. He who had the sword brake through them, (and received only two shot, not dangerous,) and escaped to the house, which was not a bow-shot off, and persuaded the other two to follow him; but they stood still till the Indians came and took them, and carried them away with their pieces. Soon after they burnt down the said house, and some outhouses and haystacks within a bow-shot of the fort, and killed a cow, and shot divers others; but they all came home with the arrows in them.

21.] Miantunnomoh, the sachem of Naragansett, (being sent for by the governor,) came to Boston with two of Canonicus's sons, and another sachem, and near twenty sanaps. Cutshamakin gave us notice the day before. The governor sent twenty musketeers to meet him at Roxbury. He came to Boston about noon. The governor had called together most of the magistrates and ministers, to give countenance to our proceedings, and to advise with them about the terms of peace. It was dinner time, and the sachems and their council dined by themselves in the same room where the governor dined, and their sanaps were sent to the inn. After dinner, Miantunnomoh declared what he had to say to us in [*blank*] propositions, which were to this effect:—That they had always loved the English, and desired firm peace with us: That they would continue in war with the Pequods and their confederates, till they were subdued; and desired we should so do: They would deliver our enemies to us, or kill them: That if any of theirs should kill our cattle, that we would not kill them, but cause them to make satisfaction: That they would now make a firm peace, and two months hence they would send us a present.

The governor told them, they should have answer the next morning.

In the morning we met again, and concluded the peace upon the articles underwritten, which the governor subscribed, and they also subscribed with their marks, and Cutshamakin also. But because we could not well make them understand the articles perfectly, we agreed to send a copy of them to Mr. Williams, who could best interpret them to them.[1] So, after dinner, they took leave, and were conveyed out of town by some musketeers, and dismissed with a volley of shot.

THE ARTICLES.

1. A firm peace between us and our friends of other plantations, (if they consent,) and their confederates, (if they will observe the articles, etc.,) and our posterities.
2. Neither party to make peace with the Pequods without the other's consent.
3. Not to harbor, etc., the Pequods, etc.
4. To put to death or deliver over murderers, etc.
5. To return our fugitive servants, etc.
6. We to give them notice when we go against the Pequods, and they to send us some guides.
7. Free trade between us.

---

[1] Roger Williams had especial skill in the Indian languages, as is evidenced by his *Key unto the Language of America* (London, 1643), reprinted in 1866 by the Narragansett Club.

8. None of them to come near our plantations during the wars with the Pequods, without some Englishman or known Indian.

9. To continue to the posterity of both parties.

The governor of Plymouth wrote to the deputy,[1] that we had occasioned a war, etc., by provoking the Pequods, and no more, and about the peace with the Naragansetts, etc. The deputy took it ill, (as there was reason,) and returned answer accordingly, and made it appear, 1. That there was as much done as could be expected, considering they fled from us, and we could not follow them in our armour, neither had any to guide us in their country. 2. We went not to make war upon them, but to do justice, etc., and having killed thirteen of them for four or five, which they had murdered of ours, and destroyed sixty wigwams, etc., we were not much behind with them. 3. They had no cause to glory over us, when they saw that they could not save themselves nor their houses and corn from so few of ours. 4. If we had left but one hundred of them living, those might have done us as much hurt as they have or are likely to do. 5. It was very likely they would have taken notice of our advantage against them, and would have sitten still, or have sought peace, if God had not deprived them of common reason.

About the middle of this month, John Tilley, master of a bark, coming down Connecticut River, went on shore in a canoe, three miles above the fort, to kill fowl; and having shot off his piece, many Indians arose out of the covert and took him, and killed one other, who was in the canoe. This Tilley was a very stout man, and of great understanding. They cut off his hands, and sent them before, and after cut off his feet. He lived three days after his hands were cut off; and themselves confessed, that he was a stout man, because he cried not in his torture.

About this time two houses were burnt, and all the goods in

---

[1] Winthrop.

them, to a great value; one was one Shaw at Watertown, and the other one Jackson of Salem, both professors, and Shaw the day before admitted of the former church. This was very observable in Shaw, that he concealed his estate, and made show as if he had been poor, and was not clear of some unrighteous passages.

One Mrs. Hutchinson,[1] a member of the church of Boston, a woman of a ready wit and bold spirit, brought over with her two dangerous errors: 1. That the person of the Holy Ghost dwells in a justified person. 2. That no sanctification can help to evidence to us our justification.—From these two grew many branches; as, 1. Our union with the Holy Ghost, so as a Christian remains dead to every spiritual action, and hath no

[1] Here begins the story of a most painful and memorable episode of our early history. No other chapter of Massachusetts history is so full of perplexities. Mrs. Hutchinson came from Lincolnshire to America, with her husband, a worthy but not notable man, and their children, drawn to America through her admiration for John Cotton, whose ministration while he was rector of St. Botolph's Church she had much enjoyed. She was a woman of kind heart and practical capacity of various kinds, possessed, too, of a fervent spirit and an intellect so keen that she was held to be the "masterpiece of woman's wit" (Johnson, *Wonder-Working Providence*, book I., ch. 42.) She attained great influence among the women of the settlement, which soon extended to the men as well; and when she denounced the ministers of the colony, excepting Cotton and her brother-in-law Wheelwright, as essentially lacking, she carried with her the Boston church, hardly any but Winthrop and Wilson the pastor withstanding her. Since the other churches of the settlement took opposite ground, a quarrel arose very bitter and dangerous, the details of which may be best learned from Winthrop. The ecclesiastical dispute as to justification by faith and justification by works is as old as the apostles Paul and James. Mrs. Hutchinson's idea was that saving grace went only to such as possessed faith, and that, this grace having been received, the recipient was above law. Hence the term "antinomian" was hurled at her and her sympathizers, a term expressly repudiated by Wheelwright, and certainly unwarranted; for the Hutchinsonians, while scorning "legalism," did not mean to cut loose from moral obligations. Undoubtedly, however, there was danger that in minds confused with the controversial jargon, Mrs. Hutchinson's ideas might be taken as countenancing licentiousness, and in one memorable case, that of John Underhill, hereafter narrated, they certainly were taken as a cloak for loose living.

Winthrop in the *Journal* tells the story only briefly; but in his other work, *A Short Story of the Rise, Reign, and Ruin of the Antinomians, Familists, and Libertines that infected the Churches of Massachusetts Bay*, a book, some extracts from which are included within the present reprint, he gives a detailed account.

gifts nor graces, other than such as are in hypocrites, nor any other sanctification but the Holy Ghost himself.

There joined with her in these opinions a brother of hers, one Mr. Wheelwright, a silenced minister sometimes in England.

25.] The other ministers in the bay, hearing of these things, came to Boston at the time of a general court, and entered conference in private with them, to the end they might know the certainty of these things; that if need were, they might write to the church of Boston about them, to prevent (if it were possible) the dangers, which seemed hereby to hang over that and the rest of the churches. At this conference, Mr. Cotton was present, and gave satisfaction to them, so as he agreed with them all in the point of sanctification, and so did Mr. Wheelwright; so as they all did hold, that sanctification did help to evidence justification. The same he had delivered plainly in public, divers times; but, for the indwelling of the person of the Holy Ghost, he held that still, as some others of the ministers did, but not union with the person of the Holy Ghost, (as Mrs. Hutchinson and others did,) so as to amount to a personal union.

Mr. Cotton, being requested by the general court, with some other ministers, to assist some of the magistrates in compiling a body of fundamental laws, did this court, present a model of Moses his judicials, compiled in an exact method, which were taken into further consideration till the next general court.[1]

30.] Some of the church of Boston, being of the opinion of Mrs. Hutchinson, had labored to have Mr. Wheelwright[2] to

---

[1] Mr. Worthington C. Ford, in *Proceedings of the Massachusetts Historical Society*, second series, XVI. 274-284, gives reasons for identifying this code drafted by Cotton with the *Abstract of the Lawes of New England* (London, 1641), reprinted in Force's *Historical Tracts*, III., but never adopted.

[2] John Wheelwright, born near the end of the sixteenth century, lived till 1679, the patriarch of the New England clergy. Educated at Cambridge, minister of Alford, near old Boston, married to a sister of Anne Hutchinson, like her

be called to be a teacher there. It was propounded the last Lord's day, and was moved again this day for resolution. One of the church stood up and said, he could not consent, etc.[1] His reason was, because the church being well furnished already with able ministers, whose spirits they knew, and whose labors God had blessed in much love and sweet peace, he thought it not fit (no necessity urging) to put the welfare of the church to the least hazard, as he feared they should do, by calling in one, whose spirit they knew not, and one who seemed to dissent in judgment, and instanced in two points, which he delivered in a late exercise there; 1. That a believer was more than a creature. 2. That the person of the Holy Ghost and a believer were united. Hereupon the governor spake, that he marvelled at this, seeing Mr. Cotton had lately approved his doctrine. To this Mr. Cotton answered, that he did not remember the first, and desired Mr. Wheelwright to explain his meaning. He denied not the points, but showed upon what occasion he delivered them. Whereupon, there being an endeavor to make a reconciliation, the first replied, that, although Mr. Wheelwright and himself might likely agree about the point, and though he thought reverendly of his godliness and abilities, so as he could be content to live under such a ministry; yet, seeing he was apt to raise doubtful disputations, he could not consent to choose him to that place. Whereupon the church gave way, that he might be called to a new church, to be gathered at Mount Woollaston, now Braintree.

he came under the influence of Cotton, and emigrated to America in 1636. In the Antinomian controversy he was a conspicuous champion of the "covenant of grace," undergoing exile at the hands of the upholders of a "covenant of works" for a fast-day sermon preached in January, 1637. This sermon is still extant, but of it and the whole Antinomian controversy we may say, with C. F. Adams, "Not only were the points obscure, but the discussion was carried on in a jargon which has become unintelligible." (*Three Episodes of Massachusetts History*, pp. 367, 439). Most of the Antinomian exiles went to Rhode Island, but Wheelwright went to New Hampshire, where he is venerated as the founder of Exeter and Hampton. In middle life, during a sojourn in England, he was made much of by Cromwell.

[1] This was no doubt Winthrop.

Divers of the brethren took offence at the said speech against Mr. Wheelwright; whereupon the same brother spake in the congregation the next day to this effect: That, hearing that some of the brethren were offended at his former speech, and for that offences were dangerous, he was desirous to give satisfaction. The offence, he said, was in three things: 1. For that he had charged the brother in public, and for a thing so long since delivered, and had not first dealt with him privately. For this he acknowledged it was a failing; but the occasion was, that, when he heard the points delivered, he took them in a good sense, as spoken figuratively, seeing the whole scope of his doctrine was sound, and savoring of the spirit of God; but hearing, very lately, that he was suspected to hold such opinions, it caused him to think, he spake as he meant. The 2d cause of offence was, that in his speech appeared some bitterness. For that he answered, that they well knew his manner of speech was always earnest in things, which he conceived to be serious; and professed, that he did love that brother's person, and did honor the gifts and graces of God in him. The 3d was, that he had charged him to have held things which he did not. For this he answered, that he had spoken since with the said brother; and for the two points, —that a believer should be more than a creature, and that there should be a personal union between the Holy Ghost and a believer,—he had denied to hold either of them; but by necessary consequence, he doth hold them both; for he holds, (said he,) that there is a real union with the person of the Holy Ghost, and then of necessity it must be personal, and so a believer must be more than a creature, viz., God-man, even Christ Jesus. For though, in a true union, the two terms may still remain the same, etc., as between husband and wife, he is a man still, and she a woman, (for the union is only in sympathy and relation,) yet in a real or personal union it is not. Now, whether this were agreeable to the doctrine of the church or not, he left to the church to judge; hoping that the Lord would direct our teacher to clear these points fully, as he had well done, in good measure, already. Withal he made this request to the brother, (which he said he did seriously and affectionately,) that, seeing these variances grew (and some estrangement withal) from some words and phrases, which were of human invention, and tended to doubtful disputation, rather than to edification, and had no footing in scripture, nor had been in use in the purest churches for three hundred years after Christ,—that, for the peace of the church, etc., they might be forborn; (he meant, person of the Holy Ghost, and real union;) and concluded, that he did not intend to dispute the matter, (as not having place or calling thereunto then;) yet, if any brother desired to see what light he walked by, he would be ready to impart it to him. How this was taken by the congregation, did not appear, for no man spake to it.

A day or two after, the same brother wrote his mind fully, with such scriptures and arguments as came to hand, and sent it to Mr. Cotton.

(9.) (*November*) 8.] A new church was gathered at Sagus, now Lynn. The governor and deputy were not there, being letted by the coming in of a ship, and other occasions. It held the company two days, Mr. Whiting,[1] who was to be the pastor, being very unskilful in church matters, and those who were to be members not fit for such a work. At last six were accepted, with Mr. Whiting, but with much ado.

12.] A commission was sent out of the chancery in England to some private men here, to examine witnesses in a cause depending there; but nothing was done in it, nor any return made.

17.] Two ships arrived here from London, and one a week before. They were full of passengers,—men, women,

[1] Samuel Whiting had been a minister at Lynn Regis, in Norfolk, and Savage surmises, gave the name to Lynn. He was a respected figure in the colonial church.

and children. One of them had been from London twenty-six weeks, and between land and land eighteen weeks; (the other two something less time;) their beer all spent and leaked out a month before their arrival, so as they were forced to stinking water (and that very little) mixed with sack or vinegar, and their other provisions very short and bad. Yet, through the great providence of the Lord, they came all safe on shore, and most of them sound and well liking. They had continual tempests, and when they were near the shore, (being brought two or three days with a strong east wind,) the weather was so thick all that time as they could not make land, and the seamen were in great perplexity, when on the sudden the fog cleared, so as they saw Cape Ann fair on their starboard bow, and presently grew thick again; yet by their compass they made their harbor. There were aboard that ship two godly ministers, Mr. Nathaniel Rogers, and Mr. Partridge,[1] and many good people in that and the other ships; and we had prayed earnestly for them; (for a small pinnace of thirty tons, which came out with them, and was come in three weeks before, brought us news of their coming). In one of the other ships, the passengers had but half a pint of drink for a day, fourteen days together; yet, through the Lord's mercy, did all well. One of the ships was overset in the night by a sudden gust, and lay so half an hour, yet righted of herself.

Cattle were grown to high rates;—a good cow, £25 or £30; a pair of bulls or oxen, £40. Corn was now at 5s. the bushel, and much rye was sown with the plough this year, for about thirty ploughs were at work. Bread was at 9 and 10s. the C.; carpenters at 3s. the day, and other workmen accordingly.

Things went not well at Connecticut. Their cattle did, many of them, cast their young, as they had done the year before.

---

[1] Rogers and Partridge were installed respectively at Ipswich and Duxbury, and are celebrated in Cotton Mather's *Magnalia*, like many more of the preachers who pass in the review.

Mons. D'Aulney,[1] captain of Penobscott or Pentagouett, returned answer to the governor's letter, wherein he professed, that they claimed no further than to Pemaquid, nor would unless he had further order; and that he supposed, that the cause why he had no order, etc., was, that the English ambassador had dealt effectually with the cardinal of France for settling the limits for our peace, etc.

The governor, Mr. Vane, a wise and godly gentleman, held, with Mr. Cotton and many others, the indwelling of the person of the Holy Ghost in a believer, and went so far beyond the rest, as to maintain a personal union with the Holy Ghost; but the deputy,[2] with the pastor and divers others, denied both; and the question proceeded so far by disputation, (in writing, for the peace sake of the church, which all were tender of,) as at length they could not find the person of the Holy Ghost in scripture, nor in the primitive churches three hundred years after Christ. So that, all agreeing in the chief matter of substance, viz. that the Holy Ghost is God, and that he doth dwell in the believers, (as the Father and Son both are said also to do,) but whether by his gifts and power only, or by any other manner of presence, seeing the scripture doth not declare it,—it was earnestly desired, that the word person might be forborn, being a term of human invention, and tending to doubtful disputation in this case.

10ber (*December*).] The governor, receiving letters from his friends in England, which necessarily required his presence there, imparted the same to the council and some others; and, being thereupon resolved of his return into England, called a court of deputies, to the end he might have free leave of the country, etc. They, being assembled in court, and himself

---

[1] Charles de Menou, Sieur d'Aulnay-Charnisé. For a detailed account of the French enterprises with which Massachusetts became connected, see C. C. Smith, "Massachusetts and the Neighboring Jurisdictions," in the *Memorial History of Boston*, I. 282 *et seqq.*

[2] Winthrop, now deputy-governor, magnanimously opens here the record of his difference with Vane, now governor, who supported Mrs. Hutchinson.

declaring the necessity of his departure, and those of the council affirming the reasons to be very urgent, though not fit to be imparted to the whole court, they desired respite to consider thereof till the morning; when one of the assistants using some pathetical passages of the loss of such a governor in a time of such danger as did hang over us, from the Indians and French, the governor brake forth into tears, and professed, that howsoever the causes propounded for his departure were such as did concern the utter ruin of his outward estate, yet he would rather have hazarded all, than have gone from them at this time, if something else had not pressed him more, viz. the inevitable danger he saw of God's judgments to come upon us for these differences and dissensions, which he saw amongst us, and the scandalous imputations brought upon himself, as if he should be the cause of all; and therefore he thought it best for him to give place for a time, etc. Upon this the court concluded that it would not be fit to give way to his departure upon these grounds. Whereupon he recalled himself, and professed, that the reasons concerning his own estate were sufficient to his own satisfaction for his departure, and therefore desired the court he might have leave to go; as for the other passage, it slipped him out of his passion, and not out of judgment. Upon this the court consented, silently, to his departure. Then the question was about supply of his place. Some were of opinion, that it should be executed by the deputy; but this scruple being cast in, that if the deputy should die, then the government would be vacant, and none have power to call any court, or to preside therein, etc., it was agreed to call a court of elections, for a new governor and deputy, in case the present deputy should be chose governor; and an order was made, (in regard of the season,) that such as would might send their votes by proxy, in papers sealed up and delivered to the deputies. And so this court was adjourned four days, and two days after the court of elections was to assemble. These things thus passed, divers of the congregation of Boston met together, and agreed that they did not apprehend the necessity of the governor's departure upon the reasons alleged, and sent some of them to declare the same to the court; whereupon the governor expressed himself to be an obedient child to the church, and therefore, notwithstanding the license of the court, yet, without the leave of the church, he durst not go away.

Whereupon a great part of the court and country, who understood hereof, declared their purpose to continue him still in his place, and therefore, so soon as the day of election came, and the country were assembled, it was thought the best way for avoiding trouble, etc., not to proceed to election, but to adjourn the court to the great general court in May. And so the court of deputies, etc., continued still, (for the other court was not called).

At this court the elders of the churches were called, to advise with them about discovering and pacifying the differences among the churches in point of opinion. The governor having declared the occasion to them, Mr. Dudley desired, that men would be free and open, etc. Another of the magistrates spake, that it would much further the end they came for, if men would freely declare what they held different from others, as himself would freely do, in what point soever he should be opposed. The governor said, that he would be content to do the like, but that he understood the ministers were about it in a church way, etc., which he spake upon this occasion: the ministers had met, a little before, and had drawn into heads all the points, wherein they suspected Mr. Cotton did differ from them, and had propounded them to him, and pressed him to a direct answer, affirmative or negative, to every one; which he had promised, and taken time for. This meeting being spoke of in the court the day before, the governor took great offence at it, as being without his privity, etc., which this day Mr. Peter told him as plainly of, (with all due reverence,) and how it had sadded the ministers' spirits, that he should be jealous of their meetings, or seem to restrain their liberty, etc. The governor excused his speech, as sudden and upon a mistake. Mr. Peter told him also, that before he came, within less than two years since, the churches were in peace, etc. The governor answered, that the light of the gospel brings a sword, and the children of the bondwoman would persecute those of the freewoman. Mr. Peter also besought him humbly to consider his youth, and short experience in the things of God, and to beware of peremptory conclusions, which he perceived him to be very apt unto. He declared further, that he had observed, both in the Low Countries and here, three principal causes of new opinions and divisions thereupon: 1. Pride, new notions lift up the mind, etc. 2. Idleness. 3. [blank.]

Mr. Wilson made a very sad speech of the condition of our churches, and the inevitable danger of separation, if these differences and alienations among brethren were not speedily remedied; and laid the blame upon these new opinions risen up amongst us, which all the magistrates, except the governor and two others, did confirm, and all the ministers but two.

In this discourse one question arose about sanctification. Mr. Cotton, in his sermon that day, had laid down this ground, that evident sanctification was an evidence of justification, and thereupon had taught, that in cases of spiritual desertion, true desires of sanctification was found to be sanctification; and further, if a man were laid so flat upon the ground, as he could see no desires, etc., but only, as a bruised reed, did wait at the feet of Christ, yet here was matter of comfort for this, as found to be true.

The question here grew, whether any of these, or evident sanctification, could be evidence to a man without a concurrent sight of his justification. The governor and Mr. Cotton denied it.

The speech of Mr. Wilson was taken very ill by Mr. Cotton and others of the same church, so as he and divers of them went to admonish him. But Mr. Wilson and some others could see no breach of rule, seeing he was called by the court about the same matter with the rest of the elders, and exhorted to deliver their minds freely and faithfully, both for discovering the danger, and the means to help; and the things he spake of were only in general, and such as were under a common fame. And being questioned about his intent, he professed he did not mean Boston church, nor the members thereof, more than others. But this would not satisfy, but they called him to answer publicly, 31; and there the governor pressed it violently against him, and all the congregation, except the deputy and one or two more, and many of them with much bitterness and reproaches; but he answered them all with words of truth and soberness, and with marvellous wisdom. It was strange to see, how the common people were led, by example, to condemn him in that, which (it was very probable) divers of them did not understand,[1] nor the rule which he was supposed to have broken; and that such as had known him so long, and what good he had done for that church, should fall upon him with such bitterness for justifying himself in a good cause; for he was a very holy, upright man, and for faith and love inferior to none in the country, and most dear to all men. The teacher joined with the church in their judgment of him, (not without some appearance of prejudice,) yet with much wisdom and moderation. They were eager to proceed to present censure, but the teacher staid them from that, telling them he might not do it, because some opposed it, but gave him a grave exhortation. The next day Mr. Wilson preached, notwithstanding, and the Lord so assisted him, as gave great satisfaction, and the governor himself gave public witness to him.

One of the brethren[2] wrote to Mr. Cotton about it, and laid before him divers failings, (as he supposed,) and some reasons

[1] It may well be believed that plain men and women were deeply embarrassed in trying to understand what Savage calls "the deadly, unintelligible opinions" to which those whom they loved and respected were giving currency.

[2] Winthrop himself, no doubt, whose suffering over being out of sympathy with Cotton, and in general over the distractions, was acute.

to justify Mr. Wilson, and dealt very plainly with him. Mr. Cotton made a very loving and gentle answer, clearing his intentions, and persisting in his judgment of Mr. Wilson's offence, laying down divers arguments for it. The said brother replied to him in like loving manner, and desired leave to show his letter to Mr. Wilson, which he readily assented unto. But for answer to his arguments, he forbore to reply to Mr. Cotton, (because he was overburdened with business,) but wrote to the two ruling elders, (whom the matter most concerned,) and, by way of defence of Mr. Wilson, answered all Mr. Cotton's arguments.

Upon these public occasions, other opinions brake out publicly in the church of Boston,—as that the Holy Ghost dwelt in a believer as he is in heaven; that a man is justified before he believes; and that faith is no cause of justification. And others spread more secretly,—as that the letter of the scripture holds forth nothing but a covenant of works; and that the covenant of grace was the spirit of the scripture, which was known only to believers; and that this covenant of works was given by Moses in the ten commandments; that there was a seed (viz., Abraham's carnal seed) went along in this, and there was a spirit and life in it, by virtue whereof a man might attain to any sanctification in gifts and graces, and might have spiritual and continual communion with Jesus Christ, and yet be damned. After, it was granted, that faith was before justification, but it was only passive, an empty vessel, etc.; but in conclusion, the ground of all was found to be assurance by immediate revelation.

All the congregation of Boston, except four or five, closed with these opinions, or the most of them; but one of the brethren[1] wrote against them, and bore witness to the truth; together with the pastor, and very few others joined with them.

About this time the rest of the ministers, taking offence at some doctrines delivered by Mr. Cotton, and especially at

[1] Winthrop himself.

some opinions, which some of his church did broach, and for he seemed to have too good an opinion of, and too much familiarity with those persons, drew out sixteen points, and gave them to him, entreating him to deliver his judgment directly in them, which accordingly he did, and many copies thereof were dispersed about. Some doubts he well cleared, but in some things he gave not satisfaction. The rest of the ministers replied to these answers, and at large showed their dissent, and the grounds thereof; and, at the next general court, held 9th of the 1st,[1] they all assembled at Boston, and agreed to put off all lectures for three weeks, that they might bring things to some issue.

One Mr. Glover of Dorchester, having laid sixty pounds of gunpowder in bags to dry in the end of his chimney, it took fire, and some went up the chimney: other of it filled the room and passed out at a door into another room, and blew up a gable end. A maid, which was in the room, having her arms and neck naked, was scorched, and died soon after. A little child, in the arms of another, was scorched upon the face, but not killed. Two men were scorched, but not much. Divers pieces, which lay charged in several places, took fire and went off, but did no harm. The room was so dark with smoke, as those in the house could neither find door nor window, and when neighbors came in, none could see each other a good time for smoke. The house was thatched, yet took not fire; yet when the smoke was gone, many things were found burnt. Another great providence was, that three little children, being at the fire a little before, they went out to play, (though it were a very cold day,) and so were preserved.

[1] March 9, 1636/7.

1637

12 mo. (*February*) 22.] The lieutenant of Saybrook, at the mouth of Connecticut, going out with nine men, armed with swords and pieces, they started three Indians, whom they pursued till they were brought into an ambush of fifty, who came upon them, and slew four of their men, and had they not drawn their swords and retired, they had been all slain. The Indians were so hardy, as they came close up to them, notwithstanding their pieces.

(11.) (*January*) 10.] Capt. Turner's house in Sagus took fire by an oven about midnight, and was burnt down, with all that was in it, save the persons. About fourteen days since, a ship called the *George* of Bristol, laden with cattle and passengers, (having been some time at the Western Islands,)[1] and having spent her mainmast about Cape Cod, and after come near Brewster's Islands, was, by N. W. winds, forced to put into Plymouth.

20.] A general fast was kept in all the churches. The occasion was, the miserable estate of the churches in Germany; the calamities upon our native country, the bishops making havock in the churches, putting down the faithful ministers, and advancing popish ceremonies and doctrines, the plague raging exceedingly, and famine and sword threatening them; the dangers of those at Connecticut, and of ourselves also, by the Indians; and the dissensions in our churches.

The differences in the said points of religion increased more and more, and the ministers of both sides (there being only Mr. Cotton of one party) did publicly declare their judgments in some of them, so as all men's mouths were full of them.

[1] Azores.

And there being, 12 mo. (*February*) 3, a ship ready to go for England, and many passengers in it, Mr. Cotton took occasion to speak to them about the differences, etc., and willed them to tell our countrymen, that all the strife amongst us was about magnifying the grace of God; one party seeking to advance the grace of God within us, and the other to advance the grace of God towards us, (meaning by the one justification, and by the other sanctification;) and so bade them tell them, that, if there were any among them that would strive for grace, they should come hither; and so declared some particulars. Mr. Wilson spake after him, and declared, that he knew none of the elders or brethren of the churches, but did labor to advance the free grace of God in justification, so far as the word of God required; and spake also about the doctrine of sanctification, and the use and necessity, etc., of it; by occasion whereof no man could tell (except some few, who knew the bottom of the matter) where any difference was: which speech, though it offended those of Mr. Cotton's party, yet it was very seasonable to clear the rest, who otherwise should have been reputed to have opposed free grace. Thus every occasion increased the contention, and caused great alienation of minds; and the members of Boston (frequenting the lectures of other ministers) did make much disturbance by public questions, and objections to their doctrines, which did any way disagree from their opinions; and it began to be as common here to distinguish between men, by being under a covenant of grace or a covenant of works, as in other countries between Protestants and papists.[1]

February 6.] A man of Weymouth (but not of the church)

[1] How hurtful to the churches the controversy was, appears from the fact that for two years, while it was raging, the records show that no member was received into the Boston church. Yet so slight were the differences that both Cotton and Wilson unite in stating the trouble in such terms, that passengers to England may make no report of discord. Stoppage of immigration and interference from the authorities were to be feared if the melancholy story of the schism were related; both sides therefore tried to put a good face on things.

fell into some trouble of mind, and in the night cried out, "Art thou come, Lord Jesus?" and with that leaped out of his bed in his shirt, and, breaking from his wife, leaped out at a high window into the snow, and ran about seven miles off, and being traced in the snow, was found dead next morning. They might perceive, that he had kneeled down to prayer in divers places.

(1.) (*March*) 9.] The general court began. When any matter about these new opinions was mentioned, the court was divided; yet the greater number far were sound. They questioned the proceeding against Mr. Wilson, for his speech in the last court, but could not fasten upon such as had prejudiced him, etc.; but, by the vote of the greater party, his speech was approved, and declared to have been a seasonable advice, and no charge or accusation.

The ministers, being called to give advice about the authority of the court in things concerning the churches, etc., did all agree of these two things: 1. That no member of the court ought to be publicly questioned by a church for any speech in the court, without the license of the court. The reason was, because the court may have sufficient reason that may excuse the sin, which yet may not be fit to acquaint the church with, being a secret of state. The second thing was, that, in all such heresies or errors of any church members as are manifest and dangerous to the state, the court may proceed without tarrying for the church; but if the opinions be doubtful, etc., they are first to refer them to the church, etc.

At this court, when Mr. Wheelwright was to be questioned for a sermon, which seemed to tend to sedition, etc., near all the church of Boston presented a petition to the court for two things: 1. That as freemen they might be present in cases of judicature. 2. That the court would declare, if they might deal in cases of conscience before the church, etc. This was taken as a groundless and presumptuous act, especially at this season, and was rejected with this answer: That the court had never used to proceed judicially but it was openly; but for matter of consultation and preparation in causes, they might and would be private.

One Stephen Greensmith, for saying that all the ministers, except A. B. C., did teach a covenant of works, was censured to acknowledge his fault in every church, and fined £40.

Mr. Wheelwright, one of the members of Boston, preaching at the last fast, inveighed against all that walked in a covenant of works, as he described it to be, viz., such as maintain sanctification as an evidence of justification, etc. and called them antichrists, and stirred up the people against them with much bitterness and vehemency. For this he was called into the court, and his sermon being produced, he justified it, and confessed he did mean all that walk in such a way. Whereupon the elders of the rest of the churches were called, and asked whether they, in their ministry, did walk in such a way. They all acknowledged they did. So, after much debate, the court adjudged him guilty of sedition, and also of contempt, for that the court had appointed the fast as a means of reconciliation of the differences, etc., and he purposely set himself to kindle and increase them.[1] The governor and some few more (who dissented) tendered a protestation, which, because it wholly justified Mr. Wheelwright, and condemned the proceedings of the court, was rejected. The church of Boston also tendered a petition in his behalf, justifying Mr. Wheelwright's sermon. The court deferred sentence till the next court, and advised with the ministers, etc., whether they might enjoin his silence, etc. They answered, that they were not clear in

---

[1] Savage quotes from Wheelwright's sermon a passage characterized not only by piety, but by a quality in those days apparently more rare—sound common sense. He in particular rejects the name "antinomian," which though not employed here by Winthrop, was by many others affixed as a stigma to the heresies of Mrs. Hutchinson and her followers. Cotton upheld Wheelwright, and in 1654, the General Court rendered to Wheelwright, who as an exile in New Hampshire effected much good, a tardy but substantial justice. See Mather, *Magnalia*, book VII., chap. III., sec. 3.

that point, but desired rather, that he might be commended to the church of Boston to take care of him, etc., which accordingly was done, and he enjoined to appear at the next court. Much heat of contention was this court between the opposite parties; so as it was moved, that the next court might be kept at Newtown. The governor refused to put it to the vote; the deputy was loath to do it, except the court would require him, because he dwelt in Boston, etc. So the court put it to Mr. Endecott.

21.] Miantunnomoh, etc., sent twenty-six, with forty fathom of wampom and a Pequod's hand. We gave four of the chief each a coat of fourteen shillings price, and deferred to return our present till after, according to their manner.

Mo. 2. (*April*) 1.] Those of Connecticut returned answer to our public letters, wherein they showed themselves unsatisfied about our former expedition against the Pequods, and their expectations of a further prosecution of the war, to which they offer to send men, and signify their unpreparedness to declare themselves in the matter of government, in regard of their engagement to attend the answer of the gentlemen of Saybrook about the same matter.

10.] Capt. Underhill was sent to Saybrook, with twenty men, to keep the fort, both in respect of the Indians, and especially of the Dutch, who, by their speeches and supplies out of Holland, gave cause of suspicion that they had some design upon it. The men were sent at the charge of the gentlemen of Saybrook, and lent by order of the council here, for fear any advantage should be taken by the adverse party, through the weakness of the place.

6.] The church of Concord kept a day of humiliation at Newtown, for ordination of their elders, and they chose Mr. Buckly[1] teacher, and Mr. Jones pastor. Upon a question moved by one sent from the church of Salem, it was resolved

---

[1] The Reverend Peter Bulkeley.

by the ministers there present, that such as had been ministers in England were lawful ministers by the call of the people there, notwithstanding their acceptance of the call of the bishops, etc., (for which they humbled themselves, acknowledging it their sin, etc.,) but being come hither, they accounted themselves no ministers, until they were called to another church, and that, upon election, they were ministers before they were solemnly ordained.

The governor, and Mr. Cotton, and Mr. Wheelwright, and the two ruling elders of Boston, and the rest of that church, which were of any note, did none of them come to this meeting. The reason was conceived to be, because they accounted these as legal preachers, and therefore would not give approbation to their ordination.

3. (*May*) 2.] Mr. Haynes, one of our magistrates, removed with his family to Connecticut.

12.] We received a letter from him and others, being then at Saybrook, that the Pequods had been up the river at Weathersfield, and had killed six men, being at their work, and twenty cows and a mare, and had killed three women, and carried away two maids.

Mr. Winslow was sent from the governor and council of Plymouth to treat with us about joining against the Pequods. He declared first their willingness to aid us; but that they could not do any thing till their general court, which was not till the first Tuesday in the 4th month. Then he made some objections: as, 1. Our refusal to aid them against the French. 2. Our people's trading at Kenebeck. 3. The injury offered them at Connecticut by those of Windsor, in taking away their land there. 4. Their own poverty, and our ability, which needed not any help from them.

To this answer was made by our governor and deputy: that, 1. We did not desire them to afford aid unto us, but to join against the common enemy, who, if he were not subdued, would prove as dangerous to them as to us, and, he prevailing, would cause all the Indians in the country to join to root out all the English. 2. For our refusal to aid them against the French, the case was not alike, for it was their private quarrel, and they were supposed to have commission from the king of France, and we thought it no wisdom for us to engage ourselves in a war with the king of France; yet we acknowledged some failing in it. For our people's trading at Kenebeck, we answered, that we gave no allowance to it, nor had we heard of more than a boat or two that had been there. For the injury done them at Connecticut, we had dealt with them to give satisfaction, but it was not in our power to do them justice in it. He alleged also, that this war did not concern them, seeing the Pequods had not killed any of theirs. We answered, that Capt. Stone, etc., for whom this war was begun, were none of ours neither. He alleged further, that, in our first undertaking, they were not acquainted with it till two or three days before our forces were to go forth. We answered, we intended at the first to send only to Block Island, and for that we thought it not needful to trouble them, and our sending them thence to the Pequods was with hope to draw them to parley, and so to some quiet end. We concluded to write further to them from our next court. And whereas they propounded to have us promise to aid them in all their occasions, etc., we answered that, seeing, when we now treated with them about joining with us, they were at liberty and might withhold, except they saw reason to move them; so we desired to be left free, that we might judge of the reason of any such occasion as might fall out. According hereunto we writ to them the 20th of the 3d month, and gave them some considerations, why they should join with us: as, 1. because, if we should be overcome, it would cost them more to help us, and be less acceptable; 2. if we should prevail without them, it would occasion ill thoughts in our people towards theirs, etc. So we left it to them.[1]

[1] This letter of Winthrop's, of May 20, 1637, is given in full by Bradford, pp. 335–337.

17.] Our court of elections was at Newtown. So soon as the court was set, being about one of the clock, a petition was preferred by those of Boston. The governor would have read it, but the deputy said it was out of order; it was a court for elections, and those must first be despatched, and then their petitions should be heard. Divers others also opposed that course, as an ill precedent, etc.; and the petition, being about pretence of liberty, etc., (though intended chiefly for revoking the sentence given against Mr. Wheelwright,) would have spent all the day in debate, etc.; but yet the governor and those of that party would not proceed to election, except the petition was read. Much time was already spent about this debate, and the people crying out for election, it was moved by the deputy, that the people should divide themselves, and the greater number must carry it. And so it was done, and the greater number by many were for election. But the governor and that side kept their place still, and would not proceed. Whereupon the deputy told him, that, if he would not go to election, he and the rest of that side would proceed. Upon that, he came from his company, and they went to election; and Mr. Winthrop was chosen governor, Mr. Dudley deputy and Mr. Endecott of the standing council; and Mr. Israel Stoughton and Mr. Richard Saltonstall were called in to be assistants; and Mr. Vane, Mr. Coddington, and Mr. Dummer, (being all of that faction,) were left quite out.

There was great danger of a tumult that day; for those of that side grew into fierce speeches, and some laid hands on others; but seeing themselves too weak, they grew quiet. They expected a great advantage that day, because the remote towns were allowed to come in by proxy; but it fell out, that there were enough beside. But if it had been otherwise, they must have put in their deputies, as other towns had done, for all matters beside elections. Boston, having deferred to choose deputies till the election was passed, went home that night, and the next morning they sent Mr. Vane, the late governor, and

Mr. Coddington, and Mr. Hoffe, for their deputies; but the court, being grieved at it, found a means to send them home again, for that two of the freemen of Boston had not notice of the election. So they went all home, and the next morning they returned the same gentlemen again upon a new choice; and the court not finding how they might reject them, they were admitted.

Upon the election of the new governor, the serjeants, who had attended the old governor to the court, (being all Boston men, where the new governor also dwelt,) laid down their halberds and went home; and whereas they had been wont to attend the former governor to and from the meetings on the Lord's days, they gave over now, so as the new governor was fain to use his own servants to carry two halberds before him; whereas the former governor had never less than four.

Divers writings were now published about these differences. Among the rest, the magistrates set forth an apology[1] to justify the sentence of the court against Mr. Wheelwright, which the adverse party had much opposed and spoken evil of, and did also set forth a remonstrance to that end, in which they did not deal fairly; for, in abbreviating Mr. Wheelwright his sermon, they clear altered both the words and meaning of such passages in it, whereat the offence was taken, and which were the ground of the court's sentence.

Mr. Wheelwright also himself set forth a small tractate about the principal doctrine of his sermon, viz., about the covenant of grace, which was also differing from his sermon.

The other ministers also set out an answer to his sermon, confuting the same by many strong arguments.

Mr. Cotton also replied to their answer very largely, and stated the differences in a very narrow scantling; and Mr. Shepherd, preaching at the day of election, brought them yet nearer, so as, except men of good understanding, and such as knew the bottom of the tenets of those of the other party, few

[1] Printed in the *Short Story*, of which more later.

could see where the difference was; and indeed it seemed so small, as (if men's affections had not been formerly alienated, when the differences were formerly stated as fundamental) they might easily have come to reconciliation. For in these particulars they agreed: 1. That justification and sanctification were both together in time; 2. That a man must know himself to be justified, before he can know himself to be sanctified; 3. That the spirit never witnesseth justification without a word and a work.

The difference was, whether the first assurance be by an absolute promise always, and not by a conditional also, and whether a man could have any true assurance, without sight of some such work in his soul as no hypocrite could attain unto.[1]

At the court Mr. Wheelwright, according as he was enjoined, did appear; but, because a general day of humiliation was appointed, and it was agreed, that all the churches should choose certain men to meet and confer about the differences, the court gave him respite to the next session, (which was appointed the first Tuesday in August,) to bethink himself, that, retracting and reforming his error, etc., the court might show him favor, which otherwise he must not expect. His answer was, that if he had committed sedition, then he ought to be put to death; and if we did mean to proceed against him, he meant to appeal to the king's court; for he could retract nothing. The court told him, that they were clear in the justice of their proceeding, and should judge of his offence as they had done, if it were to do again; but if, upon the conference among the churches, the Lord should discover any further light to them than as yet they had seen, they should gladly embrace it.

[1] The folly and pitiableness of this dissension over matters which the combatants themselves admitted to be so trifling is brought home to us in reading that in these days the Boston men gathered for the Pequot war, a most important contingent of the force, came near refusing to march, because the chaplain, John Wilson, was under a "covenant of works." And yet there has never been in New England a call for men more imperative. Palfrey, *History of New England*, I. 492.

The intent of the court in deferring the sentence was, that, being thus provoked by their tumultuous course, and divers insolent speeches, which some of that party had uttered in the court, and having now power enough to have crushed them, their moderation and desire of reconciliation might appear to all.

Having received intelligence from Miantunnomoh, that the Pequods had sent their women and children to an island for their safety, we presently sent away forty men by land to the Narigansetts, and there to take in Miantunnomoh, (and he offered to send sixteen men with ours,) and so, in the night, to set upon them.

We also provided to send one hundred and sixty[1] more after them to prosecute the war; and Mr. Stoughton, one of the magistrates, was sent with them, and Mr. Wilson, the pastor of Boston. These two were chosen thus in the open court: Three magistrates were set apart, and one was designed by a lot; also the elders set apart two; and a lot was cast between them in a solemn public invocation of the name of God.

22.] Miantunnomoh sent us word, that Capt. Mason,[2] with a company of the English upon the river, had surprised and slain eight Pequods, and taken seven squaws, and with some of them had redeemed the two English maids.

24.] By letters from Mr. Williams we were certified, (which the next day was confirmed by some who came from Saybrook,) that Capt. Mason was come to Saybrook with eighty

---

[1] The relative strength of the towns of the colony at this time may be inferred from the apportionment of this body—Boston, 26; Salem, 18; Ipswich, 17; Lynn, 16; Watertown, 14; Dorchester, 13; Charlestown, 12; Roxbury, 10; Newtown, 9; Newbury, 8; Hingham, 6; Weymouth, 5; Medford, 3; Marblehead, 3. (Savage.)

[2] Captain John Mason led the little army with great courage and skill. A better or more necessary piece of Indian fighting has perhaps never been done: it saved the colony from extinction. Sir Thomas Fairfax, Mason's old comrade in England, desired his services in the army of the Parliament. An account of the Pequot war was written by Mason himself, *Massachusetts Historical Society's Collections*, second series, VIII. 232, and another by Lyon Gardiner, *ibid.*, third series, III. 136, 173. Mason's life has been written by George E. Ellis.

English and one hundred Indians; and that the Indians had gone out there, and met with seven Pequods; five they killed; one they took alive, whom the English put to torture; and set all their heads upon the fort. The reason was, because they had tortured such of our men as they took alive.

The Dutch governor sent a sloop to Pequod to redeem the two English maids by what means soever, though it were with breach of their peace with the Pequods.[1] The sloop offered largely for their ransom; but nothing would be accepted. So the Dutch, having many Pequods aboard, stayed six of them, (the rest leaped overboard,) and with them redeemed the two maids, who had been well used by the Pequods, and no violence offered them.

The former governor and Mr. Coddington, being discontented that the people had left them out of all public service, gave further proof of it in the congregation; for they refused to sit in the magistrate's seat, (where Mr. Vane had always sitten from his first arrival,) and went and sate with the deacons, although the governor sent to desire them to come in to him. And upon the day of the general fast, they went from Boston to keep the day at the Mount with Mr. Wheelwright.

Another occasion of their discontent, and of the rest of that party, was an order, which the court had made, to keep out all such persons as might be dangerous to the commonwealth, by imposing a penalty upon all such as should retain any, etc., above three weeks, which should not be allowed by some of the magistrates; for it was very probable, that they expected many of their opinion to come out of England from Mr. Brierly his church, etc.[2]

---

[1] The humanity and bravery of the Dutch in risking a war with the Pequots to ransom the English maids, is commendable. Johnson says, *Wonder-Working Providence*, book II., chap. I., that the Pequots asked the maids if they could make gunpowder. They plainly felt their disadvantage.

[2] Winthrop wrote at this time a "Defense of the Order of the Court," to which Vane wrote "A Brief Answer," of which interchange of papers no mention is made here. The papers are preserved in *Hutchinson Papers*, I. 79, 84.

This order, and other differences between the new governor and them, was the cause, that, at his return to Boston, none of them met him; and the serjeants, which had constantly attended the former governor to all public meetings with four halberds, did now refuse to do any such office to the new, alleging that they had done it to the former voluntarily, in respect of his person, not his place. To which it was answered, that there was a double error; 1. Because the place drowns the person, be he honorable or base; 2. In that any compliment of honor, being once conferred upon an office, (though voluntarily,) cannot after be taken away without contempt and injury. The country, taking notice of this, offered to send in some from the neighboring towns to carry the halberds by course; and upon that the town of Boston offered to send some men, but not the serjeants; but the governor chose rather to make use of two of his own servants.

25.] Our English from Connecticut, with their Indians, and many of the Naragansetts, marched in the night to a fort of the Pequods at Mistick, and, besetting the same about break of the day, after two hours' fight they took it, (by firing it,) and slew therein two chief sachems, and one hundred and fifty fighting men, and about one hundred and fifty old men, women, and children, with the loss of two English, whereof but one was killed by the enemy. Divers of the Indian friends were hurt by the English, because they had not some mark to distinguish them from the Pequods, as some of them had. The story is more fully described in the next leaf.[1]

Presently upon this came news from the Naragansett, that

Vane's "Brief Answer" is memorable as containing the first adumbration of an idea for which he was afterward to struggle upon a larger stage—the idea of toleration. For the order of the court, see *Mass. Col. Records*, I. 196. From Cotton's *Way of the Congregational Churches Cleared*, a famous book, it appears that he, as well as Vane, felt outraged by the order, thus showing the more liberal spirit which in a different environment might have characterized him. He designed at this time, says Savage, to remove to Connecticut, but was dissuaded.

[1] This account has been lost, if it were ever written, but Mason's report (Ellis, *Mason*) is very vivid, recording much ruthlessness as well as valor.

all the English, and two hundred of the Indians, were cut off in their retreat, for want of powder and victuals. Three days after, this was confirmed by a post from Plymouth, with such probable circumstances, as it was generally believed. But, three days after, Mr. Williams, having gone to the Naragansetts to discover the truth, found them mourning, as being confident of it; but that night some came from the army, and assured them all was well, and that all the Pequods were fled, and had forsaken their forts. The general defeat of the Pequods at Mistick happened the day after our general fast.[1]

Mo. 4. (*June*) 3.] Two ships arrived here out of England, (Mr. Peirce was one). In them came the copy of a commission, from the commissioners for New England, to divers of the magistrates here, to govern all the people in New England till further order, etc., upon this pretence, that there was no lawful authority in force here, either mediate or immediate, from his majesty.[2]

Upon the news from Mr. Williams, that the Pequods were dispersed, and some come in and submitted to the Naragansetts, (who would not receive them before he had sent to know our mind,) the governor and council thought it needless to send so many men, and therefore sent out warrants only for one half of the two hundred; but some of the people liked not of it, and came to the governor to have all sent. He took it ill; and though three of the ministers came with them to debate the matter, he told them, that if any one, discerning an error in the proceedings of the council, had come, in a private manner, to acquaint him therewith, etc., it had been well done; but to come, so many of them, in a public and popular way, was not well, and would bring authority into contempt. This they took well at his hands, and excused their intentions.

---

[1] It was through Roger Williams that the Narragansetts were held firm to the English (Ellis, *Mason*, p. 360), a fact which Winthrop does not make clear.

[2] In addition to all the other trouble, here was a new event full of evil import.

So it was thought fit to send about forty men more, which was yielded rather to satisfy the people, than for any need that appeared.

Upon our governor's letter to Plymouth, our friends there agreed to send a pinnace, with forty men, to assist in the war against the Pequods; but they could not be ready to meet us at the first.

15.] There was a day of thanksgiving kept in all the churches for the victory obtained against the Pequods, and for other mercies.

About this time came home a small pinnace of thirty tons, which had been forth eight months, and was given for lost. She went to the Bermuda, but by continual tempests was kept from thence, and forced to bear up for the West Indies, and, being in great distress, arrived at Hispaniola, and not daring to go into any inhabited place there, but to go ashore in obscure places, and lived of turtles and hogs, etc. At last they were forced into a harbor, where lay a French man-of-war with his prize, and had surely made prize of them also, but that the providence of God so disposed, as the captain, one Petfree, had lived at Pascataquack, and knew the merchant of our bark, one Mr. Gibbons. Whereupon he used them courteously, and, for such commodities as she carried, freighted her with tallow, hides, etc., and sent home with her his prize, which he sold for a small price to be paid in New England. He brought home an aligarto, which he gave the governor.[1]

20.] Three ships arrived here from Ipswich, with three hundred and sixty passengers. The last being loath to come to an anchor at Castle Island, though hailed by the Castle boat, and required, etc., the gunner made a shot, intending to shoot before her for a warning, but the powder in the touch-hole being wet, and the ship having fresh way with wind and tide, the shot took place in the shrouds and killed a passenger,

---

[1] Mr. C. F. Adams, *Three Episodes of Massachusetts History*, p. 357, suspects that Gibbons's story masks a buccaneering venture.

an honest man. The next day the governor charged an inquest, and sent them aboard with two of the magistrates (one of them being deputed coroner) to take view of the dead body, and who, upon hearing all the evidence, etc., found that he came to his death by the providence of God.

23.] The governor went to Sagus, and so to Salem and to Ipswich, at all which places the men of the towns met him, and guarded him from town to town, (though not desired nor expected by him,) to show their respect to their governor, and also for his safety, in regard it was reported the Pequods were come this way. He returned again the 28th, being forced to travel all the night by reason of the heat, which was so extreme, as divers of those who were new come on shore, died in their travel a few miles.

26.] There arrived two ships from London, the *Hector*, and the [blank]. In these came Mr. Davenport and another minister, and Mr. Eaton and Mr. Hopkins, two merchants of London, men of fair estate and of great esteem for religion, and wisdom in outward affairs.[1]

In the *Hector* came also the Lord Ley, son and heir of the Earl of Marlborough, being about nineteen years of age, who

[1] John Davenport, Theophilus Eaton and Edward Hopkins are among the most distinguished of the Connecticut worthies. The first, like Cotton and Hooker, having achieved eminence in England, came to America a man of forty, and though urged to remain in Massachusetts, threw in his lot with the New Haven settlement, which he greatly influenced. He was remembered in his old home, and with Cotton and Hooker, was invited to sit in the Westminster Assembly. Declining this honor, he worked on in the wilderness, bravely sheltering the regicides Whalley and Goffe, at his own peril. Later in life he succeeded John Norton as minister of the First Church in Boston, for him not a happy change, dying there at the age of seventy-two. Eaton, who before his emigration had been envoy to Denmark, was for twenty years governor of New Haven, while Hopkins, his son-in-law, was, alternately with Haynes, governor of the neighboring colony of Hartford, or Connecticut. The doubling in New England colonization must be remembered or one may be misled: as in Massachusetts we find Plymouth and the Bay, so farther south we have Providence and Rhode Island, and near the great river, Connecticut and New Haven; the doubling of capitals, so long maintained in Rhode Island and Connecticut, was a survival of the early state of things. Hopkins returned to England, where he was a man of mark during the Protectorate.

came only to see the country. He was of very sober carriage, and showed much wisdom and moderation in his lowly and familiar carriage, especially in the ship, where he was much disrespected and unworthily used by the master, one Ferne, and some of the passengers; yet he bare it meekly and silently. When he came on shore the governor was from home, and he took up his lodging at the common inn. When the governor returned, he presently came to his house. The governor offered him lodging, etc., but he refused, saying, that he came not to be troublesome to any, and the house where he was, was so well governed, that he could be as private there as elsewhere.

We had news of a commission granted in England to divers gentlemen here for the governing of New England, etc.; but instead thereof we received a commission from Sir Ferdinando Gorges to govern his province of New Somersetshire, which is from Cape Elizabeth to Sagadahoc, and withal to oversee his servants and private affairs; which was observed as a matter of no good discretion, but passed in silence. We excused our not intermeddling, etc., because, being directed to six or five of them, and one of their names being mistaken, and another removed to Connecticut, there were but four in the country; as also for that it did not appear to us what authority he had to grant such a commission.[1] As for the commission from the king, we received only a copy of it, but the commission itself staid at the seal for want of paying the fees.

Mo. 5 (*July*).] The party, who procured the commission, one George Cleves, brought also a protection under the privy signet for searching out the great lake of Iracoyce,[2] and for the sole trade of beaver, and the planting of Long Island, by articles of agreement between the Earl of Sterling, Viscount

---

[1] Gorges had received a grant of this territory from the Council for New England, in February, 1635.

[2] Iroquois. This, it may be surmised, was Lake Champlain, of which the English settlers, now striking west, would be likely to hear.

Canada, and him.[1] Thus this and other gentlemen in England get large circuits of lands, etc., in this country, and are very ready to grant them out to such as will become their tenants, and, to encourage them, do procure commissions, protections, etc., which cost them nothing, but will be at no charge in any right way of plantation, which should be by coming themselves, or sending some of their children, etc.; but now, as they adventure little, so they are sure to lose nothing but their vain hope.

Capt. Stoughton and his company, having pursued the Pequots beyond Connecticut, and missing of them, returned to Pequot River, where they were advertised, that one hundred of them were newly come back to a place some twelve miles off. So they marched thither by night, and surprised them all. They put to death twenty-two men, and reserved two sachems, hoping by them to get Sasacus, (which they promised). All the rest were women and children, of whom they gave the Naragansetts thirty, and our Massachusetts Indians three, and the rest they sent hither.

A pinnace, returning, took a canoe with four Indians near Block Island. We sent to Miantunnomoh to know what they were, and after we discharged all save one, who was a Pequod, whom we gave Mr. Cutting to carry into England.

The differences grew so much here, as tended fast to a separation; so as Mr. Vane, being, among others, invited by the governor to accompany the Lord Ley at dinner, not only refused to come, (alleging by letter that his conscience withheld him,) but also, at the same hour, he went over to Nottle's Island to dine with Mr. Maverick, and carried the Lord Ley with him.

6.] There were sent to Boston forty-eight women and children. There were eighty taken, as before is expressed. These were disposed of to particular persons in the country. Some

---

[1] Sir William Alexander, Earl of Stirling, Viscount Canada, poet and courtier, had in 1635 received Long Island by grant from the Council for New England.

of them ran away and were brought again by the Indians our neighbors, and those we branded on the shoulder.

12.] Ayanemo, the sachem of Niantick, came to Boston with seventeen men. He made divers propositions, which we promised to give answer unto the next day; and then, understanding he had received many of the Pequods, submitting to him since the former defeat, we first demanded the delivery of them, which he sticking at, we refused further conference with him; but the next morning he came, and offered what we desired. So the governor referred him to treat with our captains at the Pequod, and wrote instructions to them how to deal with him, and received his present of ten fathom of wampom. He was lovingly dismissed, with some small things given him.[1]

Here came over a brother of Mrs. Hutchinson, and some other of Mr. Wheelwright's friends, whom the governor thought not fit to allow, as others, to sit down among us, without some trial of them. Therefore, to save others from the danger of the law in receiving of them, he allowed them for four months. This was taken very ill by those of the other party, and many hot speeches given forth about it, and about their removal, etc.

13.] Mr. Stoughton, with about eighty of the English, whereof Mr. Ludlow, Capt. Mason, and [*blank*,] of Connecticut, were part, sailed to the west in pursuit of Sasacus, etc. At Quinepiack,[2] they killed six, and took two. At a head of land a little short they beheaded two sachems; whereupon they called the place Sachem's Head. About this time they had given a Pequod his life to go find out Sasacus. He went, and found him not far off; but Sasacus, suspecting him, intended to kill him, which the fellow perceiving, escaped in the night,

---

[1] The severities of seventeenth-century warfare were perhaps no more marked in New than in old England, the prisoners captured at Dunbar and Worcester, for instance, faring little better than the Pequots.

[2] Now New Haven.

and came to the English. Whereupon Sasacus and Mononotto, their two chief sachems, and some twenty more, fled to the Mohawks. But eighty of their stoutest men, and two hundred others, women and children, were at a place within twenty or thirty miles of the Dutch, whither our men marched, and, being guided by a Divine Providence, came upon them, where they had twenty wigwams, hard by a most hideous swamp, so thick with bushes and so quagmiry, as men could hardly crowd into it. Into this swamp they were all gotten. Lieut. Davenport and two or three more, that entered the swamp, were dangerously wounded by the Indian arrows, and with much difficulty were fetched out. Then our men surrounded the swamp, being a mile about, and shot at the Indians, and they at them, from three of the clock in the afternoon till they desired parley, and offered to yield, and life was offered to all that had not shed English blood. So they began to come forth, now some and then some, till about two hundred women and children were come out, and amongst them the sachem of that place, and thus they kept us two hours, till night was come on, and then the men told us they would fight it out; and so they did all the night, coming up behind the bushes very near our men, and shot many arrows into their hats, sleeves, and stocks, yet (which was a very miracle) not one of ours wounded. When it was near morning, it grew very dark, so as such of them as were left crept out at one place and escaped, being (as was judged) not above twenty at most, and those like to be wounded; for in the pursuit they found some of them dead of their wounds. Here our men gat some booty of kettles, trays, wampom, etc., and the women and children were divided, and sent some to Connecticut, and some to the Massachusetts. The sachem of the place, having yielded, had his life, and his wife and children, etc. The women, which were brought home, reported that we had slain in all thirteen sachems, and that there were thirteen more left. We had now slain and taken, in all, about seven hundred. We sent fifteen of the boys and two women to Bermuda, by Mr. Peirce; but he, missing it, carried them to Providence Isle.[1]

Mo. 6 (*August*).] Mr. Stoughton sailed, with some of his company, from Pequod to Block Island. They came thither in the night, yet were discovered, and our men having killed one or two of them, and burnt some of their wigwams, etc., they came to parley, and, submitting themselves to become tributaries in one hundred fathom wampompeague, and to deliver any that should be found to have any hand in Mr. Oldham's death, they were all received, and no more harm done them.

3.] At our general court, one Greensmith, being censured for saying that all the elders, etc., except two, did preach a covenant of works, etc., he did appeal to the king; but the court, notwithstanding, committed him till, etc.

The Lord Ley, being told that one Ewre had spoken treason against the king, sent for the party, one Brooks, and inquiring of him, he told him that Ewre had said, about twelve months before, that, if the king did send any authority hither against our patent, he would be the first should resist him. This coming to the governor's knowledge, he sent for the parties, and bound them over to the general court. When they came there, Brooks brought his wife to witness with him; but her testimony agreed not with his; also three others (whom he had told it unto) reported it otherwise. So at length they all agreed, and set it under their hands, that Ewre said, that, if there came any authority out of England contrary to the patent, he would withstand it. Now, because here was no mention of the king, and because he never informed any of the magistrates of it, and for that it was evident that he bare malice to the said Ewre, we saw no cause to take any other of the parties informing, (the rather because themselves did urge it, and she re-

[1] An island in the Caribbean, off the Nicaraguan coast. In 1630 Charles I. granted it, by a patent similar to that of Massachusetts, to a company of Englishmen, mostly Puritans, who held it till 1641, when the Spaniards captured it.

fused longer to speak at all, except she might be put to her oath,) nor any offence which deserved punishment, seeing it is lawful to resist any authority, which was to overthrow the lawful authority of the king's grant; and so the governor did openly declare, in the court, as justifiable by the laws of England.

3.] The Lord Ley and Mr. Vane went from Boston to the ship, riding at Long Island, to go for England. At their departure, those of Mr. Vane's party were gathered together, and did accompany him to the boat, (and many to the ship;) and the men, being in their arms, gave him divers vollies of shot, and five pieces of ordnance, and he had five more at the castle. But the governor was not come from the court, but had left order with the captain for their honorable dismission.[1]

There was an old woman in Ipswich, who came out of England blind and deaf, yet her son could make her understand any thing, and know any man's name, by her sense of feeling. He would write upon her hand some letters of the name, and by other such motions would inform her. This the governor himself had trial of when he was at Ipswich.

5.] Mr. Hooker and Mr. Stone came, with Mr. Wilson, from Connecticut by Providence; and, the same day, Mr. Ludlow, Mr. Pincheon, and about twelve more, came the ordinary way by land, and brought with them a part of the skin and lock of hair of Sasacus and his brother, and five other Pequod sachems, who, being fled to the Mohawks for shelter, with their wampom, being to the value of five hundred pounds, were by them surprised and slain, with twenty of their best men. Mononottoh was also taken, but escaped wounded. They brought news also of divers other Pequods, which had been slain by other

---

[1] The present editor has in another work ventured to declare that Harry Vane's career in America, while characterized by shortcomings attributable largely to the immaturity of one scarcely beyond boyhood, nevertheless foreshadows the course of the able and virtuous statesman Vane afterward became. Hosmer, *Life of Young Sir Henry Vane*, 77.

Indians, and their heads brought to the English; so that now there had been slain and taken between eight and nine hundred. Whereupon letters were sent to Mr. Stoughton and the rest, to call them all home.

A woman of Boston congregation, having been in much trouble of mind about her spiritual estate, at length grew into utter desperation, and could not endure to hear of any comfort, etc., so as one day she took her little infant and threw it into a well, and then came into the house and said, now she was sure she should be damned, for she had drowned her child; but some, stepping presently forth, saved the child. See more after.

Mr. Hooker and the rest of the elders, meeting divers days, they agreed (with consent of the magistrates) upon a day of humiliation to be kept in all the churches the 24th of this month; the day for the conference to be the 30th day. At their private meetings some reconciliation was made between Mr. Cotton and Mr. Wheelwright and Mr. Wilson, he professing, that, by his speech in the court, he did not intend the doctrine of Mr. Cotton or Mr. Wheelwright delivered in the public congregation, but some opinions, (naming three or four,) which were privately carried in Boston and other parts of the country; and accordingly Mr. Cotton declared so much in the congregation the Lord's day following. And for the rest of his speech, it was agreed by all the elders to be inoffensive, considering his call thereto by the court. This sudden change was much observed by some, who were privy that Mr. Wilson had professed as much before, both privately to the elders, and publicly in the congregation, and that the said opinions had been delivered to the elders of Boston in writing as those which Mr. Wilson intended.

17.] Mr. Davenport preached at Boston (it being the lecture day) out of that in 1 Cor., I exhort you brethren, etc., that there be no division among you, etc.; wherein, as he fully set forth the nature and danger of divisions, and the disorders which were among us, etc., so he clearly discovered his judgment against the new opinions and bitter practices which were sprung up here.

Mr. Cotton, expounding that in 2 Chron. [blank] of the defection of the ten tribes from Rehoboam, and his preparations to recover them by war, and the prophet's prohibition, etc., proved from that in Numbers, 27. 21, that the rulers of the people should consult with the ministers of the churches upon occasion of any war to be undertaken, and any other weighty business, though the case should seem never so clear, as David in the case of Ziglag, and the Israelites in the case of Gibeah. Judges, etc.

26.] The captain and soldiers returned all from Pequod, having lost but one man, and he died of a flux, and another fell sick of an old infirmity, an asthma. The Indians about sent in still many Pequods' heads and hands from Long Island and other places, and [blank] sachems of Long Island came voluntarily, and brought a tribute to us of twenty fathom of wampom, each of them; and Miantunnomoh sent here some Pequod squaws, which had run from us.

31.] The Naragansetts sent us the hands of three Pequods,—one the chief of those who murdered Capt. Stone.

Twenty men went in a pinnace to kill sea horse at the Isle of Sable, and after six weeks returned home, and could not find the island; but, after another month, viz., about the [blank] of September, they set forth again with more skilful seamen, with intent to stay there all winter.

Mr. Eaton, and some others of Mr. Davenport's company, went to view Quinepiack, with intent to begin a plantation there. They had many offers here and at Plymouth, and they had viewed many places, but none could content.

Some of the magistrates and ministers of Connecticut being here, there was a day of meeting appointed to agree upon some articles of confederation, and notice was given to Plymouth, that they might join in it, (but their warning was so short as they could not come). This was concluded after. See (3.) 1643.

30.] The synod, called the assembly, began at Newtown. There were all the teaching elders through the country, and some new come out of England, not yet called to any place here, as Mr. Davenport, etc.

The assembly began with prayer, made by Mr. Shepherd, the pastor of Newtown. Then the erroneous opinions, which were spread in the country, were read, (being eighty in all;) next the unwholesome expressions; then the scriptures abused. Then they chose two moderators for the next day, viz., Mr. Buckly and Mr. Hooker, and these were continued in that place all the time of the assembly. There were about eighty opinions, some blasphemous, others erroneous, and all unsafe, condemned by the whole assembly; whereto near all the elders, and others sent by the churches, subscribed their names; but some few liked not subscription, though they consented to the condemning of them.[1]

Some of the church of Boston, and some others, were offended at the producing of so many errors, as if it were a reproach laid upon the country without cause; and called to have the persons named, which held those errors. To which it was answered and affirmed by many, both elders and others, that all those opinions could be proved, by sufficient testimony, to be held by some in the country; but it was not thought fit to name the parties, because this assembly had not to do with persons, but doctrines only. Yet this would not satisfy some, but they oft called for witnesses; and, because some of the magistrates declared to them, (when they refused to forbear

---

[1] Boston in these days was not a pleasant place to dwell in. What with the home-coming of the ministers and the notable men from the Pequot war with such gruesome trophies as the scalps of Sassacus and his tribesmen, with the weak-minded becoming insane through religious excitement, and the convening of a synod whose acts were to be marked by much severity, the harsh features of the picture are very salient. Winthrop omits many details here, but treats the subject at length in *A Short Story*, of which more presently.

speech unseasonably, though the moderators desired them), that, if they would not forbear, it would prove a civil disturbance, and then the magistrate must interpose, they objected against this, as if the magistrate had nothing to do in this assembly. So as he was forced to tell one of them, that, if he would not forbear, but make trial of it, he might see it executed. Upon this some of Boston departed from the assembly, and came no more.[1]

After the errors condemned, there were five points in question, between Mr. Cotton and Mr. Wheelwright on the one part, and the rest of the elders on the other part, which were after reduced to three, and those after put into such expressions as Mr. Cotton and they agreed, but Mr. Wheelwright did not:—

1. The first was about our union with Christ. The question was, whether we were united before we had active faith. The consent was, that there was no marriage union with Christ before actual faith, which is more than habitual.

2. The second was, about evidencing justification by sanctification. The consent was, that some saving sanctifications (as faith, etc.) were coexistent, concurrent, and coapparent (or at least might be) with the witness of the Spirit always.

3. That the new creature is not the person of a believer, but a body of saving graces in such a one; and that Christ, as a head, doth enliven or quicken, preserve and act the same, but Christ himself is no part of this new creature.

4. That though, in effectual calling, (in which the answer of the soul is by active faith, wrought at the same instant by the Spirit,) justification and sanctification be all together in

---

[1] "In his *Way of Congregational Churches*, p. 63, Cotton, answering many gross charges of Bailey's *Dissuasive*, as to his concurrence in Mrs. Hutchinson's errors, says with much force: 'Such as endeavored the healing of these distempers did seem to me to be transported with more jealousies, and heats, and paroxysms of spirit than would well stand with brotherly love, or the rule of the gospel.' Ten years after the agitations, this was his opinion; and it may safely be taken for the judgment of all succeeding time." (Savage.)

them; yet God doth not justify a man, before he be effectually called, and so a believer.

5. That Christ and his benefits may be offered and exhibited to a man under a covenant of works, but not in or by a covenant of works.

In the first handling of these questions, either party delivered their arguments in writing, which were read in the assembly, and, after, the answers to them, which spent much time without any effect; but after they came to open dispute, the questions were soon determined; for so they came to understand each other better.

Mo. 7 (*September*).] The last day of the assembly other questions were debated and resolved:—

1. That though women might meet (some few together) to pray and edify one another; yet such a set assembly, (as was then in practice at Boston,) where sixty or more did meet every week, and one woman (in a prophetical way, by resolving questions of doctrine, and expounding scripture) took upon her the whole exercise, was agreed to be disorderly, and without rule.[1]

2. Though a private member might ask a question publicly, after sermon, for information; yet this ought to be very wisely and sparingly done, and that with leave of the elders: but questions of reference, (then in use,) whereby the doctrines delivered were reproved, and the elders reproached, and that with bitterness, etc., was utterly condemned.

3. That a person, refusing to come to the assembly, to abide the censure of the church, might be proceeded against, though absent; yet it was held better, that the magistrates' help were called for, to compel him to be present.

4. That a member, differing from the rest of the church in

[1] Savage has the following characteristic note: "A *prophetical way* has been often followed, at meetings of women in Boston, and is, I think, in our days, without censure. The conduct of the female assembly in 1637, however, so much resembles party making, that the resolution of the synod is approved by the editor, though it bears hard on his great, great, great, great grandmother."

any opinion, which was not fundamental, ought not for that to forsake the ordinances there; and if such did desire dismission to any other church, which was of his opinion, and did it for that end, the church whereof he was ought to deny it for the same end.

22.] The assembly brake up; and it was propounded by the governor, that they would consider, that, seeing the Lord had been so graciously present in this assembly, that matters had been carried on so peaceably, and concluded so comfortably in all love, etc., if it were not fit to have the like meeting once a year, or, at least, the next year, to settle what yet remained to be agreed, or if but to nourish love, etc. This motion was well liked of all, but it was not thought fit to conclude it.

There was a motion made also by the governor, that, whereas there was difference among the churches about the maintenance of their ministers, it might be agreed what way was most agreeable to the rule of the gospel; but the elders did not like to deal in that, lest it should be said, that this assembly was gathered for their private advantage.

26.] Mr. Davenport (as he had been before requested by the assembly) preached out of Phil. 3:16, wherein he laid down the occasions of differences among Christians, etc., and declared the effect and fruit of the assembly, and, with much wisdom and sound argument, persuaded to unity, etc.

The diet of the assembly was provided at the country's charge, as also the fetching and sending back of those which came from Connecticut. It came to, in all, [*blank*].

28.] Two men were hanged at Boston for several murders. The one, John Williams, a ship-carpenter, who, being lately come into the country, and put in prison for theft, brake out of prison with one John Hoddy, whom, near the great pond, in the way to Ipswich, beyond Salem, he murdered, and took away his clothes and what else he had, and went in them to Ipswich, (where he had been sent to prison,) and was there again apprehended; and though his clothes were all bloody, yet he would confess nothing, till about a week after, that the body of Hoddy was found by the kine, who, smelling the blood, made such a roaring, as the cow-keeper, looking about, found the dead body covered with a heap of stones.

The other, William Schooler, was a vintner in London, and had been a common adulterer, (as himself did confess,) and had wounded a man in a duel, for which he fled into the Low Country, and from thence he fled from his captain and came into this country, leaving his wife (a handsome, neat woman) in England. He lived with another fellow at Merrimack, and there being a poor maid at Newbury, one Mary Sholy, who had desired a guide to go with her to her master, who dwelt at Pascataquack, he inquired her out, and agreed, for fifteen shillings, to conduct her thither. But, two days after, he returned, and, being asked why he returned so soon, he answered, that he had carried her within two or three miles of the place, and then she would go no farther. Being examined for this by the magistrates at Ipswich, and no proof found against him, he was let go. But, about a year after, being impressed to go against the Pequods, he gave ill speeches, for which the governor sent warrant for him, and being apprehended, (and supposed it had been for the death of the maid, some spake what they had heard, which might occasion suspicion,) he was again examined, and divers witnesses produced about it. Whereupon he was committed, arraigned, and condemned, by due proceeding. The effect of the evidence was this:—

1. He had lived a vicious life, and now lived like an atheist.

2. He had sought out the maid, and undertook to carry her to a place where he had never been.

3. When he crossed Merrimack, he landed in a place three miles from the usual path, from whence it was scarce possible she should get into the path.

4. He said he went by Winicowett house,[1] which he said stood on the contrary side of the way.

5. Being, as he said, within two or three miles of Swamscote,[2] where he left her, he went not thither to tell them of her, nor staid by her that night, nor, at his return home, did tell any body of her, till he was demanded of her.

6. When he came back, he had above ten shillings in his purse, and yet he said she would give him but seven shillings, and he carried no money with him.

7. At his return, he had some blood upon his hat, and on his skirts before, which he said was with a pigeon, which he killed.

8. He had a scratch on the left side of his nose, and, being asked by a neighbor how it came, he said it was with a bramble, which could not be, it being of the breadth of a small nail; and being asked after by the magistrate, he said it was with his piece, but that could not be on the left side.

9. The body of the maid was found by an Indian, about half a year after, in the midst of thick swamp, ten miles short of the place he said he left her in, and about three miles from the place where he landed by Merrimack, (and it was after seen, by the English,) the flesh being rotted off it, and the clothes laid all on an heap by the body.

10. He said, that soon after he left her, he met with a bear and he thought that bear might kill her, yet he would not go back to save her.

11. He brake prison, and fled as far as Powder Horn Hill, and there hid himself out of the way, for fear of pursuit, and after, when he arose to go forward, he could not, but (as himself confessed) was forced to return back to prison again.

At his death he confessed he had made many lies to excuse himself, but denied that he had killed or ravished her. He was very loath to die, and had hope he should be reprieved; but the court held him worthy of death, in undertaking the charge of a

[1] Hampton, N. H.　　　[2] Exeter, N. H.

shiftless maid, and leaving her (when he might have done otherwise) in such a place as he knew she must needs perish, if not preserved by means unknown. Yet there were some ministers and others, who thought the evidence not sufficient to take away his life.

(8.) (*October*) 7.] The *Wren*, a small pinnace, coming from Connecticut, was taken in a N. E. storm, and forced to anchor near Conyhassett, where she drave upon the rocks, and was wrecked, but all the men were saved.

12.] A day of thanksgiving kept in all the churches for our victories against the Pequods, and for the success of the assembly; but, by reason of this latter, some of Boston would not be present at the public exercises. The captains and soldiers, who had been in the late service, were feasted, and, after the sermon, the magistrates and elders accompanied them to the door of the house where they dined.

(9.) (*November*) 1.] Miantunnomoh, the Naragansett sachem, came to Boston. The governor, deputy, and treasurer, treated with him, and they parted upon fair terms. He acknowledged that all the Pequod country and Block Island were ours, and promised that he would not meddle with them but by our leave. We gave him leave to right himself for the wrongs which Janemoh and Wequash Cook had done him; and for the wrong they had done us, we would right ourselves in our own time.

A young man, coming alone in a skiff from Newtown, in a N. E. storm of wind and snow, was found dead in his boat, with a half-crown piece in his mouth.

One Jewell, master of a bark, was drowned. The manner was this. He was bound to the Isle of Sable, to relieve our men there. His bark had lain near a week at Natascott, waiting for him, but he staid at Boston drinking, and could not be gotten away. Mo. x. (*December*.) When he went, there was committed to his care a rundlet of strong water, sent to some there, he promising, that upon his life, it should not be touched;

but, as he went down in his bark's skiff, he went on shore at the castle, and there drank out about a gallon of it, and at night went away; but, it being very cold and dark, they could not find their bark, and Jewell his hat falling into the water, as they were rowing back to look for it, he fell into the water, near the shore, where it was not six feet deep, and could not be recovered.

There was great hope that the late general assembly would have had some good effect in pacifying the troubles and dissensions about matters of religion; but it fell out otherwise. For though Mr. Wheelwright and those of his party had been clearly confuted and confounded in the assembly, yet they persisted in their opinions, and were as busy in nourishing contentions (the principal of them) as before. Whereupon the general court, being assembled in the 2 of the 9th month (*November*), and finding, upon consultation, that two so opposite parties could not contain in the same body, without apparent hazard of ruin to the whole, agreed to send away some of the principal; and for this a fair opportunity was offered by the remonstrance or petition, which they preferred to the court the 9th of the 1st month (*March*), wherein they affirm Mr. Wheelwright to be innocent, and that the court had condemned the truth of Christ, with divers other scandalous and seditious speeches, (as appears at large in the proceedings of this court, which were faithfully collected and published soon after the court brake up,) subscribed by more than sixty of that faction, whereof one William Aspinwall, being one, and he that drew the said petition, being then sent as a deputy for Boston, was for the same dismissed, and after called to the court and disfranchised and banished. John Coggeshall was another deputy, who, though his hand were not to the petition, yet, professing himself to approve it, etc., was also dismissed, and after disfranchised. Then the court sent warrant to Boston to send other deputies in their room; but they intended to have sent the same men again; but Mr. Cotton, coming amongst them, dissuaded them with much ado. Then the court sent for Mr. Wheelwright, and, he persisting to justify his sermon, and his whole practice and opinions, and refusing to leave either the place or his public exercisings, he was disfranchised and banished. Upon which he appealed to the king, but neither called witnesses, nor desired any act to be made of it. The court told him, that an appeal did not lie; for by the king's grant we had power to hear and determine without any reservation, etc. So he relinquished his appeal, and the court gave him leave to go to his house, upon his promise, that, if he were not gone out of our jurisdiction within fourteen days, he would render himself to one of the magistrates.

The court also sent for Mrs. Hutchinson, and charged her with divers matters, as her keeping two public lectures every week in her house, whereto sixty or eighty persons did usually resort, and for reproaching most of the ministers (viz., all except Mr. Cotton) for not preaching a covenant of free grace, and that they had not the seal of the spirit, nor were able ministers of the New Testament; which were clearly proved against her, though she sought to shift it off. And, after many speeches to and fro, at last she was so full as she could not contain, but vented her revelations; amongst which this was one, that she had it revealed to her, that she should come into New England, and should here be persecuted, and that God would ruin us and our posterity, and the whole state, for the same. So the court proceeded and banished her; but, because it was winter, they committed her to a private house, where she was well provided, and her own friends and the elders permitted to go to her, but none else.

The court called also Capt. Underhill, and some five or six more of the principal, whose hands were to the said petition; and because they stood to justify it, they were disfranchised, and such as had public places were put from them.

The court also ordered, that the rest, who had subscribed the petition, (and would not acknowledge their fault, and which near twenty of them did,) and some others, who had been chief stirrers in these contentions, etc., should be disarmed. This troubled some of them very much, especially because they were to bring them in themselves; but at last, when they saw no remedy, they obeyed.[1]

All the proceedings of this court against these persons were set down at large, with the reasons and other observations, and were sent into England to be published there, to the end that all our godly friends might not be discouraged from coming to us, etc.

---

[1] One almost wonders that the colony survived the agitations here narrated. Aspinwall, Coddington, Coggeshall, Underhill, Wheelwright, Mrs. Hutchinson and those of her name, and many others now subjected to discipline, were people of the first distinction. It is plain that Cotton, with his disposition toward liberality and his affection for many among the heretics, was in an agonized frame of mind; while Winthrop, who not long before had been reprimanded for his lenity, must have executed with acute suffering the sentences of the court. The social order seemed rocking to destruction, and if ever there is occasion to judge men with charity, it is found here. We quote a passage from the *Colonial Records*, I. 207: "Whereas the opinions and revelations of Mr. Wheelwright and Mrs. Hutchinson have seduced and led into dangerous errors many of the people heare in Newe England, insomuch as there is just cause of suspition that they, as others in Germany, in former times, may, upon some revelation, make some suddaine irruption upon those that differ from them in judgment: for prevention whereof, it is ordered, that all those whose names are underwritten shall (upon warning given or left at their dwelling houses) before the 30th day of this month of November, deliver in at Mr. Cane's house, at Boston, all such guns, pistols, swords, powder, shot, and match as they shall bee owners of, or have in their custody, upon paine of ten pound for evry default to bee made thereof; which armes are to bee kept by Mr. Cane till this court shall take further order therein. Also it is ordered, upon like penulty of X*l*, that no man who is to render his armes by this order shall buy or borrow any guns, swords, pistols, powder, shot, or match, untill this court shall take further order therein." A list of names of those disarmed throughout the colony follows, in which are many of the best.

FROM "A SHORT STORY OF THE RISE, REIGN AND RUIN OF THE ANTINOMIANS."[1]

[THE reference in the last sentence is to the *Short Story of the Rise, Reign, and Ruin of the Antinomians, and Libertines that Infected the Churches of New England* (London, 1644), some extracts from which are here introduced. Although Savage maintained to the day of his death that the *Short Story* was the work of Thomas Welde, who from his Roxbury pastorate had gone to England in 1641, as agent of the colony, all other important authorities, Charles Deane, Samuel G. Drake, J. G. Palfrey, Joseph B. Felt, and Charles Francis Adams, assert confidently that it was the work of Winthrop, excepting the preface to which Thomas Welde signed his name. Mr. Adams in particular, who edited the document in 1894 for the Prince Society, appending to it two important papers, "The Examination of Anne Hutchinson," and "The Trial of Mrs. Hutchinson before the Church in Boston," treats the subject elaborately in his Introduction, declaring that the *Short Story* is as much a part of the *Journal* as the *Journey to the Hebrides* is part of Boswell's *Life of Samuel Johnson*, and that separation is as inappropriate in one case as the other.

In this edition the conclusion of the scholars mentioned is accepted. Savage's persistent attribution of the authorship to Welde is to be regarded as a characteristic instance of that tenacity, which though often serviceable, was sometimes perverted and ran into unreasonable obstinacy. The limits of this work forbid consideration of the question of the authorship of the *Short Story*, and also the printing of the document entire. We give only the more interesting and significant part, referring the seeker for fuller knowledge to books easily found. The whole text of the *Short Story* can be best studied in C. F. Adams's reprint, where the contemporary tracts bearing upon the matter are also given. In the same author's *Three Episodes of Massachusetts History*, the case of Anne Hutchinson is again treated, in the second division. Peter Oliver, *Puritan Commonwealth*, and

---

[1] The portion which we quote is on pp. 59–66 of the original, pp. 217–233 of Mr. C. F. Adams's Prince Society volume, *Antinomianism in the Colony of Massachusetts Bay* (Boston, 1894).

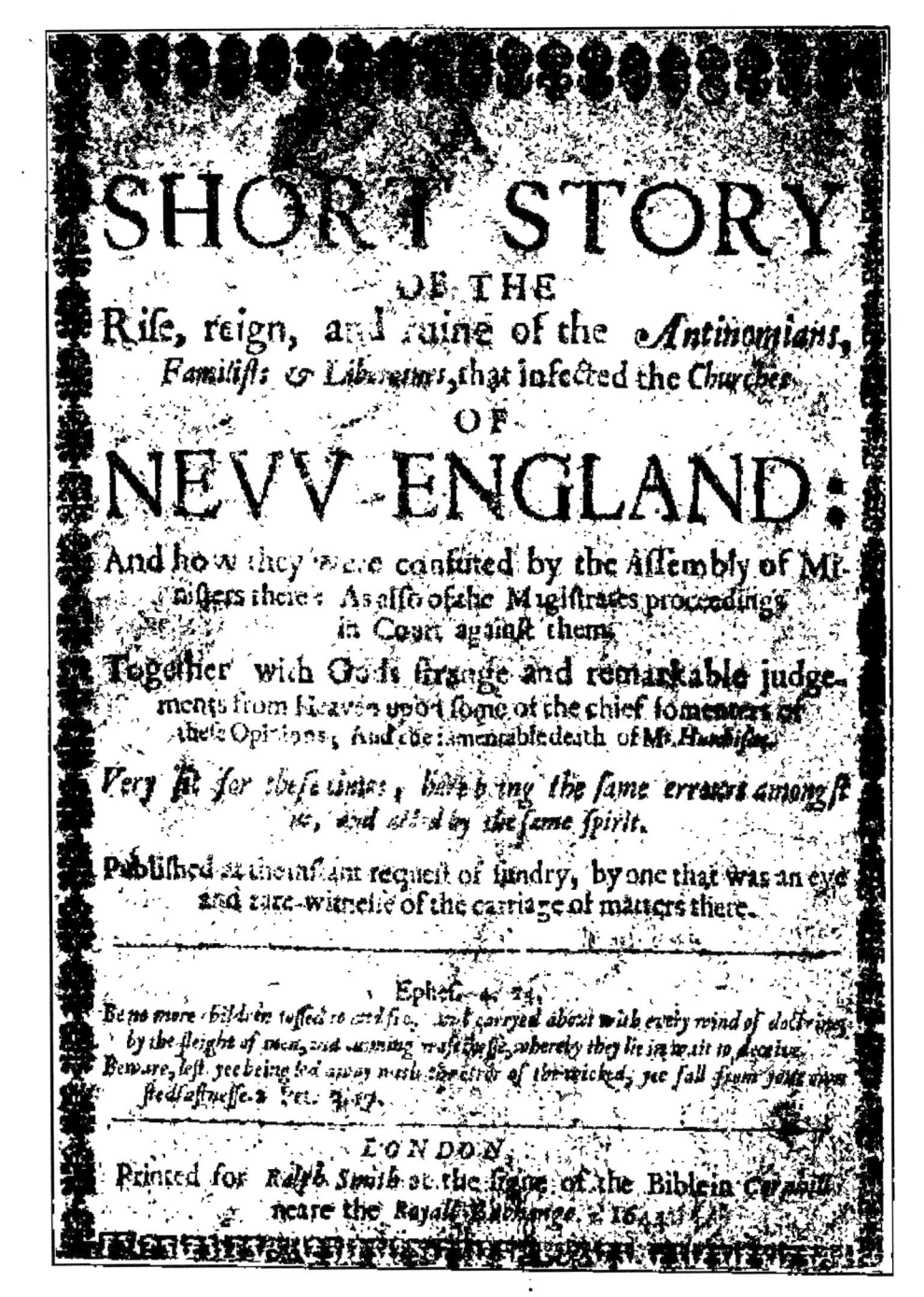

TITLE-PAGE OF "A SHORT STORY OF THE RISE, REIGN AND RUINE
OF THE ANTINOMIANS"

From a copy of the original edition in the New York Public Library (Lenox Building)

Brooks Adams, *Emancipation of Massachusetts*, handle the subject without sympathy for the party in power, while the intolerant Fathers receive at the hands of Palfrey treatment more judicial, and are sturdily championed by Henry M. Dexter, *As to Roger Williams and his Banishment from the Massachusetts Plantation*, and John A. Vinton, *The Antinomian Controversy of* 1637.

A facsimile of the title-page of the *Short Story* is given in the present volume.]

MISTRIS HUTCHISON being banished and confined, till the season of the yeere might be fit, and safe for her departure; she thought it now needlese to conceale herselfe any longer, neither would Satan lose the opportunity of making choyce of so fit an instrument, so long as any hope remained to attaine his mischievous end in darkning the saving truth of the Lord Jesus, and disturbing the peace of his Churches. Therefore she began now to discover all her mind to such as came to her, so that her opinions came abroad and began to take place among her old disciples, and now some of them raised up questions about the immortality of the soule, about the resurrection, about the morality of the Sabbath, and divers others, which the Elders finding to begin to appeare in some of their Churches, they took much paines (both in publike and private) to suppresse; and following the sent from one to another, the root of all was found to be in Mistris Hutchison; whereupon they resorted to her many times, labouring to convince her, but in vaine; yet they resorted to her still, to the end they might either reclaime her from her errours, or that they might bear witnesse against them if occasion were: For in a meeting of the Magistrates and Elders, about suppressing these new sprung errours, the Elders of Boston had declared their readinesse to deale with Mistris Hutchison in a Church way, if they had sufficient testimony: for though she had maintained some of them sometimes before them, yet they thought it not so orderly to come in as witnesses; whereupon other of the Elders, and others collecting which they had heard from her owne mouth at severall times, drew them into severall heads, and sent them to the Church of Boston, whereupon the Church (with leave of the Magistrates, because she was a prisoner) sent for her to appeare upon a Lecture day, being the fifteenth of the first moneth, and though she were at her owne house in the Towne, yet she came not into the Assembly till the Sermon and Prayer were ended, (pretending bodily infirmity). When she was come, one of the ruling Elders called her forth before the Assembly (which was very great from all the parts of the Countrey), and telling her the cause why the Church had called her, read the severall heads, which were as followeth.

1. That the soules of all men (in regard of generation) are mortall like the beasts, *Eccl.* 3. 8.

2. That in regard of Christs purchase they are immortall, so that Christ hath purchased the soules of the wicked to eternall paine, and the soules of the elect to eternall peace.

3. Those who are united to Christ have in this life new bodies, and 2 bodies, 1 *Cor.* 6. 19. she knowes not how Jesus Christ should be united to this our fleshly bodies.

4. Those who have union with Christ, shall not rise with the same fleshly bodies, 1 *Cor.* 15. 44.

5. And that the resurrection mentioned there, and in *John* 5. 28. is not meant of the resurrection of the body, but of our union here and after this life.

6. That there are no created graces in the Saints after their union with Christ, but before there are, for Christ takes them out of their hands into his owne.

7. There are no created graces in the humane nature of Christ, but he was onely acted by the power of the Godhead.

8. The Image of God wherein *Adam* was made, she could see no Scripture to warrant that it consisted in holinesse, but conceived it to be in that he was made like to Christs manhood.

9. She had no Scripture to warrant that Christs manhood is now in Heaven, but the body of Christ is his Church.

10. We are united to Christ with the same union, that his humanity on earth was with the Deity, *Jo.* 17. 21.

11. She conceived the Disciples before Christ his death were not converted, *Matth.* 18. 3.

12. There is no evidence to be had of our good estate, either from absolute or conditionall promises.

13. The Law is no rule of life to a Christian.

14. There is no Kingdome of Heaven in Scripture but onely Christ.

15. There is first engraffing into Christ before union, from which a man might fall away.

16. The first thing God reveales to assure us is our election.

17. That Abraham was not in a saving estate till the 22. chap. of *Gen.* when hee offered Isaac, and saving the firmenesse of Gods election, he might have perished notwithstanding any work of grace that was wrought in him till then.

18. That union to Christ is not by faith.

19. That all commands in the word are Law, and are not a way of life, and the command of faith is a Law, and therefore killeth; she supposed it to be a Law from *Rom.* 3. 27.

20. That there is no faith of Gods elect but assurance, there is no faith of dependance but such as an hypocrite may have and fall away from, proved *John* 15. for by that she said they are in Christ, but Christ is not in them.

21. That an hypocrite may have Adams righteousnesse and perish, and by that righteousnes he is bound to the Law, but in union with Christ, Christ comes into the man, and he retaines the seed, and dieth, and then all manner of grace in himselfe, but all in Christ.

22. There is no such thing as inherent righteousness.

23. We are not bound to the Law, no not as a rule of life.

24. We are dead to all acts in spirituall things, and are onely acted by Christ.

25. Not being bound to the Law, it is not transgression against the Law to sinne, or breake it, because our sinnes they are inward and spirituall, and so are exceeding sinfull, and onely are against Christ.

26. Sanctification can be no evidence at all of our good estate.

27. That her particuler revelations about future events are as infallible as any part of Scripture, and that she is bound as much to believe them, as the Scripture, for the same holy Ghost is the author of them both.

28. That so farre as a man is in union with Christ, he can doe no duties perfectly, and without the communion of the unregenerate part with the regenerate.

29. That such exhortations as these, to worke out our salvation with feare, to make our calling and election sure, &c. are spoken onely to such, as are under a Covenant of workes.

All which she did acknowledge she had spoken, (for a coppy of them had been sent to her divers dayes before, and the witnesses hands subscribed, so as she saw it was in vaine to deny them). Then she asked by what rule such an Elder could come to her pretending to desire light, and indeede to entrappe her, to which the same Elder answered that he had beene twice with her, and that he told her indeed at St. Ives, that he had beene troubled at some of her speeches in the Court, wherein he did desire to see light for the ground and meaning of them, but he professed in the presence of the Lord, that he came not to entrap her, but in compassion to her Soule, to helpe her out of those snares of the Devill, wherein he saw she was entangled, and that before his departure from her he did beare witnesse against her opinions, and against her spirit, and did leave it sadly upon her from the word of God; then presently she grew into passion against her Pastor[1] for his speech against her at the Court after the sentence was

---
[1] John Wilson.

passed, which he gave a full answer unto, shewing his zeale against her errors, whereupon she asked for what errors she had beene banished, professing withall that she held none of these things she was now charged with, before her imprisonment; (supposing that whatsoever should be found amisse, would be imputed to that, but it was answered as the truth was, that she was not put to durance, but onely a favourable confinement, so as all of her Family and divers others, resorted to her at their pleasure). But this allegation was then proved false, (and at her next convention more fully) for there were divers present, who did know she spake untruth. Her answer being demanded to the first Articles, she maintained her assertion that the Soules were mortall, &c. alledging the place in the *Eccles.* cited in the Article, and some other Scriptures nothing to the purpose, she insisted much upon that in *Gen.* 1. In the day thou eatest, &c. thou shalt dye, she could not see how a Soule could be immortally miserable, though it might be eternally miserable, neither could shee distinguish betweene the Soule and the Life; and though she were pressed by many Scriptures and reasons alleadged by the Elders of the same, and other Churches, so as she could not give any answer to them, yet she stood to her opinion, till at length a stranger[1] being desired to speake to the point, and hee opening to her the difference betweene the Soule and the Life, the first being a spirituall substance, and the other the union of that with the body; she then confessed she saw more light then before, and so with some difficulty was brought to confesse her error in that point. Wherein was to be observed that though he spake

[1] "The 'stranger' was probably the Rev. John Davenport, at the time a guest of John Cotton. . . . He came to New England in 1637, reaching Boston on the 26th of June, in the midst of the Antinomian excitement. He took an active part in the Cambridge Synod of the following September; but in March, 1638, at the time of the occurrence of the events referred to in the text, having perfected all his arrangements, was about to migrate to Connecticut in company with many of those who had come with him from England, being, in the language of Cotton Mather, 'more fit for Zebulon's ports than for Issachar's tents.'" (C. F. Adams.)

to very good purpose, and so clearly convinced her as she could not gainsay, yet it was evident shee was convinced before, but she could not give the honour of it to her owne Pastor or teacher, nor to any of the other Elders, whom she had so much slighted.

Then they proceeded to the third, fourth, and fifth Articles, about the body and the resurrection of the dead, which she maintained according to the Articles, and though shee were not able to give any reasonable answer to the many places of the Scripture, and other arguments which were brought to convince her, yet shee still persisted in her errour, giving froward speeches to some that spake to her, as when one of the Elders used this argument, that if the resurrection were only our union with Christ, then all that are united, are the children of the resurrection, and therefore are neither to marry, nor to give in marriage, and so by consequence, there ought to be community of women; shee told him that hee spake like the Pharisees, who said that Christ had a devill, because that Abraham were dead and the Prophets, and yet hee had said, that those which eate his flesh, should never dye, not taking the speech in the true meaning, so did hee (said shee) who brought that argument, for it is said there, they should bee like the Angels, &c. The Elders of Boston finding her thus obstinate, propounded to the Church for an admonition to bee given her, to which all the Church consented, except two of her sons, who because they persisted to defend her, were under admonition also. Mr. Cotton gave the admonition, and first to her sons, laying it sadly upon them, that they would give such way to their naturall affection, as for preserving her honour, they should make a breach upon the honour of Christ, and upon their Covenant with the Church, and withall teare the very bowels of their soule, by hardning her in her sin: In this admonition to her, first, hee remembred her of the good way shee was in at her first comming, in helping to discover to divers, the false bottom they stood upon, in trusting to legall works without Christ; then hee shewed her, how by falling into these grosse and fundamentall errors, she had lost the honour of her former service, and done more wrong to Christ and his Church, then formerly shee had done good, and so laid her sin to her conscience with much zeale and solemnity. Hee admonished her also of the height of spirit, then hee spake to the sisters of the Church, and advised them to take heed of her opinions, and to with-hold all countenance and respects from her, lest they should harden her in her sin: so shee was dismissed and appointed to appeare againe that day sevennight.

The Court had ordered that shee should return to Roxbury again, but upon intimation that her spirit began to fall, shee was permitted to remain at Mr. Cottons house (where Davenport was also kept) who before her next appearing, did both take much pains with her, and prevailed so far, that shee did acknowledge her errour in all the Articles (except the last) and accordingly she wrote down her answers to them all. When the day came, and shee was called forth and the Articles read again to her, shee delivered in her answers in writing, which were also read, and being then willing to speak to the Congregation for their further satisfaction, shee did acknowledge that shee had greatly erred, and that God had left her to her self herein, because she had so much under-natured his Ordinances, both in slighting the Magistrates at the Court, and also the Elders of the Church, and confessed that when shee was at the Court, shee looked only at such failings as shee apprehended in the Magistrates proceedings, without having regard to the place they were in, and that the speeches shee then used about her revelations were rash, and without ground, and shee desired the prayers of the Church for her.

Thus farre shee went on well, and the Assembly conceived hope of her repentance, but in her answers to the severall articles, shee gave no satisfaction, because in diverse of them shee answered by circumlocutions, and seemed to lay all the faults in her expressions, which occasioned some of the Elders to desire she might expresse her self more cleerly, and for that ever shee was demanded about the Article, whether she were not, or had not been of that judgement, that there is no inherent righteousnesse in the Saints, but those gifts and graces which are ascribed to them that are only in Christ as the subject? to which shee answered, that shee was never of that judgement, howsoever by her expressions shee might seem to bee so; and this shee affirmed with such confidence as bred great astonishment in many, who had known the contrary, and diverse alledged her own sayings and reasonings, both before her confinement and since, which did manifest to all that were present, that shee knew that shee spake untruth, for it was proved that shee had alledged that in *Esay*[1] 53. By his knowledge shall my righteous servant justifie many; which shee had maintained to bee meant of a knowledge in Christ, and not in us; so likewise that in *Galatians*,[2] I live by the faith of the Son of God, which shee said was the faith of Christ, and not any faith inherent in us; also, that shee had maintained, that Christ is our sanctification in the same sort that hee is our justification, and that shee had said, that shee would not pray for grace, but for Christ, and that (when she had been pressed with diverse Scriptures, which spake of washing and creating a new heart, and writing the Law in the heart, etc.) shee had denyed, that they did mean any sanctification in us: There were diverse women also with whom shee had dealt about the same point, who (if their modesty had not restrained them) would have born witnesse against her herein (as themselves after confessed), wherefore the Elders pressed her very earnestly to remember her self, and not to stand so obstinately to maintain so manifest an untruth, but she was deafe of that eare, and would not acknowledge that shee had been at any time of that judge-

---

[1] Isaiah. [2] ii. 20.

ment, howsoever her expressions were; Then Mr. Cotton told the Assembly, that whereas shee had been formerly dealt with for matter of doctrine, he had (according to the duty of his place being the teacher of that Church) proceeded against unto admonition, but now the case being altered, and she being in question for maintaining of untruth, which is matter of manners, he must leave the businesse to the Pastor, Mr. Wilson, to goe on with her, but withall declared his judgement in the case from that in *Revel.* 22. that such as make and maintaine a lye, ought to be cast out of the Church; and whereas two or three pleaded that she might first have a second admonition, according to that in *Titus* 3. 10.[1] he answered that that was onely for such as erred in point of doctrine, but such as shall notoriously offend in matter of conversation, ought to be presently cast out, as he proved by Ananias and Saphira,[2] and the incestuous Corinthian,[3] (and as appeares by that of Simon Magus)[4] and for her owne part though she heard this moved in her behalfe, that she might have a further respite, yet she her selfe never desired it: so the Pastor went on, and propounding it to the Church, to know whether they were all agreed, that she should be cast out, and a full consent appearing (after the usuall manner) by their silence, after a convenient pause he proceeded, and denounced the sentence of excommunication against her, and she was commanded to depart out of the Assembly. In her going forth, one standing at the dore, said, The Lord sanctifie this unto you, to whom she made answer, The Lord judgeth not as man judgeth, better to be cast out of the Church then to deny Christ.

Thus it hath pleased the Lord to have compassion of his poore Churches here, and to discover this great imposter, an instrument of Satan so fitted and trained to his service for interrupting the passage [of the] Kingdome in this part of the world, and poysoning the Churches here planted, as no

---

[1] "A man that is an heretick after the first and second admonition reject."
[2] *Acts*, v. 1–11.   [3] 1 *Corinthians*, v. 5.   [4] *Acts*, viii. 18–24.

story records the like of a woman, since that mentioned in the *Revelation*; it would make a large volume to lay downe all passages, I will onely observe some few, which were obvious to all that knew her course.

1. In her entrance I observe, (1. Her entrance.
(2. Her progresse.
(3. Her downfall.

1. The foundation she laid was (or rather seemed to be) Christ and Free-Grace.

2. Rule she pretended to walke by, was onely the Scripture.

3. The light to discerne this rule, was onely the holy Ghost.

4. The persons she conversed with were (for the most part) Christians in Church Covenant.

5. Her ordinary talke was about the things of the Kingdome of God.

6. Her usuall conversation was in the way of righteousnesse and kindnesse.

Thus she entred and made up the first act of her course.

In her progresse I observe,

First, her successe, she had in a short time insinuated her selfe into the hearts of much of the people (yea of many of the most wise and godly) who grew into so reverent an esteeme of her godlinesse, and spirituall gifts, as they looked at her as a Prophetesse, raised up of God for some great worke now at hand, as the calling of the Jewes, &c. so as she had more resort to her for counsell about matter of conscience, and clearing up mens spirituall estates, then any Minister (I might say all the Elders) in the Country.

Secondly, Pride and Arraigning of her spirit.

1. In framing a new way of conversation and evidencing thereof, carried along in the distinction betweene the Covenant of workes, which she would have no otherwise differenced, but by an immediate Revelation of the Spirit.

2. In despising all (both Elders and Christians) who went not her way, and laying them under a Covenant of workes.

3. In taking upon her infallibly to know the election of others, so as she would say, that if she had but one halfe houres talke with a man, she would tell whether he were elect or not.

4. Her impatience of opposition, which appeares in divers passages before.

Thirdly, Her skill and cunning to devise.

1. In that she still pretended she was of Mr. Cottons judgement in all things.

2. In covering her errors by doubtfull expressions.

3. In shadowing the true end, and abuse of her weekely meetings under the name of repeating Mr. Cottons Sermons.

4. In her method of practise to bring the conscience under a false terror, by working that an argument of a Covenant of workes, which no Christian can have comfort without, viz. of sanctification, or qualifications, (as she termed it.)

5. In her confident profession of her owne good estate, and the clearnesse and comfort of it, obtained in the same way of waiting for immediate Revelation which she held out to others.

In her downefall there may be observed the Lords faithfulnesse in honouring and justifying his owne Ordinances.

1. In that hee made her to cleare the justice of the Court, by confessing the vanity of her revelations, &c. and her sinne in despising his Ministers.

2. In that the judgement and sentence of the Church hath concurred with that of the Court in her rejection, so that she is cast out of both as an unworthy member of either.

3. The Justice of God in giving her up to those delusions, and to that impudency in venting and maintaining them, as should bring her under that censure, which (not long before) she had endeavoured and expected to have brought upon some other, who opposed her proceedings.

4. That she who was in such esteeme in the Church for soundnesse of Judgement and sincerity of heart (but a few moneths before) should now come under admonition for

many foule and fundamentall errors, and after be cast out for notorious lying.

5. That shee who was wont to bee so confident of her spirituall good estate, and ready (undesired) to hold it forth to others (being pressed now at her last appearance before the Church to give some proofs of it) should bee wholly silent in that matter.

6. Whereas upon the sentence of the Court against her, shee boasted highly of her sufferings for Christ, &c. it was noted by one of the Elders (who bare witnesse against her errors) that the spirit of glory promised in *Pet.*[1] to those who suffer for well-doing, did not come upon her, but a spirit of delusion, and damnable error, which as it had possessed her before, so it became more effectuall and evident by her sufferings.

7. Here is to bee seen the presence of God in his Ordinances, when they are faithfully attended according to his holy will, although not free from human infirmities: This American Jesabel kept her strength and reputation, even among the people of God, till the hand of Civill Justice laid hold on her, and then shee began evidently to decline, and the faithfull to bee freed from her forgeries; and now in this last act, when shee might have expected (as most likely shee did) by her seeming repentance of her errors, and confessing her undervaluing of the Ordinances of Magistracy and Ministracy, to have redeemed her reputation in point of sincerity, and yet have made good all her former work, and kept open a back doore to have returned to her vomit again, by her paraphrasticall retractions, and denying any change in her judgement, yet such was the presence and blessing of God in his own Ordinance, that this subtilty of Satan was discovered to her utter shame and confusion, and to the setting at liberty of many godly hearts, that had been captivated by her to that day; and that Church which by her means was brought

---

[1] 1 *Peter*, iii. 17; iv. 14.

under much infamy, and neere to dissolution, was hereby sweetly repaired, and a hopefull way of establishment, and her dissembled repentance cleerly detected, God giving her up since the sentence of excommunication, to that hardnesse of heart, as shee is not affected with any remorse, but glories in it, and feares not the vengeance of God, which she lyes under, as if God did work contrary to his own word, and loosed from heaven, while his Church had bound upon earth.[1]

[1] As to the accounts in the *History* and the *Short Story* Mr. Adams remarks: "The inference is strong that both accounts were prepared by the same hand; but while that in the *Short Story* was written at once and hurried off to England in some vessel then about to sail, that in the *History* was set down subsequently and more at leisure. This also would account for the greater warmth of expression in the *Short Story*—a thing not characteristic of Winthrop."

(WINTHROP'S JOURNAL RESUMED.)

AFTER this, many of the church of Boston, being highly offended with the governor for this proceeding,[1] were earnest with the elders to have him called to account for it; but they were not forward in it, and himself, understanding their intent, thought fit to prevent such a public disorder, and so took occasion to speak to the congregation to this effect:—

1. That if he had been called, etc., he would have desired, first, to have advised with the elders, whether the church had power to call in question the proceedings of the civil court.

2. He would have consulted with the rest of the court, whether he might discover the counsels of the court to this assembly.

3. Though he knew, that the elders and some others did know, that the church could not inquire into the justice and proceedings of the court, etc.; yet, for the satisfaction of such as did not, and were willing to be satisfied, he would declare his mind herein.

4. He showed, that, if the church had such power, they must have it from Christ, but Christ had disclaimed it in his practice and by rule, as Luke [blank,] Matt. [blank;] and the scripture holds not out any rule or example for it; and though Christ's kingly power be in his church, yet that is not that kingly power whereby he is King of kings and Lord of lords, for by that kings reign and princes, etc. It is true, indeed, that magistrates, as they are church members, are accountable to the church for their failings, but that is when they are out of their calling; for we have examples of the highest magistrates in the same kind, as Uzzia, when he would go offer incense in the temple, the officers of the church called him to account, and

[1] The proceedings of the court against the Hutchinsonians.

withstood him. But when Asa put a prophet in prison, and when Salam put out Abiathar from the priesthood, (the one being a good act and the other ill,) yet the officers of the church did not call either of them to account for it. If a magistrate shall, in a private way, take away a man's goods or his servants, etc., the church may call him to account for it; but if he doth thus in pursuing a course of justice, (though the thing be unjust,) yet he is not accountable, etc.

5. For himself, he did nothing in the cases of the brethren, but by the advice and direction of our teacher and other of the elders. For in the oath, which was administered to him and the rest, etc., there was inserted, by his advice, this clause,— In all causes wherein you are to give your vote, etc., you are to give your vote as in your judgment and conscience you shall see to be most for the public good, etc.; and so for his part he was persuaded, that it would be most for the glory of God, and the public good, to pass sentence as they did.

6. He would give them one reason, which was a ground for his judgment, and that was, for that he saw, that those brethren, etc., were so divided from the rest of the country in their judgment and practice, as it could not stand with the public peace, that they should continue amongst us. So, by the example of Lot in Abraham's family, and after Hagar and Ishmael, he saw they must be sent away.[1]

---

[1] Winthrop's justification of himself is interesting as coming from one naturally candid and gentle who in a great strait, in a fierce contest between liberal and illiberal minds, provides for the public good as well as he can according to his lights.

1638

Mo. 11 (*January*).] The church at Roxbury dealt with divers of their members, (who had their hands to the petition,) and spent many days in public meetings to have brought them to see their sin in that, as also in the corrupt opinions which they held, but could not prevail with them. So they proceeded to two or three admonitions, and, when all was in vain, they cast them out of the church. In their dealing with them, they took some of them in plain lies and other foul distempers.

9.] Divers of the elders went to Weymouth, to reconcile the differences between the people and Mr. Jenner, whom they had called thither with intent to have him their pastor. They had good success of their prayers.

13.] About thirty persons of Boston going out in a fair day to Spectacle Island to cut wood, (the town being in great want thereof,) the next night the wind rose so high at N. E. with snow, and after at N. W. for two days, and then it froze so hard, as the bay was all frozen up, save a little channel. In this twelve of them gate to the Governor's Garden, and seven more were carried in the ice in a small skiff out at Broad Sound, and kept among Brewster's Rocks, without food or fire, two days, and then the wind forbearing, they gate to Pullin Point, to a little house there of Mr. Aspenwall's. Three of them gate home the next day over the ice, but their hands and feet frozen. Some lost their fingers and toes, and one died. The rest went from Spectacle Island to the main, but two of them fell into the ice, yet recovered again.[1]

In this extremity of weather, a small pinnace was cast away

---

[1] Since most of the localities of Boston harbor retain the old names, the story will be easily followed.

upon Long Island by Natascott, but the men were saved and came home upon the ice.

16.] The powder and arms of the country, which were kept at Boston, were, by order of the last court, carried to Roxbury and Newtown.

This year a plantation was begun at Tecticutt by a gentlewoman, an ancient maid, one Mrs. Poole. She went late thither, and endured much hardship, and lost much cattle. Called, after, Taunton.[1]

Another plantation was begun (and called Sandwich) about fifteen miles beyond Plymouth, towards Cape Cod, by many families, which removed from Sagus, otherwise Lynn.

Upon occasion of the censures of the court upon Mrs. Hutchinson and others, divers other foul errors were discovered, which had been secretly carried by way of inquiry, but after were maintained by Mrs. Hutchinson and others; and so many of Boston were tainted with them, as Mr. Cotton, finding how he had been abused, and made (as himself said) their stalking horse, (for they pretended to hold nothing but what Mr. Cotton held, and himself did think the same,) did spend most of his time, both publicly and privately, to discover those errors, and to reduce such as were gone astray. And also the magistrates, calling together such of the elders as were near, did spend two days in consulting with them about the way to help the growing evils.

Some of the secret opinions were these:—

That there is no inherent righteousness in a child of God.

That neither absolute nor conditional promises belong to a Christian.

That we are not bound to the law, not as a rule, etc.

That the Sabbath is but as other days.

That the soul is mortal, till it be united to Christ, and then it is annihilated, and the body also, and a new given by Christ.

That there is no resurrection of the body.

[1] The foundress is still held in honor in Taunton.

Mo. 12 (*February*).] Divers gentlemen and others, being joined in a military company, desired to be made a corporation, etc. But the council, considering (from the example of the Pretorian band among the Romans, and the Templars in Europe) how dangerous it might be to erect a standing authority of military men, which might easily, in time, overthrow the civil power, thought fit to stop it betimes. Yet they were allowed to be a company, but subordinate to all authority.[1]

About this time the Indians, which were in our families, were much frightened with Hobbamock (as they call the devil) appearing to them in divers shapes, and persuading them to forsake the English, and not to come at the assemblies, nor to learn to read, etc.

26.] Mr. Peirce, in the Salem ship, the *Desire*, returned from the West Indies after seven months. He had been at Providence,[2] and brought some cotton, and tobacco, and negroes, etc., from thence, and salt from Tertugos. Dry fish and strong liquors are the only commodities for those parts. He met there two men-of-war, set forth by the lords, etc., of Providence[3] with letters of mart, who had taken divers prizes from the Spaniard, and many negroes.

Mo. 1 (*March*).] While Mrs. Hutchinson continued at Roxbury, divers of the elders and others resorted to her, and finding her to persist in maintaining those gross errors beforementioned, and many others, to the number of thirty or thereabout, some of them wrote to the church at Boston, offering to make proof of the same before the church, etc., 15; whereupon she was called, (the magistrates being desired to give her license to come,) and the lecture was appointed to begin at ten. (The general court being then at Newtown, the governor and the treasurer, being members of Boston, were permitted to come

---

[1] Here we have the origin of the Ancient and Honorable Artillery Company, still a cherished and flourishing organization.

[2] In the Caribbean. We here have plain evidence of a trade in slaves.

[3] See *ante*, p. 228, note 1.

down, but the rest of the court continued at Newtown.) When she appeared, the errors were read to her. The first was, that the souls of men are mortal by generation, but, after, made immortal by Christ's purchase. This she maintained a long time; but at length she was so clearly convinced by reason and scripture, and the whole church agreeing that sufficient had been delivered for her conviction, that she yielded she had been in an error. Then they proceeded to three other errors: 1. That there was no resurrection of these bodies, and that these bodies were not united to Christ, but every person united hath a new body, etc. These were also clearly confuted, but yet she held her own; so as the church (all but two of her sons) agreed she should be admonished, and because her sons would not agree to it, they were admonished also.

Mr. Cotton pronounced the sentence of admonition with great solemnity, and with much zeal and detestation of her errors and pride of spirit.[1] The assembly continued till eight at night, and all did acknowledge the special presence of God's spirit therein; and she was appointed to appear again the next lecture day.

While the general court sate, there came a letter, directed to the court, from John Greene of Providence, who, not long before, had been imprisoned and fined, for saying that the

[1] Nothing in Cotton's life is so hard to excuse as his pronouncing sentence at this time upon Anne Hutchinson. Her affection for him brought her across the sea; it was under his ministrations that her ideas developed; while condemning the teaching of the ministers in general, she always made an exception of him. On his side, too, his sympathy with her was so strong that his standing had been much imperilled. It would be wrong to believe that in turning against her now he was selfishly thinking of himself. In his honest opinion she had gone too far, endangering the material and spiritual welfare of her environment. The situation is full of pathos. The strong, well-purposed man, bound by many limitations, yearning no doubt toward the pupil he had moulded, but alarmed at her perverseness, sits in the judgment-seat confronting the enthusiast against whom the world is turning. Though many of her utterances are scarcely intelligible to modern readers, an occasional light breaks forth of wisdom before her age; she was brave, sincere, and possessed of womanly sweetness. The world will always with tender thoughts follow her sad fortunes to their tragic close.

magistrates had usurped upon the power of Christ in his church, and had persecuted Mr. Williams and another, whom they had banished for disturbing the peace by divulging their opinions against the authority of the magistrates, etc.; but upon his submission, etc., his fine was remitted; and now, by his letter, he retracted his former submission, and charged the court as he had done before. Now, because the court knew, that divers others of Providence were of the same ill affection to the court, and were probably suspected to be confederate in the same letter, the court ordered, that, if any of that plantation were found within our jurisdiction, he should be brought before one of the magistrates, and if he would not disclaim the charge in the said letter, he should be sent home, and charged to come no more into this jurisdiction, upon pain of imprisonment and further censure.[1]

At this court, divers of our chief military officers, who had declared themselves favorers of the familistical persons and opinions, were sent for, and being told, that the court having some jealousy of them for the same, and therefore did desire some good satisfaction from them, they did ingenuously acknowledge, how they had been deceived and misled by the pretence, which was held forth, of advancing Christ, and debasing the creature, etc., which since they have found to be otherwise, and that their opinions and practices tended to disturbance and delusions; and so blessed God, that had so timely discovered their error and danger to them.

At this court, a committee was appointed, of some magistrates, some ministers, and some others, to compile a body of fundamental laws.

Also the elders (who had been requested to deliver their judgments concerning the law of adultery, about which three had been kept long in prison) returned their answer, with the reasons thereof, to this effect: That, if the law had been suffi-

[1] From John Greene was descended the revolutionary general Nathaniel Greene.

ciently published, they ought to be put to death.[1] Whereupon the court, considering that there had been some defect in that point, and especially for that it had been oft questioned among the deputies and others, whether that law were of force or not, being made by the court of assistants by allowance of the general court; therefore it was thought safest, that these three persons should be whipped and banished; and the law was confirmed and published.

The Castle Island being found to be very chargeable to maintain the garrison there, and of little use, but only to have some command of ships, which should come hither with passengers, etc., there was a committee appointed to dispose of the ammunition there, etc.

22.] Mrs. Hutchinson appeared again; (she had been licensed by the court, in regard she had given hope of her repentance, to be at Mr. Cotton's house, that both he and Mr. Davenport might have the more opportunity to deal with her;) and the articles being again read to her, and her answer required, she delivered it in writing, wherein she made a retractation of near all, but with such explanations and circumstances as gave no satisfaction to the church; so as she was required to speak further to them. Then she declared, that it was just with God to leave her to herself, as he had done, for her slighting his ordinances, both magistracy and ministry; and confessed that what she had spoken against the magistrates at the court (by way of revelation) was rash and ungrounded; and desired the church to pray for her. This gave the church good hope of her repentance; but when she was examined about some particulars, as that she had denied inherent righteousness, etc., she affirmed that it was never her judgment; and though it was proved by many testimonies, that she had been of that judgment, and so had persisted, and maintained it by argument against divers, yet she impudently persisted in her

[1] The reference is to a law passed in October, 1631, providing death for both parties.

affirmation, to the astonishment of all the assembly. So that, after much time and many arguments had been spent to bring her to see her sin, but all in vain, the church, with one consent, cast her out. Some moved to have her admonished once more; but, it being for manifest evil in matter of conversation, it was agreed otherwise; and for that reason also the sentence was denounced by the pastor, matter of manners belonging properly to his place.

After she was excommunicated, her spirits, which seemed before to be somewhat dejected, revived again, and she gloried in her sufferings, saying, that it was the greatest happiness, next to Christ, that ever befel her. Indeed, it was a happy day to the churches of Christ here, and to many poor souls, who had been seduced by her, who, by what they heard and saw that day, were (through the grace of God) brought off quite from her errors, and settled again in the truth.

At this time the good providence of God so disposed, divers of the congregation (being the chief men of the party, her husband being one) were gone to Naragansett to seek out a new place for plantation, and taking liking of one in Plymouth patent, they went thither to have it granted them; but the magistrates there, knowing their spirit, gave them a denial, but consented they might buy of the Indians an island in the Naragansett Bay.[1]

After two or three days, the governor sent a warrant to Mrs. Hutchinson to depart this jurisdiction before the last of this month, according to the order of court, and for that end set her at liberty from her former constraint, so as she was not to go forth of her own house till her departure; and upon the 28th she went by water to her farm at the Mount, where she was to take water, with Mr. Wheelwright's wife and family, to go to Pascataquack; but she changed her mind, and went by land to Providence, and so to the island in the Naragansett Bay,

---

[1] Here we find the beginnings of the colony of Rhode Island as distinguished from Providence, to which we have seen Roger Williams depart.

which her husband and the rest of that sect had purchased of the Indians, and prepared with all speed to remove unto. For the court had ordered, that, except they were gone with their families by such a time, they should be summoned to the general court, etc.

30.] Mr. Davenport and Mr. Prudden, and a brother of Mr. Eaton, (being ministers also,) went by water to Quinepiack; and with them many families removed out of this jurisdiction to plant in those parts, being much taken with the opinion of the fruitfulness of that place, and more safety (as they conceived) from danger of a general governor, who was feared to be sent this summer; which, though it were a great weakening to these parts, yet we expected to see a good providence of God in it, (for all possible means had been used to accommodate them here; Charlestown offered them largely, Newbury their whole town, the court any place which was free,) both for possessing those parts which lay open for an enemy, and for strengthening our friends at Connecticut, and for making room here for many, who were expected out of England this year, and for diverting the thoughts and intentions of such in England as intended evil against us, whose designs might be frustrate by our scatterings so far; and such as were now gone that way were as much in the eye of the state of England as we here.[1]

There came letters from Connecticut to the governor of the Massachusetts, to desire advice from the magistrates and elders here about Sequin and the Indians of the river, who had, underhand, (as was conceived,) procured the Pequods to do that onslaught at Weathersfield the last year. The case fell out to be this: Sequin gave the English land there, upon contract that he might sit down by them, and be protected, etc. When he came to Weathersfield, and had set down his wigwam, they drave him away by force. Whereupon, he not being of

[1] New Haven must be distinguished from the enterprise of Hooker and Haynes at Hartford, or Connecticut.

strength to repair this injury by open force, he secretly draws in the Pequods. Such of the magistrates and elders as could meet on the sudden returned this answer, viz.: That, if the cause were thus, Sequin might, upon this injury first offered by them, right himself either by force or fraud, and that by the law of nations; and though the damage he had done them had been one hundred times more than what he sustained from them, that is not considerable in point of a just war; neither was he bound (upon such an open act of hostility publicly maintained) to seek satisfaction first in a peaceable way; it was enough, that he had complained of it as an injury and breach of covenant. According to this advice, they proceeded and made a new agreement with the Indians of the river.

Another plantation was now in hand at Mattakeese,[1] six miles beyond Sandwich. The undertaker of this was one Mr. Batchellor, late pastor at Sagus, (since called Lynn,) being about seventy-six years of age; yet he walked thither on foot in a very hard season.

He and his company, being all poor men, finding the difficulty, gave it over, and others undertook it.

27.] The Indians of Block Island sent three men with ten fathom of wampom for part of their tribute.

The wife of one William Dyer, a milliner in the New Exchange, a very proper and fair woman, and both of them notoriously infected with Mrs. Hutchinson's errors, and very censorious and troublesome, (she being of a very proud spirit, and much addicted to revelations,) had been delivered of [a] child some few months before, October 17, and the child buried, (being stillborn,) and viewed of none but Mrs. Hutchinson and the midwife, one Hawkins's wife, a rank familist also; and another woman had a glimpse of it, who, not being able to keep counsel, as the other two did, some rumor began to spread, that the child was a monster. One of the

[1] Later Yarmouth.

elders, hearing of it, asked Mrs. Hutchinson, when she was ready to depart; whereupon she told him how it was, and said she meant to have it chronicled,[1] but excused her concealing of it till then, (by advice, as she said, of Mr. Cotton,) which coming to the governor's knowledge, he called another of the magistrates and that elder, and sent for the midwife, and examined her about it. At first she confessed only, that the head was defective and misplaced, but being told that Mrs. Hutchinson had revealed all, and that he intended to have it taken up and viewed, she made this report of it, viz.: It was a woman child, stillborn, about two months before the just time, having life a few hours before; it came hiplings till she turned it; it was of ordinary bigness; it had a face, but no head, and the ears stood upon the shoulders and were like an ape's; it had no forehead, but over the eyes four horns, hard and sharp; two of them were above one inch long, the other two shorter; the eyes standing out, and the mouth also; the nose hooked upward; all over the breast and back full of sharp pricks and scales, like a thornback; the navel and all the belly, with the distinction of the sex, were where the back should be, and the back and hips before, where the belly should have been; behind, between the shoulders, it had two mouths, and in each of them a piece of red flesh sticking out; it had arms and legs as other children; but, instead of toes, it had on each foot three claws, like a young fowl, with sharp talons.

The governor speaking with Mr. Cotton about it, he told him the reason why he advised them to conceal it: 1. Because he saw a providence of God in it, that the rest of the women, which were coming and going in the time of her travail, should then be absent. 2. He considered, that, if it had been his own case, he should have desired to have had it concealed. 3. He had known other monstrous births, which had been concealed, and that he thought God might intend only the in-

---

[1] Public registration of births, marriages and deaths was maintained in the Bay colony with great care.

struction of the parents, and such other to whom it was known, etc. The like apology he made for himself in public, which was well accepted.[1]

(2.) (*April.*)] The governor, with advice of some other of the magistrates and of the elders of Boston, caused the said monster to be taken up, and though it were much corrupted, yet most of those things were to be seen, as the horns and claws, the scales, etc. When it died in the mother's body, (which was about two hours before the birth,) the bed whereon the mother lay did shake, and withal there was such a noisome savor, as most of the women were taken with extreme vomiting and purging, so as they were forced to depart; and others of them their children were taken with convulsions, (which they never had before nor after,) and so were sent for home, so as by these occasions it came to be concealed.

Another thing observable was, the discovery of it, which was just when Mrs. Hutchinson was cast out of the church. For Mrs. Dyer going forth with her, a stranger asked, what young woman it was. The others answered, it was the woman which had the monster; which gave the first occasion to some that heard it to speak of it. The midwife, presently after this discovery, went out of the jurisdiction; and indeed it was time for her to be gone, for it was known, that she used to give young women oil of mandrakes and other stuff to cause conception; and she grew into great suspicion to be a witch, for it was credibly reported, that, when she gave any medicines, (for she practised physic,) she would ask the party, if she did believe, she could help her, etc.

Another observable passage was, that the father of this monster, coming home at this very time, was, the next Lord's day, by an unexpected providence, questioned in the church for divers monstrous errors, as for denying all inherent right-

[1] The repulsive notion that the displeasure of Heaven was revealed by monstrous births was entertained by men of the best intelligence.

eousness, etc., which he maintained, and was for the same admonished.[1]

12.] A general fast was kept through all the churches, by advice from the court, for seeking the Lord to prevent evil, that we feared to be intended against us from England by a general governor; for the safe arrival of our friends from thence, (very many being expected;) and for establishment of peace and truth amongst us.

21.] Owsamekin, the sachem of Acooemeck, on this side Connecticut, came to the governor and brought a present of eighteen skins of beaver from himself and the sachems of Mohegan beyond Connecticut and Pakontuckett. The occasion was, (as he said,) it was reported, that we were angry with him, and intended to war upon them; so they came to seek peace. The governor received the present, and (having none of the other magistrates at hand to advise with) answered them, that if they had done no wrong to the English, nor aided our enemies, we would be at peace with them; and accordingly signified so much to the magistrates at Connecticut. They took this answer well, and departed with the letter.

23.] This was a very hard winter. The snow lay, from November 4th to March 23d, half a yard deep about the Massachusetts, and a yard deep beyond Merrimack, and so the more north the deeper, and the spring was very backward. This day it did snow two hours together, (after much rain from N. E.) with flakes as great as shillings. This was in the year 1637.

24.] The governor and deputy went to Concord to view some land for farms, and, going down the river about four miles, they made choice of a place for one thousand acres for each of them. They offered each other the first choice, but because the deputy's was first granted, and himself had store

---

[1] The putting to death of Mary Dyer, the Quakeress, who now in this sad fashion emerges into history, is the tragedy of a later time. Her execution took place in 1660.

of land already, the governor yielded him the choice. So, at the place where the deputy's land was to begin, there were two great stones, which they called the Two Brothers, in remembrance that they were brothers by their children's marriage, and did so brotherly agree, and for that a little creek near those stones was to part their lands. At the court in the 4th month after, two hundred acres were added to the governor's park.[1]

26.] Mr. Coddington (who had been an assistant from the first coming over of the government, being, with his wife, taken with the familistical opinions) removed to Aquiday Island in the Naragansett Bay.

(3.) (*May*) 2.] At the court of elections, the former governor, John Winthrop, was chosen again. The same day, at night, he was taken with a sharp fever, which brought him near death; but many prayers were put up to the Lord for him, and he was restored again after one month.

This court the name of Newtown was altered, and it was called Cambridge.[2]

The spring was so cold, that men were forced to plant their corn two or three times, for it rotted in the ground; but, when we feared a great dearth, God sent a warm season, which brought on corn beyond expectation.

(4.) (*June*) 1.] Between three and four in the afternoon, being clear, warm weather, the wind westerly, there was a great earthquake. It came with a noise like a continued thunder or the rattling of coaches in London, but was presently gone. It was at Connecticut, at Naragansett, at Pascataquack,

---

[1] The "Two Brothers" still hold their place on the river-bank. See photograph in Augustine Jones, *Thomas Dudley*. The reconciliation between Winthrop and Dudley seems to have been complete.

[2] Savage estimates that there were forty or fifty Cambridge men dwelling in the colony, and not a few from Oxford. The college was established by order of the General Court in October, 1636; Rev. John Harvard died later in this year 1638; the name Harvard College was bestowed in March, 1639, in recognition of his bequest.

and all the parts round about. It shook the ships, which rode in the harbor, and all the islands, etc. The noise and the shakings continued about four minutes. The earth was unquiet twenty days after, by times.

5.] Unkus, alias Okoco, the Monahegan sachem in the twist of Pequod River,[1] came to Boston with thirty-seven men. He came from Connecticut with Mr. Haynes, and tendered the governor a present of twenty fathom of wampom. This was at the court, and it was thought fit by the council to refuse it, till he had given satisfaction about the Pequods he kept, etc. Upon this he was much dejected, and made account we would have killed him; but, two days after, having received good satisfaction of his innocency, etc., and he promising to submit to the order of the English touching the Pequods he had, and the differences between the Naragansetts and him, we accepted his present. And, about half an hour after, he came to the governor, and entertained him with these compliments: This heart (laying his hand upon his breast) is not mine, but yours; I have no men; they are all yours; command me any difficult thing, I will do it; I will not believe any Indians' words against the English; if any man shall kill an Englishman, I will put him to death, were he never so dear to me. So the governor gave him a fair, red coat, and defrayed his and his men's diet, and gave them corn to relieve them homeward, and a letter of protection to all men, etc., and he departed very joyful.

Many ships arrived this year, with people of good quality and estate, notwithstanding the council's order, that none such should come without the king's license; but God so wrought, that some obtained license, and others came away without. The troubles which arose in Scotland about the book of common prayer, and the canons, which the king would have forced upon the Scotch churches, did so take up

---

[1] The Mohegans lay west of the Pequot territory, as the Narragansetts lay to the east.

the king and council, that they had neither heart nor leisure to look after the affairs of New England; yet, upon report of the many thousands, which were preparing to come away, the archbishops caused all the ships to be stayed. But, upon the petition of the masters, and suggestion of the great damage it would be to the commonwealth in hindering the Newfoundland trade, which brought in much money, etc., they were presently released. And in this and other passages it plainly appeared, that near all the lords of the council did favor this plantation; and all the officers of the custom house were very ready to further it, for they never made search for any goods, etc., but let men bring what they would, without question or control. For sure the Lord awed their hearts, and they and others (who savored not religion) were amazed to see men of all conditions, rich and poor, servants and others, offering themselves so readily for New England, when, for furnishing of other plantations, they were forced to send about their stalls,[1] and when they had gotten any, they were forced to keep them as prisoners from running away.

Mo. (6.) (*August*) 3.] In the night was a very great tempest or hiracano at S. W. which drave a ship on ground at Charlestown, and brake down the windmill there, and did much other harm. It flowed twice in six hours, and about Naragansett it raised the tide fourteen or fifteen foot above the ordinary spring tides, upright.

Janemoh, the sachem of Niantick,[2] had gone to Long Island and rifled some of those Indians, which were tributaries to us. The sachem complained to our friends of Connecticut, who wrote us about it, and sent Capt. Mason, with seven men, to require satisfaction. The governor of the Massachusetts wrote also to Mr. Williams to treat with Miantunnomoh about satisfaction, or otherwise to bid them look for war.

[1] Decoys.
[2] The Niantics were a tribe near and closely allied to the Narragansetts, in territory towards which the English were now departing.

Upon this Janemoh went to Connecticut, and made his peace, and gave full satisfaction for all injuries.

Two ships, which came over this year much pestered, lost many passengers, and some principal men, and many fell sick after they were landed, and many of them died.

Four servants of Plymouth ran from their masters, and, coming to Providence, they killed an Indian. He escaped, after he was deadly wounded in the belly, and gat to other Indians. So, being discovered, they fled and were taken at the Isle Aquiday.[1] Mr. Williams gave notice to the governor of Massachusetts, and desired advice. He returned answer, that, seeing they were of Plymouth, they should certify Plymouth of them, and, if they would send for them, to deliver them; otherwise, seeing no English had jurisdiction in the place where the murder was committed, neither had they at the Island any government established, it would be safest to deliver the principal, who was certainly known to have killed the party, to the Indian his friends, with caution that they should not put him to torture, and to keep the other three to further consideration.

After this, Plymouth men sent for them, (but one had escaped,) and the governor there wrote to the governor here for advice, especially for that he heard they intended to appeal into England. The governor returned answer of encouragement to proceed notwithstanding, seeing no appeal did lie, for that they could not be tried in England, and that the whole country here were interested in the case, and would expect to have justice done.[2] Whereupon they proceeded as appears after.

Many of Boston and others, who were of Mrs. Hutchinson's judgment and party, removed to the Isle of Aquiday; and

---

[1] Aquiday, Aquidneck, or Rhode Island, now becoming important as the seat of the new plantation beyond Providence.

[2] See Bradford, pp. 344–346. The Plymouth governor at this time was Thomas Prence.

others, who were of the rigid separation, and savored anabaptism, removed to Providence, so as those parts began to be well peopled.

There came over this summer twenty ships, and at least three thousand persons,[1] so as they were forced to look out new plantations. One was begun at Merrimack, and another four or five miles above Concord, and another at Winicowett.

The three prisoners, being brought to Plymouth, and there examined, did all confess the murder, and that they did it to get his wampom, etc.; but all the question was about the death of the Indian, for no man could witness that he saw him dead. But Mr. Williams and Mr. James of Providence made oath, that his wound was mortal, etc. At last two Indians, who, with much difficulty, were procured to come to the trial, (for they still feared that the English were conspired to kill all the Indians,) made oath after this manner, viz.: that if he were not dead of that wound, then they would suffer death. Upon this they three were condemned and executed. Two of them died very penitently, especially Arthur Peach, a young man of good parentage and fair conditioned, and who had done very good service against the Pequods.

The fourth escaped to Pascataquack. The governor sent after him, but those of Pascataquack conveyed him away, and openly withstood his apprehension. It was their usual manner (some of them) to countenance, etc., all such lewd persons as fled from us to them.

(7.) (*September.*) The general court was assembled, in which it was agreed, that, whereas a very strict order was sent from the lords commissioners for plantations for the sending home our patent, upon pretence that judgment had passed against it upon a quo warranto, a letter should be written by the governor, in the name of the court, to excuse our not sending of it; for it was resolved to be best not to send it, because

---

[1] The immigration, which two years later suddenly ceased, was now at its height.

then such of our friends and others in England would conceive it to be surrendered, and that thereupon we should be bound to receive such a governor and such orders as should be sent to us, and many bad minds, yea, and some weak ones, among ourselves, would think it lawful, if not necessary, to accept a general governor. The copy of the letter is reserved, etc., in form of a petition. See the after fol. 74.[1]

At this court a law was made about such as should continue excommunicated six months, and for public thankgiving for the arrival of the ships, and for the coming on of harvest beyond expectation, etc. This law was after repealed.

At this court, also, Capt. Underhill (being about to remove to Mr. Wheelwright) petitioned for three hundred acres of land promised him formerly; by occasion whereof he was questioned about some speeches he had used in the ship lately, in his return out of England, viz., that he should say, that we were zealous here, as the Scribes and Pharisees were, and as Paul was before his conversion, etc., which he denying, they were proved to his face by a sober, godly woman, whom he had seduced in the ship, and drawn to his opinions, (but she was after freed again). Among other passages, he told her how he came to his assurance, and that was thus: He had lain under a spirit of bondage and a legal way five years, and could get no assurance, till at length, as he was taking a pipe of tobacco, the Spirit set home an absolute promise of free grace with such assurance and joy, as he never since doubted of his good estate, neither should he, though he should fall into sin. He would not confess nor deny this, but took exceptions at the court for crediting one witness against him, etc., and withal said, that he was still of the same opinion he had been, etc. Whereupon he was demanded, if he were of the same opinion

[1] It was important in this age, that a charter should be beyond the control of the grantor, not lightly to be set aside, but only after *quo warranto* proceedings embarrassing to those in power. See Brooks Adams, *Emancipation of Massachusetts*, p. 17. Winthrop refers to a page in his second note-book where Savage found nothing.

he had been in about the petition or remonstrance. He answered, yes, and that his retractation was only of the manner, not of the matter. Whereupon his retractation (which he had lately delivered to the governor, to be presented to this court) was read, wherein he professeth how the Lord had brought him to see his sin in condemning the court, and passing the bounds of modesty and submission, which is required in private persons, etc., and in what trouble of spirit he had been for it, etc. Upon this, the court committed him for abusing the court with a show of retractation, and intending no such thing; and the next day he was called again and banished. The Lord's day following, he made a speech in the assembly, showing that, as the Lord was pleased to convert Paul as he was in persecuting, etc., so he might manifest himself to him as he was taking the moderate use of the creature called tobacco. He professed withal, that he knew not wherein he had deserved the sentence of the court, and that he was sure that Christ was his, etc. The elders reproved him for this speech; and Mr. Cotton told him, that he brake a rule in condemning publicly the sentence of the court, before he had privately convinced the magistrates, or some of them; and told him, also, that, although God doth often lay a man under a spirit of bondage, when he is walking in sin, as Paul was, yet he never sends such a spirit of comfort but in an ordinance, as he did to the same Paul by Ananias; and ergo advised him well to examine the revelation and joy which he had.

The next Lord's day, the same Capt. Underhill, having been privately dealt with upon suspicion of incontinency with a neighbor's wife, and not harkening to it, was publicly questioned, and put under admonition. The matter was, for that the woman being young, and beautiful, and withal of a jovial spirit and behavior, he did daily frequent her house, and was divers times found there alone with her, the door being locked on the inside. He confessed it was ill, because it had an appearance of evil in it; but his excuse was, that the woman was in great trouble of mind, and sore temptations, and that he resorted to her to comfort her; and that when the door was found locked upon them, they were in private prayer together. But this practice was clearly condemned also by the elders, affirming, that it had not been of good report for any of them to have done the like, and that they ought, in such case, to have called in some brother or sister, and not to have locked the door, etc. They also declared, that once he procured them to go visit her, telling them that she was in great trouble of mind; but when they came to her, (taking her, it seems, upon the sudden,) they perceived no such thing.[1] See the issue of this after, (9,) 1638, and (10,) 13, 38.

Mrs. Hutchinson, being removed to the Isle of Aquiday, in the Naragansett Bay, after her time was fulfilled, that she expected deliverance of a child, was delivered of a monstrous birth, which, being diversely related in the country, (and, in the open assembly at Boston, upon a lecture day, declared by Mr. Cotton to . . . signify her error in denying inherent righteousness, but that all was Christ in us, and nothing of ours in our faith, love, etc.) hereupon the governor wrote to Mr. Clarke, a physician and a preacher to those of the island, to know the certainty thereof.[2] . . .

21.] A ship of Barnstaple arrived with about eighty passengers, near all western people. There came with them a godly minister, one Mr. Matthews.

Here arrived a small Spanish frigate with hides and tallow. She was a prize taken by Capt. Newman, who was

---

[1] This passage makes it plain that the Hutchinsonian doctrines admitted of a perilous interpretation. John Underhill was a dangerous character in the community. As the successful soldier of the colony he had great prestige, and his bad example would work evil. Being a subject of the "covenant of grace," he made it a cloak for licentiousness. His acknowledgments of sin and professions of repentance were justly held in suspicion. He was long an object of fear in New England.

[2] The repulsive details which Winthrop took pains to gather are here omitted. They are not inaccessible, and they only show how far bigotry could carry a mind naturally noble and magnanimous.

set out with letters of mart by the lords, etc., of the Isle of Providence.[1]

This year there came a letter from Mr. Thomas Mewtis, clerk of the council in England, directed to Mr. Winthrop, (the present governor,) and therein an order from the lords commissioners for foreign plantations, (being all of the council,) wherein they straightly required the patent to be sent home by the first ship, etc. This letter and order were produced at the general court last past, and there agreed not to send home the patent, but to return answer to the lords by way of humble petition, which was drawn up and sent accordingly. These instruments are all among the governor's papers, and the effect of them would be here inserted.[2]

25.] Being the third day of the week, and two days before the change, the wind having blown at N. E. all the day, and rainy in the night, was a mighty tempest, and withal the highest tide, which had been seen since our coming into this country; but, through the good providence of God, it did little harm. About fourteen days after, the wind having been at N. W. and then calm here, came in the greatest eastern sea, which had been in our time. Mr. Peirce (who came in a week after) had that time a very great tempest three days at N. E.

A remarkable providence appeared in a case, which was tried at the last court of assistants. Divers neighbors of Lynn, by agreement, kept their cattle by turns. It fell out to the turn of one Gillow to keep them, and, as he was driving them forth, another of these neighbors went along with him, and kept him so earnestly in talk, that his cattle strayed and gate in the corn. Then this other neighbor left him, and would not help him recover his cattle, but went and told another how he had kept Gillow in talk, that he might lose his cattle, etc. The

---

[1] The context always shows, when "Providence" is named, whether the spot in New England or that in the Caribbean Sea is intended. See *ante*, p. 228, note 1.

[2] See Hubbard's *New England*, pp. 268–271, for their text.

cattle, getting into the Indian corn, eat so much ere they could be gotten out, that two of them fell sick of it, and one of them died presently; and these two cows were that neighbor's who had kept Gillow in talk, etc. The man brings his action against Gillow for his cow, (not knowing that he had witness of his speech); but Gillow, producing witness, etc., barred him of his action, and had good costs, etc.

The court, taking into consideration the great disorder general through the country in costliness of apparel, and following new fashions, sent for the elders of the churches, and conferred with them about it, and laid it upon them, as belonging to them, to redress it, by urging it upon the consciences of their people, which they promised to do. But little was done about it; for divers of the elders' wives, etc., were in some measure partners in this general disorder.

8ber (*October*).] About two years since one Mr. Bernard, a minister at Batcomb in Somersetshire in England, sent over two books in writing, one to the magistrates, and the other to the elders, wherein he laid down arguments against the manner of our gathering our churches, etc., which the elders could not answer till this time, by reason of the many troubles about Mrs. Hutchinson's opinions, etc. Mr. Cotton also answered another book sent over in defence of set form of prayer. This I suppose was Mr. Ball's book.

About this time was very much rain and snow, in six weeks together; scarce two days without rain or snow. This was observed by some as an effect of the earthquake.

(9.) (*November*) 8.] A church was gathered at Dedham with good approbation; and, 28th, Mr. Peck ordained teacher at Hingham.

By order of the last general court, the governor wrote a letter to Mr. Burdet,[1] Mr. Wiggin, and others of the planta-

---

[1] Burdet was a minister who, finding the Salem atmosphere too strict, went north to Piscataqua, there joining Wiggin, agent of the Puritan Lords Saye and Brooke, who had the power of a governor thereabouts.

tion of Pascataquack, to this effect: That, whereas there had been good correspondency between us formerly, we could not but be sensible of their entertaining and countenancing, etc., some that we had cast out, etc., and that our purpose was to survey our utmost limits, and make use of them. Mr. Burdet returned a scornful answer, and would not give the governor his title, etc. This was very ill taken, for that he was one of our body, and sworn to our government, and a member of the church of Salem; so as the governor was purposed to summon him to appear at our court to answer his contempt; but, advising with the deputy about it, he was dissuaded from it, the rather for that, if he should suffer in this cause, it would ingratiate him more with the archbishops, (with whom he had intelligence, etc.) but his council was rather to undermine him by making him thoroughly known, etc., to his friends in Pascataquack, and to take them from him. Whereupon the governor wrote to Edward Hilton, declaring his ill dealing, (and sent a copy of his letter,) and advising them to take heed how they put themselves into his power, etc., but rather to give us a proof of their respect towards us, etc.—He intimated withal how ill it would relish, if they should advance Capt. Underhill, whom we had thrust out for abusing the court with feigning a retractation both of his seditious practice and also of his corrupt opinions, and after denying it again, and for casting reproach upon our churches, etc.; signifying withal, that he was now found to have been an unclean person, (for he was charged by a godly young woman to have solicited her chastity under pretence of Christian love, and to have confessed to her, that he had his will oftentimes of the cooper's wife, and all out of strength of love,) and the church had sent for him, and sent him a license to come and go, under the hands of the governor and deputy; but he refused to come, excusing himself, by letters to the elders, that the license was not sufficient, etc., and, by letters to the governor, that he had no rule to come and answer to any offence, except his banishment were released; but to the matter he was charged with, he gave no answer, but sought an evasion. Pascataquack men had chosen him their governor before the letter came to them.

13.] The governor went by water to Salem where he was entertained with all the respect that they could show him. The 12 he returned by land, and they sent six of their chief military officers with carbines to guard him to Boston.

17.] Roger Herlakenden,[1] one of our magistrates, about thirty years of age, second son of [blank] Herlakenden of Earl's Colne in Essex, Esq., died at Cambridge of the small pox. He was a very godly man, and of good use both in the commonwealth and in the church. He was buried with military honor, because he was lieutenant colonel. He left behind a virtuous gentlewoman and two daughters. He died in great peace, and left a sweet memorial behind him of his piety and virtue.

10. (*December*) 2.] Ezekiel Rogers, son of Richard Rogers of Weathersfield in Essex, a worthy son of so worthy a father, lying at Boston with some who came out of Yorkshire with him, where he had been a painful preacher many years, being desirous to partake in the Lord's supper with the church of Boston, did first impart his desire to the elders, and having given them satisfaction, they acquainted the church with it, and before the sacrament, being called forth by the elders, he spoke to this effect, viz.: that he and his company (viz. divers families, who came over with him this summer) had, of a good time, withdrawn themselves from the church communion of England, and that for many corruptions which were among them. But, first, he desired, that he might not be mistaken, as if he did condemn all there; for he did acknowledge a special presence of God there in three things: 1, in the soundness of

---

[1] This young magistrate, whose promise for usefulness was so prematurely blighted, was of noble lineage, his line running to the Plantagenets. His sister Mabel married John Haynes, governor of Massachusetts and Connecticut, from which union came a long and distinguished line.

doctrine in all fundamental truths; 2, in the excellency of ministerial gifts; 3, in the blessing upon the same, for the work of conversion and for the power of religion, in all which there appeared more, etc., in England than in all the known world besides. Yet there are such corruptions, as, since God let them see some light therein, they could not, with safe conscience, join any longer with them. The first is, their national church; second, their hierarchy, wholly antichristian; third, their dead service; fourth, their receiving (nay, compelling) all to partake of the seals; fifth, their abuse of excommunications, wherein they enwrap many a godly minister, by causing him to pronounce their sentence, etc., they not knowing that the fear of the excommunication lies in that. Hereupon they bewailed before the Lord their sinful partaking so long in those corruptions, and entered a covenant together, to walk together in all the ordinances, etc.[1]

1639. 10. (*December*) 3.] Being settled at Rowley, they renewed their church covenant, and their call [*blank*] of Mr. Rogers to the office of pastor, according to the course of other churches, etc.

(10.) (*December*) 6.] Dorothy Talbye was hanged at Boston for murdering her own daughter, a child of three years old. She had been a member of the church of Salem, and of good esteem for godliness, etc.; but, falling at difference with her husband, through melancholy or spiritual delusions, she sometimes attempted to kill him, and her children, and herself, by refusing meat, saying it was so revealed to her, etc. After much patience, and divers admonitions not prevailing, the church cast her out. Whereupon she grew worse; so as the magistrate caused her to be whipped. Whereupon she was reformed for a time, and carried herself more dutifully to her

[1] Ezekiel Rogers stood a powerful figure in the New England church. Rowley, of which he was the first minister, took its name from the Yorkshire village from which he came, and his influence was felt far and wide. He is especially commemorated in the *Magnalia* of Cotton Mather. The ensuing item of 1639 is inserted by Winthrop, out of place, to complete the story.

husband, etc.; but soon after she was so possessed with Satan, that he persuaded her (by his delusions, which she listened to as revelations from God) to break the neck of her own child, that she might free it from future misery. This she confessed upon her apprehension; yet, at her arraignment, she stood mute a good space, till the governor told her she should be pressed to death, and then she confessed the indictment. When she was to receive judgment, she would not uncover her face, nor stand up, but as she was forced, nor give any testimony of her repentance, either then or at her execution. The cloth, which should have covered her face, she plucked off and put between the rope and her neck. She desired to have been beheaded, giving this reason, that it was less painful and less shameful. After a swing or two, she catched at the ladder. Mr. Peter, her late pastor, and Mr. Wilson, went with her to the place of execution, but could do no good with her. Mr. Peter gave an exhortation to the people to take heed of revelations, etc., and of despising the ordinance of excommunication as she had done; for when it was to have been denounced against her, she turned her back, and would have gone forth, if she had not been stayed by force.

One Capt. Newman, being set forth with commission from the Earl of Holland, governor of the Westminster company, and the Earl of Warwick, and others of the same company,[1] to spoil the Spaniard within the limits of their grant in the West Indies, after he had taken many of their small vessels, etc., returned home by the Massachusetts in a small pinnace, with which he had taken all his prizes, (for his great ship was of no use for that purpose). He brought many hides and much tallow. The hides he sold here for £17.10 the score; the tallow at 29s. the hundred; and set sail for England (10,) 1. He was after cast away at Christopher's with a very rich prize, in the great hyrracano, 1642.

13.] A general fast was kept upon the motion of the elders

[1] The Company of the Isle of Providence. See p. 228, note 1.

to the governor and council. The chief occasion was, the much sickness of pox and fevers spread through the country, (yet it was to the east and south also,) the apparent decay of power of religion, and the general declining of professors to the world, etc. Mr. Cotton, in his exercise that day at Boston, did confess and bewail, as the churches', so his own security, sloth, and credulity, whereupon so many and dangerous errors had gotten up and spread in the church; and went over all the particulars, and showed how he came to be deceived; the errors being framed (in words) so near the truths which he had preached and the falsehood of the maintainers of them, who usually would deny to him what they had delivered to others, etc. He acknowledged, that such as had been seducers of others (instancing in some of those of the Island, though he named them not) had been justly banished. Yet he said, that such as had been only misled, and others, who had done any thing out of a misguided conscience, (not being grossly evil,) should be borne withal, and first referred to the church, and if that could not heal them, they should rather be imprisoned, fined, or, etc., than banished, *qua* it was likely no other church would receive them.[1]

Those who were gone with Mrs. Hutchinson to Aquiday fell into new errors daily. One Nicholas Easton, a tanner, taught, that gifts and graces were that antichrist mentioned Thess., and that which withheld, etc., was the preaching of the law; and that every of the elect had the Holy Ghost and also the devil indwelling. Another, one Herne, taught, that women had no souls, and that Adam was not created in true holiness, etc., for then he could not have lost it.

Those who went to the falls at Pascataquack, gathered a church, and wrote to our church to desire us to dismiss Mr.

---

[1] In this passage we see the mental suffering of Cotton. Such cases as that of Underhill no doubt appalled him, and he was driven to strictness. The concluding sentences show that his heart was tender toward those who wandered, and averse to severe discipline.

Wheelwright to them for an officer; but, because he desired it not himself, the elders did not propound it. Soon after came his own letter, with theirs, for his dismission, which thereupon was granted. Others likewise (upon their request) were also dismissed thither.

The governor's letter to Mr. Hilton, about Mr. Burdet and Capt. Underhill, was by them intercepted and opened; and thereupon they wrote presently into England against us, discovering what they knew of our combination to resist any authority, that should come out of England against us, etc.; for they were extremely moved at the governor's letter, but could take no advantage by it, for he made account, when he wrote it, that Mr. Hilton would show it them. And, upon this, Capt. Underhill wrote a letter to Mr. Cotton, full of high and threatening words against us; but he wrote another, at the same time, to the governor in very fair terms, entreating an obliterating of all that was past, and a bearing with human infirmities, etc., disavowing all purpose of revenge, etc. See after, (1,) 1639.

The devil would never cease to disturb our peace, and to raise up instruments one after another. Amongst the rest, there was a woman in Salem, one Oliver his wife, who had suffered somewhat in England for refusing to bow at the name of Jesus, though otherwise she was conformable to all their orders. She was (for ability of speech, and appearance of zeal and devotion) far before Mrs. Hutchinson, and so the fitter instrument to have done hurt, but that she was poor and had little acquaintance. She took offence at this, that she might not be admitted to the Lord's supper without giving public satisfaction to the church of her faith, etc., and covenanting or professing to walk with them according to the rule of the gospel; so as, upon the sacrament day, she openly called for it, and stood to plead her right, though she were denied; and would not forbear, before the magistrate, Mr. Endecott, did threaten to send the constable to put her forth. This woman was brought to the court for disturbing the peace in the church, etc., and there she gave such peremptory answers, as she was committed till she should find sureties for her good behavior. After she had been in prison three or four days, she made means to the governor, and submitted herself, and acknowledged her fault in disturbing the church; whereupon he took her husband's bond for her good behavior, and discharged her out of prison. But he found, after, that she still held her former opinions, which were very dangerous, as, 1. That the church is the heads of the people, both magistrates and ministers, met together, and that these have power to ordain ministers, etc. 2. That all that dwell in the same town, and will profess their faith in Christ Jesus, ought to be received to the sacraments there; and that she was persuaded, that, if Paul were at Salem, he would call all the inhabitants there saints. 3. That excommunication is no other but when Christians withdraw private communion from one that hath offended.

About five years after, this woman was adjudged to be whipped for reproaching the magistrates. She stood without tying, and bare her punishment with a masculine spirit, glorying in her suffering. But after (when she came to consider the reproach, which would stick by her, etc.) she was much dejected about it. She had a cleft stick put on her tongue half an hour, for reproaching the elders, (6,) 1646.

At Providence, also, the devil was not idle. For whereas, at their first coming thither, Mr. Williams and the rest did make an order, that no man should be molested for his conscience, now men's wives, and children, and servants, claimed liberty hereby to go to all religious meetings, though never so often, or though private, upon the week days; and because one Verin refused to let his wife go to Mr. Williams so oft as she was called for, they required to have him censured. But there stood up one Arnold, a witty man of their own company, and withstood it, telling them that, when he consented to that order, he never intended it should extend to the breach of any ordinance of God, such as the subjection of wives to their husbands, etc., and gave divers solid reasons against it. Then one Greene (who hath married the wife of one Beggerly, whose husband is living, and no divorce, etc., but only it was said, that he had lived in adultery, and had confessed it) he replied, that, if they should restrain their wives, etc., all the women in the country would cry out of them, etc. Arnold answered him thus: Did you pretend to leave the Massachusetts, because you would not offend God to please men, and would you now break an ordinance and commandment of God to please women? Some were of opinion, that if Verin would not suffer his wife to have her liberty, the church should dispose her to some other man, who would use her better. Arnold told them, that it was not the woman's desire to go so oft from home, but only Mr. Williams's and others. In conclusion, when they would have censured Verin, Arnold told them, that it was against their own order, for Verin did that he did out of conscience; and their order was, that no man should be censured for his conscience.

Another plot the old serpent had against us, by sowing jealousies and differences between us and our friends at Connecticut, and also Plymouth. This latter was about our bounds. They had planted Scituate, and had given out all the lands to Conyhassett. We desired only so much of the marshes there, as might accommodate Hingham, which being denied, we caused Charles River to be surveyed, and found it come so far southward as would fetch in Scituate and more; but this was referred to a meeting between us.

The differences between us and those of Connecticut were divers; but the ground of all was their shyness of coming under our government, which, though we never intended to make them subordinate to us, yet they were very jealous, and therefore, in the articles of confederation, which we propounded to them, and whereby order was taken, that all differences, which might fall out, should be ended by a way of peace, and never to come to a necessity or danger of force,—they did so alter the chief article, as all would have come to nothing. For whereas the article was, That, upon any matter of difference, two, three, or more commissioners of every of the confederate colonies should assemble, and have absolute power (the greater number of them) to determine the matter,— they would have them only to meet, and if they could agree, so; if not, then to report to their several colonies, and to return with their advice, and so to go on till the matter might be agreed; which, beside that it would have been infinitely tedious and extreme chargeable, it would never have attained the end; for it was very unlikely, that all the churches in all the plantations would ever have accorded upon the same propositions.[1]

These articles, with their alterations, they sent to our general court at Newtown, the [blank] of the 5th, by Mr. Haynes, Mr. Pincheon, and John Steele. The court, finding their alteration, and the inconveniences thereof, would take the like liberty to add and alter; (for the articles were drawn only by some of the council, and never allowed by the court). This they excepted against, and would have restrained us of that liberty, which they took themselves; and one of their three commissioners, falling in debate with some of our deputies, said, that they would not meddle with any thing that was within our limits; which being reported to the court, they thought it seasonable we should stand upon our right, so as, though we were formerly willing that Agawam (now Springfield) should have fallen into their government, yet, seeing they would not be beholden to us for any thing, we intended to keep it; and accordingly we put it in as an article, that the line between us should be, one way, the Pequod River, (viz. south and north,) and the other way, (viz. east and west,) the limits

---

[1] Though the relations of Connecticut with the parent colony were here inharmonious the emigrants at first remembered with affection their old homes. Hartford was originally called Newtown, whence most of the settlers were drawn; Windsor was Dorchester, and Westfield, Watertown.

of our own grant. And this article we added: That we, etc., should have liberty to pass to and fro upon Connecticut, and they likewise. To these articles all their commissioners offered to consent, but it was thought by our court, (because of the new articles,) that they should first acquaint their own court with it. And so their commissioners departed.

After this, we understood that they went on to exercise their authority at Agawam.[1] Whereupon the governor wrote to them to desire them to forbear until the line was laid out, with advice about some other things, as by the copy of the letter appears. After a long time, Mr. Ludlow (in the name of their court) returned answer, which was very harsh; and in fine declared, that they thought it not fit to treat any further before they had advice from the gentlemen of Saybrook, etc. The governor acquainted the council and magistrates with this letter; and, because they had tied our hands (in a manner) from replying, he wrote a private letter to Mr. Haynes, wherein he lays open their mistakes (as he called them) and the apparent causes of offence, which they had given us; as by disclaiming to their Naragansetts to be bound by our former agreement with them, (which they would never make till the wars were ended,) by making a treaty of agreement with the Naragansetts and Monhigans, without joining us, or mentioning us to that end, (though we had by letter given them liberty to take us in,) and by binding all the Indians (who had received any Pequods) to pay tribute for them all to them at Connecticut, etc. (All these things are clearly to be seen in the letters.) These and the like miscarriages in point of correspondency were conceived to arise from these two errors in their government: 1. They chose divers *scores* men, who had no learning nor judgment, which might fit them for those affairs, though otherwise men holy and religious. 2. By occasion hereof, the main burden for managing of state business fell upon some one or other of their ministers, (as the phrase and style of these

[1] Agawam, or Springfield; also the Indian name of Ipswich.

letters will clearly discover,) who, though they were men of singular wisdom and godliness, yet, stepping out of their course, their actions wanted that blessing, which otherwise might have been expected.[1]

[August 28, 1638. In my letter to Mr. Hooker, I complain of three things:—

1. That they told the Narragansetts, that they were not tied to the agreement we made with the Indians; and that they did this, to advance their own reputation with the Indians, and to abase ours; that it was a point of state policy in them not to dissent, while the war was at their doors, for they had need of our help, etc.; that it was done without any pressing occasion; that it was done unseasonably, after their own commissioners had propounded that before the Indians we should in all things appear as one.

2. That they altered the articles of confederation in the most material point, and all because some preëminence was therein yielded to the Massachusetts, and being again agreed, (only referred to consent, etc.) in three months we had no answer from them; that the way which they would have taken, of referring differences to the churches, would occasion infinite trouble and expense, and yet leave the issue to the sword.

I expostulated about the unwarrantableness and unsafeness of referring matter of counsel or judicature to the body of the people, quia the best part is always the least, and of that best part the wiser part is always the lesser. The old law was, choose ye out judges, etc., and thou shalt bring the matter to the judge, etc.

3. That they did still exercise jurisdiction at Agawam, though one of their commissioners disclaimed to intermeddle in our line, and thither we challenged our right, and it was agreed so, and I had wrote to them to desire them to forbear until, etc., that Mr. Pincheon had small encouragement to be under them; that if his relation were true, I could not see the justice of their proceeding against him, etc.

That the end of my writing to him was, that he might help quench these sparks of contention; that I did open our grievances to him in

---

[1] Savage's note here gives an idea of the care with which his transcript, adopted in the present edition, was made. "These lines were so effectually erased, that, for some years, my desire of decyphering them was baffled; but, after twice abandoning the task, I gradually obtained, with the aid of a gentleman much skilled in reading difficult MS., a sufficient confidence in all but one word."

their most true and reasonable intendment; that though I be strict for our right in public, quia their magistrates are so, yet I am willing to listen to advice, and my aim is the common good.]¹

15.] The wind at N. E., there was so great a tempest of wind and snow all the night and the next day, as had not been since our time. Five men and youths perished between Mattapan and Dorchester, and a man and a woman between Boston and Roxbury. Anthony Dick, in a bark of thirty tons, cast away upon the head of Cape Cod. Three were starved to death with the cold; the other two got some fire and so lived there, by such food as they saved, seven weeks, till an Indian found them, etc. Two vessels bound for Quinipiack were cast away at Aquiday, but the people saved. Much other harm was done in staving of boats, etc., and by the great tides, which exceeded all before. This happened the day after a general fast, which occasioned some of our ministers to stir us up to seek the Lord better, because he seemed to discountenance the means of reconciliation. Whereupon the next general court, by advice of the elders, agreed to keep another day, and to seek further into the causes of such displeasure, etc.; which accordingly was performed.

---

[1] This passage was written by Winthrop in another part of the manuscript volume, but we are apparently warranted in treating it as a portion of the *Journal*. The letter here summarized, though described as addressed to Hooker, not Haynes, is plainly a part of the correspondence mentioned in the paragraph to which we have subjoined this extract.

1639

(11.) (*January*) 14.] The earthquake, which had continued at times since the 1st of the 4th, was more generally felt, and the same noise heard in many places.

30.] A church was gathered at Weymouth with approbation of the magistrates and elders. It is observable, this church, having been gathered before, and so that of Lynn, could not hold together, nor could have any elders join or hold with them. The reason appeared to be, because they did not begin according to the rule of the gospel, which when Lynn had found and humbled themselves for it, and began again upon a new foundation, they went on with a blessing.

The people of this town of Weymouth had invited one Mr. Lenthall to come to them, with intention to call him to be their minister. This man, though of good report in England, coming hither, was found to have drank in some of Mrs. Hutchinson's opinions, as of justification before faith, etc., and opposed the gathering of our churches in such a way of mutual stipulation as was practised among us. From the former he was soon taken off upon conference with Mr. Cotton; but he stuck close to the other, that only baptism was the door of entrance into the church, etc., so as the common sort of people did eagerly embrace his opinions, and some labored to get such a church on foot as all baptized ones might communicate in without any further trial of them, etc. For this end they procured many hands in Weymouth to a blank, intending to have Mr. Lenthall's advice to the frame of their call; and he likewise was very forward to become a minister to them in such a way, and did openly maintain the cause. But the magistrates, hearing of this disturbance and combination, thought it needful to stop it betimes, and ergo they called

Mr. Lenthall, and some of the chief of the faction, to the next general court in the 1 month, where Mr. Lenthall, having before conferred with some of the magistrates and of the elders, and being convinced both of his error in judgment, and of his sin in practice to the distrubance of our peace, etc., did openly and freely retract, with expression of much grief of heart for his offence, and did deliver his retractation in writing, under his hand, in the open court; whereupon he was enjoined to appear at the next court, and in the mean time to make and deliver the like recantation in some public assembly at Weymouth. So the court stopped for any further censure by fine, or, etc., though it was much urged by some.

At the same court one Smith was convicted and fined £20 for being a chief stirrer in the business; and one Silvester was disfranchised; and one Britton, who had spoken reproachfully of the answer, which was sent to Mr. Barnard his book against our church covenant, and of some of our elders, and had sided with Mr. Lenthall, etc., was openly whipped, because he had no estate to answer, etc.

Mo. 1 (*March*).] A printing house was begun at Cambridge by one Daye, at the charge of Mr. Glover, who died on sea hitherward. The first thing which was printed was the freemen's oath; the next was an almanac made for New England by Mr. William Peirce, mariner; the next was the Psalms newly turned into metre.[1]

A plantation was begun by Sandwich, and was called Yarmouth, in Plymouth jurisdiction.

Another plantation was begun upon the north side of Merrimack, called Sarisbury, now Colchester;[2] another at Winicowett, called Hampton, which gave occasion of some difference between us and some of Pascataquack, which grew thus:

---

[1] See R. F. Roden, *The Cambridge Press*, 1638-1692 (New York, 1905). William Peirce, maker of the almanac, was the active and versatile captain of the *Lion* and other ships, who has been often mentioned. Though this was the first press of New England, the Spaniards had been printing in Mexico since 1539.   [2] Now Salisbury.

Mr. Wheelwright, being banished from us, gathered a company and sat down by the falls of Pascataquack, and called their town Exeter; and for their enlargement they dealt with an Indian there, and bought of him Winicowett, etc., and then wrote to us what they had done, and that they intended to lot out all these lands in farms, except we could show a better title. They wrote also to those whom we had sent to plant Winicowett to have them desist, etc. These letters coming to the general court, they returned answer, that they looked at this their dealing as against good neighborhood, religion, and common honesty; that, knowing we claimed Winicowett as within our patent, or as vacuum domicilium, and had taken possession thereof by building an house there above two years since, they should now go and purchase an unknown title, and then come to inquire of our right. It was in the same letter also manifestly proved, that the Indians having only a natural right to so much land as they had or could improve, so as the rest of the country lay open to any that could and would improve it, as by the said letter more at large doth appear.

In this year one James Everell, a sober, discreet man, and two others, saw a great light in the night at Muddy River.[1] When it stood still, it flamed up, and was about three yards square; when it ran, it was contracted into the figure of a swine: it ran as swift as an arrow towards Charlton, and so up and down about two or three hours. They were come down in their lighter about a mile, and, when it was over, they found themselves carried quite back against the tide to the place they came from. Divers other credible persons saw the same light, after, about the same place.

The general court, in the 7th mo. (*September*) last, gave order to the governor to write to them of Pascataquack, to signify to them, that we looked at it as an unneighborly part, that they should encourage and advance such as we had cast

---

[1] Muddy River became Brookline, Massachusetts.

out from us for their offences, before they had inquired of us the cause, etc. (The occasion of this letter was, that they had aided Mr. Wheelwright to begin a plantation there, and intended to make Capt. Underhill their governor in the room of Mr. Burdett, who had thrust out Capt. Wiggin, set in there by the lords, etc.) Upon this, Capt. Underhill (being chosen governor there) wrote a letter to a young gentleman, (who sojourned in the house of our governor,) wherein he reviles the governor with reproachful terms and imprecations of vengeance upon us all. This letter being showed to the governor and council, the governor, by advice, wrote the letter to Edward Hilton as is before mentioned, page [blank], mo. 10, (*December*) 13. The captain was so nettled with this letter, and especially because his adulterous life with the cooper's wife at Boston was now discovered, and the church had called him to come and make answer to it; but he made many excuses, as want of liberty, being a banished man, (yet the governor and council had sent him a safe conduct,) and upon his pretence of the insufficiency of that, the general court sent him another for three months. But, instead of coming, he procured a new church at Pascataquack of some few loose men (who had chosen one Mr. Knolles,[1] a weak minister, lately come out of England, and rejected by us for holding some of Mrs. Hutchinson's opinions) to write to our church at Boston in his commenda-

---

[1] This was Hanserd Knollys, famous among the early Baptists. A Lincolnshire man, of Cambridge training, he found a patron in the liberal Bishop Williams of Lincoln, through whom he obtained a living as a Church of England priest. Becoming a separatist he fled to New England, and appears in Winthrop's *Journal* as minister of Dover, on the Piscataqua. Returning to England after a few disturbed years of sojourn, he found the tolerant spirit of the Commonwealth congenial. As schoolmaster and preacher, he was successful and obtained offices lucrative and influential. After the Restoration he was persecuted, undergoing banishment, imprisonment and confiscation of property. He lived to the age of 92, preaching even when he could no longer stand, and writing much. Though stigmatized as weak, he played a conspicuous part, and was buried in Bunhill Fields with many other great non-conformists. See Gordon, in the *Dictionary of National Biography, s. v.* He appears to poor advantage in Winthrop, who could hardly be a candid judge of such a man.

tion, wherein they style him the right worshipful, their honored governor; all which notwithstanding, the church of Boston proceeded with him; and, in the mean time, the general court wrote to all the chief inhabitants of Pascataquack, and sent them a copy of his letters, (wherein he professeth himself to be an instrument ordained of God for our ruin,) to know, whether it were with their privity and consent, that he sent us such a defiance, etc., and whether they would maintain him in such practices against us, etc.

Those of Pascataquack returned answer to us by two several letters. Those of the plantation disclaimed to have any hand in his miscarriages, etc., and offered to call him to account, etc., whensoever we would send any to inform against him. The others at the river's mouth disclaimed likewise, and showed their indignation against him for his insolences, and their readiness to join in any fair course for our satisfaction; only they desired us to have some compassion of him, and not to send any forces against him.

After this, Capt. Underhill's courage was abated, for the chiefest in the river fell from him, and the rest little regarded him, so as he wrote letters of retractation to divers; and, to show his wisdom, he wrote a letter to the deputy and the court, (not mentioning the governor,) wherein he sent the copies of some of the governor's letters to Pascataquack, supposing that something would appear in them either to extenuate his fault, or to lay blame upon the governor; but he failed in both, for the governor was able to make good what he had written.

16.] There was so violent a wind at S. S. E. and S. as the like was not since we came into this land. It began in the evening, and increased till midnight. It overturned some new, strong houses; but the Lord miraculously preserved old, weak cottages. It tare down fences,—people ran out of their houses in the night, etc. There came such a rain withal, as raised the waters at Connecticut twenty feet above their meadows etc.

The Indians near Aquiday being pawwawing in this tempest, the devil came and fetched away five of them. Quere.[1]

At Providence things grew still worse; for a sister of Mrs. Hutchinson, the wife of one Scott, being infected with Anabaptistry, and going last year to live at Providence, Mr. Williams was taken (or rather emboldened) by her to make open profession thereof, and accordingly was rebaptized by one Holyman,[2] a poor man late of Salem. Then Mr. Williams rebaptized him and some ten more. They also denied the baptizing of infants, and would have no magistrates.

At Aquiday, also, Mrs. Hutchinson exercised publicly, and she and her party (some three or four families) would have no magistracy. She sent also an admonition to the church of Boston; but the elders would not read it publicly, because she was excommunicated. By these examples we may see how dangerous it is to slight the censures of the church; for it was apparent, that God had given them up to strange delusions. Those of Aquiday also had entertained two men, whom the church of Roxbury had excommunicated, and one of them did exercise publicly there. For this the church of Boston called in question such of them as were yet their members; and Mr. Coddington, being present, not freely acknowledging his sin, (though he confessed himself in some fault,) was solemnly admonished.

This is further to be observed in the delusions which this people were taken with: Mrs. Hutchinson and some of her adherents happened to be at prayer when the earthquake was at Aquiday, etc., and the house being shaken thereby, they were persuaded, (and boasted of it,) that the Holy Ghost did shake it in coming down upon them, as he did upon the apostles.

(2.) (*April.*)] A plantation was begun between Ipswich

---

[1] "Quere" here is the interpolation of a later hand.
[2] Ezekiel Holiman, one of eleven who founded the first Baptist church in America, a helper of Roger Williams and an honored man. Magistracy was not wholly rejected either in Providence Plantation, or on Rhode Island, though government was in most particulars reduced to its lowest terms.

and Newbury. The occasion was this: Mr. Eaton and Mr. Davenport having determined to sit down at Quinipiack, there came over one Mr. Ezekiel Rogers,[1] second son of that truly faithful servant of God, Mr. Richard Rogers of Weathersfield in England, and with him some twenty families, godly men, and most of them of good estate. This Mr. Rogers, being a man of special note in England for his zeal, piety, and other parts, they labored by all means to draw with them to Quinipiack, and had so far prevailed with him, being newly come, and unacquainted with the state of the country, as they had engaged him; yet, being a very wise man, and considering that many of quality in England did depend upon his choice of a fit place for them, he agreed upon such propositions and cautions, as, though they promised to fulfil them all, (whereupon he sent divers of his people thither before winter,) yet, when it came to, they were not able to make good what they had promised. Whereupon he consulted with the elders of the bay, and, by their advice, etc., holding his former engagement released, he and his people took that place by Ipswich; and because some farms had been granted by Ipswich and Newbury, which would be prejudicial to their plantation, they bought out the owners, disbursing therein about £800; and he sent a pinnace to Quinipiack to fetch back the rest of his people; but Mr. Eaton and Mr. Davenport, and others of Connecticut, (being impatient of the loss of him and his people,) staid the pinnace, and sent a messenger with letters of purpose to recover him again. This made him to desire the elders to assemble again, and he showed them the letters they sent, (which wanted no arguments, though some truth;) but he made the case so clear, by letters which had passed between them, etc., as they held him still free from all engagement; and so he returned answer to them, and went on with his plantation.

[1] Ezekiel Rogers, already mentioned, preferred Massachusetts to Quinipiack (New Haven). founding Rowley as described.

The Indians of Block Island sent, for their tribute this year, ten fathom of wampompeak.

One Mr. Howe, of Lynn, a godly man, and a deputy of the last general court, after the court was ended, and he had dined, being in health as he used to be, went to pass over to Charlestown, and, being alone, he was presently after found dead upon the strand, being there (as it seemed) waiting for the boat, which came soon after.

(3.) (*May*) 2.] Mr. Cotton, preaching out of the 8 of Kings, 8, taught, that when magistrates are forced to provide for the maintenance of ministers, etc., then the churches are in a declining condition. There he showed, that the ministers' maintenance should be by voluntary contribution, not by lands, or revenues, or tithes, etc.; for these have always been accompanied with pride, contention, and sloth, etc.[1]

11.] The two chief sachems of Naragansett sent the governor a present of thirty fathom of wampom, and Sequin, the sachem of Connecticut, sent ten fathom.

At Aquiday the people grew very tumultuous, and put out Mr. Coddington and the other three magistrates, and chose Mr. William Hutchinson only, a man of a very mild temper and weak parts, and wholly guided by his wife, who had been the beginner of all the former troubles in the country, and still continued to breed disturbance.[2]

They also gathered a church in a very disordered way; for they took some excommunicated persons, and others who were members of the church of Boston and not dismissed.

6.] The two regiments in the bay were mustered at Bos-

---

[1] Cotton's adoption of Congregationalism was gradual, but now he had been long thoroughly committed to its principles.

[2] Probably William Hutchinson does not deserve such contemptuous treatment. Though no doubt less able and forceful than his wife, he stood by her loyally as did their children. He had the respect of his neighbors, as this election to high office shows, and was the progenitor of one of the most illustrious of Massachusetts families. Savage, in a "protracted note," gives reasons for doubting the accuracy of this picture of affairs in Aquiday.

ton, to the number of one thousand soldiers, able men, and well armed and exercised. They were led, the one by the governor, who was general of all, and the other by the deputy, who was colonel, etc. The captains, etc., showed themselves very skilful and ready in divers sorts of skirmishes and other military actions, wherein they spent the whole day.[1]

One of Pascataquack, having opportunity to go into Mr. Burdet his study, and finding there the copy of his letter to the archbishops, sent it to the governor, which was to this effect: That he did delay to go into England, because he would fully inform himself of the state of the people here in regard of allegiance; and that it was not discipline that was now so much aimed at, as sovereignty; and that it was accounted perjury and treason in our general courts to speak of appeals to the king.[2]

The first ships, which came this year, brought him letters from the archbishops and the lords commissioners for plantations, wherein they gave him thanks for his care of his majesty's service, etc., and that they would take a time to redress such disorders as he had informed them of, etc., but, by reason of the much business now lay upon them, they could not, at present, accomplish his desire. These letters lay above fourteen days in the bay, and some moved the governor to open them; but himself and others of the council thought it not safe to meddle with them, nor would take any notice of them; and it fell out well, by God's good providence; for the letters, (by some means) were opened, (yet without any of their privity or consent,) and Mr. Burdet threatened to complain of it to the lords; and afterwards we had knowledge of the contents of them by some of his own friends.

The governor received letters from Mr. Cradock, and in them another order from the lords commissioners, to this effect:

---

[1] For an interesting contemporary account of the military organization of early Massachusetts, see Johnson, *Wonder-Working Providence*, book II., chap. XXVI.   [2] The temper of the colonists is not misrepresented here.

That, whereas they had received our petition upon their former order, etc., by which they perceived, that we were taken with some jealousies and fears of their intentions, etc., they did accept of our answer, and did now declare their intentions to be only to regulate all plantations to be subordinate to the said commission; and that they meant to continue our liberties, etc., and therefore did now again peremptorily require the governor to send them our patent by the first ship; and that, in the mean time, they did give us, by that order, full power to go on in the government of the people until we had a new patent sent us; and, withal, they added threats of further course to be taken with us, if we failed.

This order being imparted to the next general court, some advised to return answer to it. Others thought fitter to make no answer at all, because, being sent in a private letter, and not delivered by a certain messenger, as the former order was, they could not proceed upon it, because they could not have any proof that it was delivered to the governor; and order was taken, that Mr. Cradock's agent, who delivered the letter to the governor, etc., should, in his letters to his master, make no mention of the letters he delivered to the governor, seeing his master had not laid any charge upon him to that end.

Mr. Haynes, the governor of Connecticut, and Mr. Hooker, etc., came into the bay, and staid near a month. It appeared by them, that they were desirous to renew the treaty of confederation with us, and though themselves would not move it, yet, by their means, it was moved to our general court, and accepted; for they were in some doubt of the Dutch, who had lately received a new governor, a more discreet and sober man than the former,[1] and one who did complain much of the injury done to them at Connecticut, and was very forward to hold correspondency with us, and very inquisitive how things stood between us and them of Connecticut, which occasioned us the more readily to renew the former treaty, that the

[1] The new Dutch governor was William Kieft.

Dutch might not take notice of any breach or alienation between us.

22.] The court of elections was; at which time there was a small eclipse of the sun. Mr. Winthrop was chosen governor again, though some laboring had been, by some of the elders and others to have changed, not out of any dislike of him, (for they all loved and esteemed him,) but out of their fear lest it might make way for having a governor for life, which some had propounded as most agreeable to God's institution and the practice of all well ordered states. But neither the governor nor any other attempted the thing; though some jealousies arose which were increased by two occasions. The first was, there being want of assistants, the governor and other magistrates thought fit (in the warrant for the court) to propound three, amongst which Mr. Downing, the governor's brother-in-law,[1] was one, which they conceived to be done to strengthen his party, and therefore, though he were known to be a very able man, etc., and one who had done many good offices for the country, for these ten years, yet the people would not choose him. Another occasion of their jealousy was, the court, finding the number of deputies to be much increased by the addition of new plantations, thought fit, for the ease both of the country and the court, to reduce all towns to two deputies. This occasioned some to fear, that the magistrates intended to make themselves stronger, and the deputies weaker, and so, in time, to bring all power into the hands of the magistrates; so as the people in some towns were much displeased with their deputies for yielding to such an order. Whereupon, at the next session, it was propounded to have the number of deputies restored; and allegations were made, that it was an infringement of their liberty; so as, after much debate, and such reasons given for diminishing the number of deputies, and clearly proved that their liberty consisted not in the num-

[1] Emanuel Downing and his wife Lucy, sister of the governor, arrived shortly before, and were properly held in great consideration.

ber, but in the thing, divers of the deputies, who came with intent to reverse the last order, were, by force of reason, brought to uphold it; so that, when it was put to the vote, the last order for two deputies only was confirmed. Yet, the next day, a petition was brought to the court from the freemen of Roxbury, to have the third deputy restored. Whereupon the reasons of the court's proceedings were set down in writing, and all objections answered, and sent to such towns as were unsatisfied with this advice, that, if any could take away those reasons, or bring us better for what they did desire, we should be ready, at the next court, to repeal the said order.

The hands of some of the elders (learned and godly men) were to this petition, though suddenly drawn in, and without due consideration, for the lawfulness of it may well be questioned: for when the people have chosen men to be their rulers, and to make their laws, and bound themselves by oath to submit thereto, now to combine together (a lesser part of them) in a public petition to have any order repealed, which is not repugnant to the law of God, savors of resisting an ordinance of God; for the people, having deputed others, have no power to make or alter laws, but are to be subject; and if any such order seem unlawful or inconvenient, they were better prefer some reasons, etc., to the court, with manifestation of their desire to move them to a review, than peremptorily to petition to have it repealed, which amounts to a plain reproof of those whom God hath set over them, and putting dishonor upon them, against the tenor of the fifth commandment.

There fell out at this court another occasion of increasing the people's jealousy of their magistrates, viz.: One of the elders, being present with those of his church, when they were to prepare their votes for the election, declared his judgment, that a governor ought to be for his life, alleging for his authority the practice of all the best commonwealths in Europe, and especially that of Israel by God's own ordinance. But this was opposed by some other of the elders with much zeal, and so notice was taken of it by the people, not as a matter of dispute, but as if there had been some plot to put it in practice, which did occasion the deputies, at the next session of this court, to deliver in an order drawn to this effect: That, whereas our sovereign lord, King Charles, etc., had, by his patent, established a governor, deputy and assistants, that therefore no person, chosen a counsellor for life, should have any authority as a magistrate, except he were chosen in the annual elections to one of the said places of magistracy established by the patent. This being thus bluntly tendered, (no mention being made thereof before,) the governor took time to consider of it, before he would put it to vote. So, when the court was risen, the magistrates advised of it, and drew up another order to this effect: That whereas, at the court in [blank,] it was ordered, that a certain number of magistrates should be chosen to be a standing council for life, etc., whereupon some had gathered that we had erected a new order of magistrates not warranted by our patent, this court doth therefore declare, that the intent of the order was, that the standing council should always be chosen out of the magistrates, etc.; and therefore it is now ordered, that no such counsellor shall have any power as a magistrate, nor shall do any act as a magistrate, etc., except he be annually chosen, etc., according to the patent; and this order was after passed by vote. That which led those of the council to yield to this desire of the deputies was, because it concerned themselves, and they did more study to remove these jealousies out of the people's heads, than to preserve any power or dignity to themselves above others; for till this court those of the council, viz., Mr. Endecott, had stood and executed as a magistrate, without any annual election, and so they had been reputed by the elders and all the people till this present. But the order was drawn up in this form, that it might be of less observation and freer from any note of injury to make this alteration rather by way of explanation of the fundamental order, than without any cause shown to repeal that which had been established by serious advice of the elders, and had been in practice two or three years without any inconvenience. And here may be observed, how strictly the people would seem to stick to their patent, where they think it makes for their advantage, but are content to decline it, where it will not warrant such liberties as they have taken up without warrant from thence, as appears in their strife for three deputies, etc., when as the patent allows them none at all, but only by inference, etc., voting by proxies, etc.[1]

The governor acquainted the general court, that, in these two last years of his government, he had received from the Indians, in presents, to the value of about £40, and that he had spent about £20 in entertainments of them and in presents to their sachems, etc. The court declared, that the presents were the governor's due, but the tribute was to be paid to the treasurer.

15.] Mr. Endecott and Mr. Stoughton, commissioners for us, and Mr. Bradford and Mr. Winslow for Plymouth, met at Hingham about deciding the difference between us concerning our bounds. Our commissioners had full power to determine, etc.; but theirs had not, although they had notice of it long before, and themselves had appointed the day. Whereupon the court ordered, that those of Hingham should make use of all the land near Conyhassett[2] to the creek next Scituate, till the court should take further order; and a letter was directed to the governor of Plymouth to the same effect, with declaration of the reasons of our proceeding, and readiness to give them a further meeting. The charges of their commissioners'

[1] At the Court at which Vane was elected a Council for Life, appointed from the magistrates, was determined upon, following a suggestion of Lord Saye and Sele. Into this council were put Winthrop, Dudley, and a year later Endicott. Palfrey thinks this aristocratic innovation was set up in the hope of attracting over some high-born men. But it found no favor with the people and dropped out of the polity. Palfrey, *History of New England*, I. 441, 555, 614.

[2] Conyhasset, now Cohasset. See Bradford's account of the dispute, *History of Plymouth Plantation*, pp. 349, 350.

diet was defrayed by us, because they met us within our own jurisdiction.

Those of Exeter replied to our answer, standing still to maintain the Indians' right, and their interest thereby. But, in the mean time, we had sent men to discover Merrimack, and found some part of it about Penkook[1] to lie more northerly than forty-three and a half. So we returned answer to them, that, though we would not relinquish our interest by priority of possession for any right they could have from the Indians, yet, seeing they had professed not to claim any thing which should fall within our patent, we would look no further than that in respect of their claim.

One Mr. Ryall, having gotten a patent at Sagadahoc out of the grand patent,[2] wrote to our governor and tendered it to our government, so as we would send people to possess it. The governor acquainted the general court with it, but nothing was done about it, for we were not ready for such a business, having enough to do at home.

26.] Mr. Hooker being to preach at Cambridge, the governor and many others went to hear him, (though the governor did very seldom go from his own congregation upon the Lord's day). He preached in the afternoon, and having gone on, with much strength of voice and intention of spirit, about a quarter of an hour, he was at a stand, and told the people, that God had deprived him both of his strength and matter, etc., and so went forth, and about half an hour after returned again, and went on to very good purpose about two hours.

There was at this time a very great drouth all over the country, both east and west, there being little or no rain from the 26th of the 2d month to the 10th of the 4th; so as the corn generally began to wither, and great fear there was it would all be lost. Whereupon the general court conferred with the

---

[1] Penkook or Pennacook, now Concord, N. H.

[2] Presumably the royal patent of April 3, 1639, by which Maine was granted to Gorges.

elders, and agreed upon a day of humiliation about a week after. The very day after the fast was appointed there fell a good shower, and, within one week after the day of humiliation was past, we had such store of rain, and so seasonably, as the corn revived and gave hope of a very plentiful harvest. When the court and the elders were met about it, they considered of such things as were amiss, which might provoke God against us, and agreed to acquaint their churches therewith, that they might be stirred up to bewail and reform them.

(4.) (*June*.)] We were much afraid this year of a stop in England, by reason of the complaints which had been sent against us, and the great displeasure which the archbishops and others, the commissioners for plantations, had conceived and uttered against us, both for those complaints, and also for our not sending home our patent. But the Lord wrought for us beyond all expectation; for the petition, which we returned in answer of the order sent for our patent, was read before the lords and well accepted, as is before expressed; and ships came to us from England and divers other parts with great store of people and provisions of all sorts.

About this time our people came from Isle Sable. A bark went for them, on the 2 of the 1 month, but by foul weather she was wrecked there, and of her ruins they made a small one, wherein they returned. It was found to be a great error to send thither before the middle of the 2 month. They had gotten store of seal oil and skins, and some horse teeth and black fox skins; but the loss of the vessel, etc., overthrew the hope of the design.

The island is very healthful and temperate. We lost not one man in two years, nor any sick, etc.

(5.) (*July*.)] The rent at Connecticut grew greater, notwithstanding the great pains which had been taken for healing it; so as the church of Weathersfield itself was not only divided from the rest of the town, etc., but, of those seven which were the church, four fell off; so as it was conceived, that thereby the church was dissolved, which occasioned the church of Watertown here (which had divers of their members there, not yet dismissed) to send two of their church to look after their members, and to take order with them. But the contention and alienation of minds was such, as they could not bring them to any other accord than this, that the one party must remove to some other place, which they both consented to, but still the difficulty remained; for those three, who pretended themselves to be the church, pleaded that privilege for their stay, and the others alleged their multitude, etc., so as neither would give place, whereby it seemed, that either they minded not the example of Abraham's offer to Lot, or else they wanted Abraham's spirit of peace and love.

This controversy having called in Mr. Davenport and others of Quilipiack, for mediation, and they not according with those of Connecticut about the case, gave advantage to Satan to sow some seeds of contention between those plantations also; but, being godly and wise men on both parts, things were easily reconciled.

In this month there arrived two ships at Quilipiack. One was of three hundred and fifty tons, wherein came Mr. Fenwick[1] and his lady and family to make a plantation at Saybrook upon the mouth of Connecticut. Two other plantations were begun beyond Quilipiack, and every plantation intended a peculiar government.

There were also divers new plantations begun this summer here and at Plymouth, as Colchester[2] upon Merrimack, Sudbury by Concord, (Winicowett was named Hampton,) Yarmouth and Barnstaple by Cape Cod.

Capt. Underhill, having been dealt with and convinced of

[1] George Fenwick, a man of high birth and fortune, had, as a wife, Savage believes, a daughter of Sir Arthur Haselrig, a statesman and soldier of much note in the English Commonwealth. His part in Connecticut was important, but his name fails of frequent mention, perhaps because of his return to England, where he attained distinction. See Hutchinson, *History of Massachusetts Bay*, I. 100.   [2] Colchester soon became Salisbury.

his great sin against God and the churches and state here, etc., returned to a better mind, and wrote divers letters to the governor and deputy, etc., bewailing his offences, and craving pardon. See after, (1,) 5, 39, and (7,) 3, 40.[1]

There was sent to the governor the copy of a letter written into England by Mr. Hansard Knolles of Pascataquack, wherein he had most falsely slandered this government, as that it was worse than the high commission, etc., and that here was nothing but oppression, etc., and not so much as a face of religion. The governor acquainted one of Pascataquack, Mr. Knolles his special friend,[2] with it. Whereupon Mr. Knolles became very much perplexed, and wrote to the governor, acknowledging the wrong he had done us, and desired that his retractation might be published.[3] The governor sent his letter into England, and kept a copy of it. See more of this after, (12,) 20, 1639.[4]

At Providence matters went after the old manner. Mr. Williams and many of his company, a few months since, were in all haste rebaptized, and denied communion with all others, and now he was come to question his second baptism, not being able to derive the authority of it from the apostles, otherwise than by the ministers of England, (whom he judged to be ill authority,) so as he conceived God would raise up some apostolic power. Therefore he bent himself that way, expecting (as was supposed) to become an apostle; and having, a little before, refused communion with all, save his own wife, now he would preach to and pray with all comers. Whereupon some of his followers left him and returned back from whence they went.

(6.) (*August*) 27.] Here came a small bark from the West

---

[1] *I. e.*, March 5, 1639/40, and September 3, 1640. See those dates, *post*, the former under February 20.   [2] *I. e.*, Mr. Knolles's special friend.

[3] Hanserd Knollys had grounds for criticism, as the *Journal* shows. Retractation seems to have been common among these heretics and dissentients, when brought to account; but exile, prison, the "bilbowes," and the whip were terrifying penalties.   [4] *I. e.*, February 20, 1639/40.

Indies, one Capt. Jackson [?] in her, with commission from the Westminster company to take prize, etc., from the Spaniard. He brought much wealth in money, plate, indico, and sugar. He sold his indico and sugar here for £1400, wherewith he furnished himself with commodities, and departed again for the West Indies.

A fishing trade was begun at Cape Ann by one Mr. Maurice Tomson, a merchant of London; and an order was made, that all stocks employed in fishing should be free from public charge for seven years. This was not done to encourage foreigners to set up fishing among us, (for all the gains would be returned to the place where they dwelt,) but to encourage our own people to set upon it, and in expectation that Mr. Tomson, etc., would, ere long, come settle with us.

(7.) (*September*.)] Here was such store of exceeding large and fat mackerel upon our coast this season, as was a great benefit to all our plantations. Some one boat with three men would take, in a week, ten hogsheads, which was sold at Connecticut for £3.12 the hogshead.

There were such swarms of small flies, like moths, came from the southward, that they covered the sea, and came flying like drifts of snow; but none of them were seen upon the land.

(7.) (*September*) 17.] A church was gathered at the Mount.[1]

4.] At the general court at Boston, one Mr. Nathaniel Eaton, brother to the merchant at Quilipiack,[2] was convented and censured. The occasion was this: He was a schoolmaster, and had many scholars, the sons of gentlemen and others of best note in the country, and had entertained one Nathaniel Briscoe, a gentleman born, to be his usher, and to do some other things for him, which might not be unfit for a scholar. He had not been with him above three days but he fell out with him for a very small occasion, and, with reproachful terms, discharged him, and turned him out of his doors; but, it being then about eight of the clock after the Sabbath,

---

[1] Mount Wollaston.   [2] *I. e.*, to Theophilus Eaton of New Haven.

he told him he should stay till next morning, and, some words growing between them, he struck him and pulled him into his house. Briscoe defended himself, and closed with him, and, being parted, he came in and went up to his chamber to lodge there. Mr. Eaton sent for the constable, who advised him first to admonish him, etc., and if he could not, by the power of a master, reform him, then he should complain to the magistrate. But he caused his man to fetch him a cudgel, which was a walnut tree plant, big enough to have killed a horse, and a yard in length, and, taking his two men with him, he went up to Briscoe, and caused his men to hold him till he had given him two hundred stripes about the head and shoulders, etc., and so kept him under blows (with some two or three short intermissions) about the space of two hours, about which time Mr. Shepherd and some others of the town came in at the outcry, and so he gave over. In this distress Briscoe gate out his knife, and struck at the man that held him, but hurt him not. He also fell to prayer, (supposing he should have been murdered,) and then Mr. Eaton beat him for taking the name of God in vain. After this Mr. Eaton and Mr. Shepherd (who knew not then of these passages) came to the governor and some other of the magistrates, complaining of Briscoe for his insolent speeches, and for crying out murder and drawing his knife, and desired that he might be enjoined to a public acknowledgment, etc. The magistrates answered, that they must first hear him speak, and then they would do as they should see cause. Mr. Eaton was displeased at this, and went away discontented, etc., and, being after called into the court to make answer to the information, which had been given by some who knew the truth of the case, and also to answer for his neglect and cruelty, and other ill usage towards his scholars, one of the elders (not suspecting such miscarriages by him) came to the governor, and showed himself much grieved, that he should be publicly produced, alleging, that it would derogate from his authority and reverence among his scholars, etc.

But the cause went on notwithstanding, and he was called, and these things laid to his charge in the open court. His answers were full of pride and disdain, telling the magistrates, that they should not need to do any thing herein, for he was intended to leave his employment. And being asked, why he used such cruelty to Briscoe his usher, and to other his scholars, (for it was testified by another of his ushers and divers of his scholars, that he would give them between twenty and thirty stripes at a time, and would not leave till they had confessed what he required,) his answer was, that he had this rule, that he would not give over correcting till he had subdued the party to his will. Being also questioned about the ill and scant diet of his boarders, (for, though their friends gave large allowance, yet their diet was ordinarily nothing but porridge and pudding, and that very homely,) he put it off to his wife.[1] So the court dismissed him at present, and commanded him to

[1] Savage gives here a curious paper, apparently the confession of Mrs. Eaton, detailing the hardships of old-time students. Of this we quote some portions. "For their breakfast, that it was not so well ordered, the flour not so fine as it might, nor so well boiled or stirred, at all times that it was so, it was my sin of neglect, and want of that care that ought to have been in one that the Lord had intrusted with such a work. . . . And that they had not so good or so much provision in my husband's absence as presence, I conceived it was, because he would call sometimes for butter or cheese, when I conceived there was no need of it; yet, forasmuch as the scholars did otherways apprehend, I desire to see the evil that was in the carriage of that as well as in the other, and to take shame to myself for it. And that they sent down for more, when they had not enough, and the maid should answer, if they had not, they should not, I must confess, that I have denied them cheese, when they have sent for it, and it have been in the house; for which I shall humbly beg pardon of them, and own the shame, and confess my sin. . . . For the Moor [probably a slave] his lying in Sam. Hough's sheet and pillow-bier, it hath a truth in it: he did so one time, and it gave Sam. Hough just cause of offence; and that it was not prevented by my care and watchfulness, I desire [to] take the shame and the sorrow for it. . . . For beer and bread, that it was denied them by me betwixt meals, truly I do not remember, that ever I did deny it unto them; and John Wilson will affirm that, generally, the bread and beer was free for the boarders to go unto. . . . And for their wanting beer, betwixt brewings, a week or half a week together, I am sorry that it was so at any time, and should tremble to have it so, were it in my hands to do again." Hough and Wilson, mentioned in the passage, were sons respectively of a magistrate and elder, and the institution was Harvard College.

attend again the next day, when, being called, he was commanded to the lower end of the table, (where all offenders do usually stand,) and, being openly convict of all the former offences, by the oaths of four or five witnesses, he yet continued to justify himself; so, it being near night, he was committed to the marshall till the next day. When the court was set in the morning, many of the elders came into the court, (it being then private for matter of consultation,) and declared how, the evening before, they had taken pains with him, to convince him of his faults; yet, for divers hours, he had still stood to his justification; but, in the end, he was convinced, and had freely and fully acknowledged his sin, and that with tears; so as they did hope he had truly repented, and therefore desired of the court that he might be pardoned, and continued in his employment, alleging such further reasons as they thought fit. After the elders were departed, the court consulted about it, and sent for him, and there, in the open court, before a great assembly, he made a very solid, wise, eloquent, and serious (seeming) confession, condemning himself in all the particulars, etc. Whereupon, being put aside, the court consulted privately about his sentence, and, though many were taken with his confession, and none but had a charitable opinion of it; yet, because of the scandal of religion, and offence which would be given to such as might intend to send their children hither, they all agreed to censure him, and put him from that employment. So, being called in, the governor, after a short preface, etc., declared the sentence of the court to this effect, viz.: that he should give Briscoe £30, fined 100 marks, and debarred teaching of children within our jurisdiction. A pause being made, and expectation that (according to his former confession) he would have given glory to God, and acknowledged the justice and clemency of the court, the governor giving him occasion, by asking him if he had ought to say, he turned away with a discontented look, saying, "If sentence be passed, then it is to no end to speak." Yet the court remitted his fine to £20, and willed Briscoe to take but £20.

The church at Cambridge, taking notice of these proceedings, intended to deal with him. The pastor moved the governor, if they might, without offence to the court, examine other witnesses. His answer was, that the court would leave them to their own liberty; but he saw not to what end they should do it, seeing there had been five already upon oath, and those whom they should examine should speak without oath, and it was an ordinance of God, that by the mouths of two or three witnesses every matter should be established. But he soon discovered himself; for, ere the church could come to deal with him, he fled to Pascataquack, and, being pursued and apprehended by the governor there, he again asknowledged his great sin in flying, etc., and promised (as he was a Christian man) he would return with the messengers. But, because his things he carried with him were aboard a bark there, bound to Virginia, he desired leave to go fetch them, which they assented unto, and went with him (three of them) aboard with him. So he took his truss and came away with them in the boat; but, being come to the shore, and two of them going out of the boat, he caused the boatsmen to put off the boat, and because the third man would not go out, he turned him into the water, where he had been drowned, if he had not saved himself by swimming. So he returned to the bark, and presently they set sail and went out of the harbor. Being thus gone, his creditors began to complain; and thereupon it was found, that he was run in debt about £1000, and had taken up most of this money upon bills he had charged into England upon his brother's agents, and others whom he had no such relation to. So his estate was seized, and put into commissioners' hands, to be divided among his creditors, allowing somewhat for the present maintenance of his wife and children. And, being thus gone, the church proceeded and cast him out. He had been sometimes initiated among the Jesuits, and, coming into England, his friends drew him from them, but, it was very probable, he now intended to return to them again, being at this time about thirty years of age, and upwards. See after.

7. (*September*) 17.] Mount Woollaston had been formerly laid to Boston; but many poor men having lots assigned them there, and not able to use those lands and dwell still in Boston, they petitioned the town first to have a minister there, and after to have leave to gather a church there, which the town at length (upon some small composition) gave way unto. So, this day, they gathered a church after the usual manner, and chose one Mr. Tomson, a very gracious, sincere man, and Mr. Flint, a godly man also, their ministers.

Mo. 9 (*November*).] At a general court holden at Boston, great complaint was made of the oppression used in the country in sale of foreign commodities; and Mr. Robert Keaine,[1] who kept a shop in Boston, was notoriously above others observed and complained of; and, being convented, he was charged with many particulars; in some, for taking above six-pence in the shilling profit; in some above eight-pence; and, in some small things, above two for one; and being hereof convict, (as appears by the records,) he was fined £200, which came thus to pass: The deputies considered, apart, of his fine, and set it at £200; the magistrates agreed but to £100. So, the court being divided, at length it was agreed, that his fine should be £200, but he should pay but £100, and the other should be respited to the further consideration of the next general court. By this means the magistrates and deputies were brought to an accord, which otherwise had not been likely, and so much trouble might have grown, and the offender escaped censure. For the cry of the country was so great against oppression, and

[1] Robert Keayne, here disciplined for extortion, lived long in the colony, a rich and well connected man. His daughter married a son of Thomas Dudley, and he himself was brother-in-law of John Wilson. He appears again in the story, sometimes falling into disfavor, though commonly a man well at the front.

some of the elders and magistrates had declared such detestation of the corrupt practice of this man (which was the more observable, because he was wealthy and sold dearer than most other tradesmen, and for that he was of ill report for the like covetous practice in England, that incensed the deputies very much against him). And sure the course was very evil, especial circumstances considered: 1. He being an ancient professor of the gospel: 2. A man of eminent parts: 3. Wealthy, and having but one child: 4. Having come over for conscience' sake, and for the advancement of the gospel here: 5. Having been formerly dealt with and admonished, both by private friends and also by some of the magistrates and elders, and having promised reformation; being a member of a church and commonwealth now in their infancy, and under the curious observation of all churches and civil states in the world. These added much aggravation to his sin in the judgment of all men of understanding. Yet most of the magistrates (though they discerned of the offence clothed with all these circumstances) would have been more moderate in their censure: 1. Because there was no law in force to limit or direct men in point of profit in their trade. 2. Because it is the common practice, in all countries, for men to make use of advantages for raising the prices of their commodities. 3. Because (though he were chiefly aimed at, yet) he was not alone in this fault. 4. Because all men through the country, in sale of cattle, corn, labor, etc., were guilty of the like excess in prices. 5. Because a certain rule could not be found out for an equal rate between buyer and seller, though much labor had been bestowed in it, and divers laws had been made, which, upon experience, were repealed, as being neither safe nor equal. Lastly, and especially, because the law of God appoints no other punishment but double restitution; and, in some cases, as where the offender freely confesseth, and brings his offering, only half added to the principal. After the court had censured him, the church of Boston called him also in question, where (as before he had done in the court) he did, with tears, acknowledge and bewail his covetous and corrupt heart, yet making some excuse for many of the particulars, which were charged upon him, as partly by pretence of ignorance of the true price of some wares, and chiefly by being misled by some false principles, as 1. That, if a man lost in one commodity, he might help himself in the price of another. 2. That if, through want of skill or other occasion, his commodity cost him more than the price of the market in England, he might then sell it for more than the price of the market in New England, etc. These things gave occasion to Mr. Cotton, in his public exercise the next lecture day, to lay open the error of such false principles, and to give some rules of direction in the case.

Some false principles were these:—

1. That a man might sell as dear as he can, and buy as cheap as he can.

2. If a man lose by casualty of sea, etc., in some of his commodities, he may raise the price of the rest.

3. That he may sell as he bought, though he paid too dear, etc., and though the commodity be fallen, etc.

4. That, as a man may take the advantage of his own skill or ability, so he may of another's ignorance or necessity.

5. Where one gives time for payment, he is to take like recompense of one as of another.

The rules for trading were these:—

1. A man may not sell above the current price, i. e., such a price as is usual in the time and place, and as another (who knows the worth of the commodity) would give for it, if he had occasion to use it; as that is called current money, which every man will take, etc.

2. When a man loseth in his commodity for want of skill, etc., he must look at it as his own fault or cross, and therefore must not lay it upon another.

3. Where a man loseth by casualty of sea, or, etc., it is a loss cast upon himself by providence, and he may not ease

himself of it by casting it upon another; for so a man should seem to provide against all providences, etc., that he should never lose; but where there is a scarcity of the commodity, there men may raise their price; for now it is a hand of God upon the commodity, and not the person.

4. A man may not ask any more for his commodity than his selling price, as Ephron to Abraham, the land is worth thus much.[1]

The cause being debated by the church, some were earnest to have him excommunicated; but the most thought an admonition would be sufficient. Mr. Cotton opened the causes, which required excommunication, out of that in 1 Cor. 5. 11. The point now in question was, whether these actions did declare him to be such a covetous person, etc. Upon which he showed, that it is neither the habit of covetousness, (which is in every man in some degree,) nor simply the act, that declares a man to be such, but when it appears, that a man sins against his conscience, or the very light of nature, and when it appears in a man's whole conversation. But Mr. Keaine did not appear to be such, but rather upon an error in his judgment, being led by false principles; and, beside, he is otherwise liberal, as in his hospitality, and in church communion, etc. So, in the end, the church consented to an admonition.

Upon this occasion a question grew, whether an admonition did bar a man from the sacrament, etc. Of this more shall be spoken hereafter.

Being now about church matters, I will here insert another passage in the same church, which fell out about the same time. Their old meeting-house, being decayed and too small, they sold it away, and agreed to build another, which workmen undertook to set up for £600. Three hundred they had for the old, and the rest was to be gathered by voluntary contributions, as other charges were. But there grew a great difference among the brethren, where this new one should stand. Some

[1] This laying down by John Cotton of commercial ethics is interesting.

were for the green, (which was the governor's first lot, and he had yielded it to the church, etc.;) others, viz., the tradesmen, especially, who dwelt about the market place, desired it might stand still near the market, lest in time it should divert the chief trade from thence. The church referred it to the judgment and determination of five of the brethren, who agreed, that the fittest place (all things considered) would be near the market; but, understanding that many of the brethren were unsatisfied, and desired rather it might be put to a lot, they declared only their opinions in writing, and respited the full determination to another general meeting, thinking it very unsafe to proceed with the discontent of any considerable part of the church. When the church met, the matter was debated to and fro, and grew at length to some earnestness, etc.; but, after Mr. Cotton had cleared it up to them, that the removing it to the green would be a damage to such as dwelt by the market, who had there purchased and built at great charge, but it would be no damage to the rest to have it by the market, because it would be no less, but rather more convenient for them, than where the former stood, they all yielded to have it set by the market place; and, though some remained still in their opinion, that the green were the fitter place, yet, for peace sake, they yielded to the rest by keeping silence while it passed.[1] This good providence and overruling hand of God caused much admiration and acknowledgment of special mercy to the church, especially considering how long the like contention had held in some other churches, and with what difficulty they had been accorded.

(7.) (*September.*)] At the court of assistants, one Marmaduke Percy, of Salem, was arraigned for the death of one [blank], his apprentice. The great inquest found the bill for murder; the jury of life and death could not agree; so they were adjourned to the next court, and Percy was let to bail by

---

[1] The Green included the present site of the Old South Church. The new church was finally placed at the head of the present State Street.

the governor and some other of the magistrates, after the court. At the court in 10ber (*December*), the prisoner appeared, and the jury being called, had further evidence given them, which tended to the clearing of Percy; yet two of the jury dissented from the rest, who were all agreed to acquit him. In the end it had this issue, that these two were silent, and so the verdict was received. The cause was this: The boy was ill disposed, and his master gave him unreasonable correction, and used him ill in his diet. After, the boy gate a bruise on his head, so as there appeared a fracture in his skull, being dissected after his death. Now, two things were in the evidence, which made the case doubtful; one, the boy his charging his master, before his death, to have given him that wound with his meatyard[1] and with a broomstaff (for he spake of both at several times;) the other was, that he had told another, that his hurt came with the fall of a bough from a tree; and other evidence there was none.

4.] At the general court, etc., the inhabitants of the upper part of Pascataquack, viz. Dover, etc., had written to the governor to offer themselves to come under our government. Answer was returned them, that, if they sent two or three of their company, with full commission, under all their hands, to conclude, etc., it was like the court would agree to their propositions. And now, at this court, came three with commission to agree upon certain articles annexed to their commission, which being read, the court appointed three to treat with them; but, their articles being not reasonable, they stood not upon them, but confessed that they had absolute commission to conclude by their discretion. Whereupon the treaty was brought to a conclusion to this effect: That they should be as Ipswich and Salem, and have courts there, etc., as by the copy of the agreement remaining with the recorder doth appear. This was ratified under our public seal, and so delivered to them: only they desired a promise from the court, that, if the people

---

[1] Meteyard, a stick for meting or measuring.

did not assent to it, (which yet they had no fear of,) they might be at liberty, which was granted them.

Those of Exeter sent the like propositions to the court; but not liking (it seems) the agreement, which those of Dover had made, they repented themselves, and wrote to the court, that they intended not to proceed.[1]

At this court there fell out some contestation between the governor and the treasurer.[2] Nicholas Trerice being defendant in a cause, wherein Mr. Hibbins,[3] brother-in-law to the treasurer, was plaintiff, for £500, which the searchers took from him in the ship, whereof Trerice was master, and the defendant having answered upon oath to certain interrogatories ministered unto him, (and which were read to him before he took his oath,) and the treasurer pressing him again with the same interrogatory, the governor said, he had answered the same directly before. The treasurer thereupon said, (angrily,) Sir, I speak not to you. The governor replied, that time was very precious, and, seeing the thing was already answered, it was fit to proceed. Thereupon the treasurer stood up, and said, if he might not have liberty to speak, he would no longer sit there. The governor replied, that it was his place to manage the proceedings of the court, etc. The treasurer then said, You have no more to do in managing the business here than I. At which the governor took offence, as at an injury done to his place, and appealed to the court to declare, whether he might not enjoin any of the magistrates silence, if he saw cause. The deputy governor, at first apprehension, gainsaid it; but, presently, both himself and the rest of the magistrates (for the deputies were without, staying till this cause should be ended) did agree, that he might so do for a particular time;

---

[1] Here we see the stirrings of an impulse to come together which before long brought about the confederation of the colonies, at which we shall soon glance.   [2] The treasurer was Bellingham, afterward governor.

[3] William Hibbins was a citizen of repute whose wife attained a tragic notoriety. Disordered in mind, as Hubbard relates, *General History of New England*, p. 574, she was put to death as a witch in 1656.

and if the party, so enjoined silence, were unsatisfied, he might appeal to the whole court, who might give him liberty to speak, though the governor had restrained him. So the governor pressed it no further, yet expected that the court would not have suffered such a public affront to the governor to have passed without due reproof, etc. But nothing was done, save only the secretary and some one other spake somewhat of their dislike of it; neither did it occasion any falling out between the governor and treasurer, for the governor held himself sufficiently discharged, after he had referred it to the consideration of the court, so as, if they did not look at it as a public injury, he was willing to account of it accordingly.

There happened a memorable thing at Plymouth about this time. One Keysar, of Lynn, being at Plymouth in his boat, and one Dickerson with him, a professor, but a notorious thief, was coming out of the harbor with the ebb, and the wind southerly, a fresh gale; yet, with all their skill and labor, they could not, in three hours, get the boat above one league, so as they were forced to come to an anchor, and, at the flood, to go back to the town; and, as soon as they were come in, the said Dickerson was arrested upon suspicion of a gold ring and some other pieces of gold, which, upon search, were found about him, and he was there whipped for it.

The like happened at Boston about two years before. Schooler, who was executed for murder, as before is mentioned, had broke prison and was escaped beyond Winisemett, but there he was taken with such an astonishment, etc., as he could go no further, but was forced to return to Boston. These and many other examples of discovering hypocrites and other lewd persons, and bringing them under their deserved punishments, do (among other things) show the presence and power of God in his ordinances, and his blessing upon his people, while they endeavor to walk before him with uprightness.

At Kennebeck, the Indians wanting food, and there being store in the Plymouth trading house, they conspired to kill the

English there for their provisions; and some Indians coming into the house, Mr. Willet,[1] the master of the house, being reading in the Bible, his countenance was more solemn than at other times, so as he did not look cheerfully upon them, as he was wont to do; whereupon they went out and told their fellows, that their purpose was discovered. They asked them, how it could be. The others told them, that they knew it by Mr. Willet's countenance, and that he had discovered it by a book that he was reading. Whereupon they gave over their design.

The people had long desired a body of laws,[2] and thought their condition very unsafe, while so much power rested in the discretion of magistrates. Divers attempts had been made at former courts, and the matter referred to some of the magistrates and some of the elders; but still it came to no effect; for, being committed to the care of many, whatsoever was done by some, was still disliked or neglected by others. At last it was referred to Mr. Cotton and Mr. Nathaniel Warde, etc., and each of them framed a model, which were presented to this general court, and by them committed to the governor and deputy and some others to consider of, and so prepare it for the court in the 3d month next. Two great reasons there were, which caused most of the magistrates and some of the elders not to be very forward in this matter. One was, want of sufficient experience of the nature and disposition of the people, considered with the condition of the country and other circumstances, which made them conceive, that such laws would

[1] Thomas Willett, afterward the first mayor of New York.

[2] *The Body of Liberties*, which at length came into existence in response to the desire of the people here referred to, is a code of great interest, esteemed in its time comparable only to Magna Charta and the Common Law of England, and important in the history of constitutional development. It was mainly the work of Nathaniel Ward, of Ipswich, a man of bright mind, well versed in the law; though Cotton had a hand in it. A work of value here is Whitmore, *The Colonial Laws of Massachusetts* (Boston, 1889). See also *Old South Leaflets*, no. 164, *The Massachusetts Body of Liberties*, with scholarly annotation by Edwin D. Mead.

be fittest for us, which should arise pro re nata upon occasions, etc., and so the laws of England and other states grew, and therefore the fundamental laws of England are called customs, consuetudines. 2. For that it would professedly transgress the limits of our charter, which provide, we shall make no laws repugnant to the laws of England, and that we were assured we must do. But to raise up laws by practice and custom had been no transgression; as in our church discipline, and in matters of marriage, to make a law, that marriages should not be solemnized by ministers, is repugnant to the laws of England; but to bring it to a custom by practice for the magistrates to perform it, is no law made repugnant, etc. At length (to satisfy the people) it proceeded, and the two models were digested with divers alterations and additions, and abbreviated and sent to every town, (12,) to be considered of first by the magistrates and elders, and then to be published by the constables to all the people, that if any man should think fit, that any thing therein ought to be altered, he might acquaint some of the deputies therewith against the next court.

By this time there appeared a great change in the church of Boston; for whereas, the year before, they were all (save five or six) so affected to Mr. Wheelwright and Mrs. Hutchinson, and those new opinions, as they slighted the present governor and the pastor, looking at them as men under a covenant of works, and as their greatest enemies; but they bearing all patiently, and not withdrawing themselves, (as they were strongly solicited to have done,) but carrying themselves lovingly and helpfully upon all occasions, the Lord brought about the hearts of all the people to love and esteem them more than ever before, and all breaches were made up, and the church was saved from ruin beyond all expectation; which could hardly have been, (in human reason,) if those two had not been guided by the Lord to that moderation, etc. And the church (to manifest their hearty affection to the governor, upon occasion of some strait he was brought into through his bailiff's unfaithfulness) sent him £200.

There was now a church gathered at the Mount, and Mr. Tomson (a very holy man, who had been an instrument of much good at Acomenticus) was ordained the pastor the 19th of the 9th month.

(10.) (*December.*)] At the general court, an order was made to abolish that vain custom of drinking one to another, and that upon these and other grounds:

1. It was a thing of no good use.

2. It was an inducement to drunkenness, and occasion of quarrelling and bloodshed.

3. It occasioned much waste of wine and beer.

4. It was very troublesome to many, especially the masters and mistresses of the feast, who were forced thereby to drink more oft than they would, etc. Yet divers (even godly persons) were very loath to part with this idle ceremony, though (when disputation was tendered) they had no list, nor, indeed, could find any arguments, to maintain it. Such power hath custom, etc.[1]

Mr. Ezekiel Rogers, of whose gathering of a church in England mentioned was made before, being now settled with his company at Rowley, was there ordained pastor, etc.

3.] There were so many lectures now in the country, and many poor persons would usually resort to two or three in the week, to the great neglect of their affairs, and the damage of the public. The assemblies also were (in divers churches) held till night, and sometimes within the night, so as such as dwelt far off could not get home in due season, and many weak bodies could not endure so long, in the extremity of the heat or cold, without great trouble, and hazard of their health. Whereupon the general court ordered, that the elders should be desired to

---

[1] We have frequent occasion to remark in Winthrop superstition and limitation of various kinds. With all this he had also strong good sense, and that appears in this passage relating to the drink habit.

give a meeting to the magistrates and deputies, to consider about the length and frequency of church assemblies, and to make return to the court of their determinations, etc. This was taken in ill part by most of the elders and other of the churches, so as that those who should have met at Salem, did not meet, and those in the bay, when they met with the magistrates, etc., at Boston, expressed much dislike of such a course, alleging their tenderness of the church's liberties, (as if such a precedent might enthrall them to the civil power, and as if it would cast a blemish upon the elders, which would remain to posterity, that they should need to be regulated by the civil magistrate, and also raise an ill savor of the people's coldness, that would complain of much preaching, etc.,—when as liberty for the ordinances was the main end (professed) of our coming hither). To which it was answered, 1. That the order was framed with as much tenderness and respect as might be in general words, without mentioning sermons or lectures, so as it might as well be taken for meetings upon other occasions of the churches, which were known to be very frequent. 2. It carried no command, but only an expression of a desire. 3. It concluded nothing, but only to confer and consider. 4. The record of such an order will be rather an argument of the zeal and forwardness of the elders and churches, as it was of the Israelites', when they offered so liberally to the service of the tabernacle, as Moses was forced to restrain them. Upon this interpretation of the court's intent, the elders were reasonably satisfied, and the magistrates finding how hardly such propositions would be digested, and that, if matters should be further pushed, it might make some breach, or disturbance at least, (for the elders had great power in the people's hearts, which was needful to be upheld, lest the people should break their bonds through abuse of liberty, which divers, having surfeited of, were very forward to incite others to raise mutinies and foment dangerous and groundless jealousies of the magistrates, etc., which the wisdom and care of the elders did still prevail against; and indeed the people themselves, generally, through the churches, were of that understanding and moderation, as they would easily be guided in their way by any rule from scripture or sound reason:) in this consideration, the magistrates and deputies, which were then met, thought it not fit to enter any dispute or conference with the elders about the number of lectures, or for appointing any certain time for the continuance of the assemblies, but rested satisfied with their affirmative answer to these two propositions: 1. That their church assemblies might ordinarily break up in such season, as people that dwell a mile or two off might get home by daylight. 2. That, if they were not satisfied in the declaration of our intentions in this order of court, that nothing was attempted herein against the church's liberties, etc., they would truly acquaint us with the reasons of their unsatisfiedness; or, if we heard not from them before the next court, we should take it for granted, that they were fully satisfied. They desired, that the order might be taken off the record; but for that it was answered, that it might not be done without consent of the general court; only it was agreed unto, that the secretary might defer to enter it in the book till the mind of the court might be known.

1640

(12.) (*February*) 20.] One Mr. Hanserd Knolles, a minister in England, who came over the last summer in the company of our familistical opinionists, and so being suspected and examined, and found inclining that way, was denied residence in the Massachusetts; whereupon he went to Pascataquack, where he began to preach; but Mr. Burdett, being then their governor and preacher, inhibited him. But, he being after removed to Acomenticus, the people called Mr. Knolles, and in short time he gathered some of the best minded into a church body, and became their pastor, and Capt. Underhill being their governor, they called their town Dover. But this Mr. Knolles, at his first coming thither, wrote a letter to his friends in London, wherein he bitterly inveighed against us, both against our magistrates and churches, and against all the people in general, (as by the copy of his letter sent over to our governor may appear). The governor gave him notice thereof, and, being brought to a better judgment by further consideration and more experience, he saw the wrong he had done us, and was deeply humbled for it, and wrote to the governor to that effect, and desired a safe conduct, that he might come into the bay to give satisfaction, etc., for he could have no rest in his spirit until, etc.; which being sent him under the governor his hand, (with consent of the council,) he came, and, upon a lecture day at Boston, (most of the magistrates and elders in the bay being there assembled,) he made a very free and full confession of his offence, with much aggravation against himself, so as the assembly were well satisfied. He wrote also a letter to the same effect to his said friends in England, which he left with the governor to be sent to them.

Capt. Underhill, also, being struck with horror and remorse

for his offences, both against the church and civil state, could have no rest till he had obtained a safe conduct to come and give satisfaction; and accordingly, (1,) 5, at a lecture at Boston, (it being then the court time,) he made a public confession both of his living in adultery with Faber's wife, (upon suspicion whereof the church had before admonished him,) and attempting the like with another woman, and also the injury he had done to our state, etc., and acknowledged the justice of the court in their proceeding against him, etc. Yet all his confessions were mixed with such excuses and extenuations, as did not give satisfaction of the truth of his repentance, so as it seemed to be done rather out of policy, and to pacify the sting of his conscience, than in sincerity. But, however, his offences being so foul and scandalous, the church presently cast him out; which censure he seemed to submit unto, and, for the time he staid in Boston, (being four or five days) he was very much dejected, etc.; but, being gone back, he soon recovered his spirits again, or, at least, gave not that proof of a broken heart, as he gave hope of at Boston. For (to ingratiate himself with the state of England, and with some gentlemen at the river's mouth, who were very zealous that way, and had lately set up common prayer, etc.) he sent thirteen men armed to Exeter to fetch one Gabriel Fish, who was detained in the officer's hands for speaking against the king, the magistrates of Exeter being then in the bay to take advice what to do with him; and besides, when the church and people of Dover desired him to forbear to come to the next court, till they had considered of his case, and he had promised so to do, yet, hearing that they were consulting to remove him from his government, he could not refrain, but came and took his place in the court; and though he had offered to lay down his place, yet, when he saw they went about it, he grew passionate, and expostulated with them, and would not stay to receive his dismission, nor would be seen to accept it, when it was sent after him. Yet they proceeded, and chose one Roberts to be president of the court, and, soon after, they returned back Fish to Exeter, which was considerately done of them, for it had been a dangerous precedent against them, being a weak plantation, if the commissioners from the lords of the council, who were daily expected, should have taken occasion to have done the like by them, though they held themselves to be out of that province, which was granted to Sir Ferdinando Gorges. Besides this, in the open court he committed one of his fellow magistrates for rising up and saying he would not sit with an adulterer, etc. But the chief matter, which they produced against him, was, that, whereas he himself was the mover of them to break off their agreement with us, he had written to our governor, and laid it upon the people, especially upon some among them; and for this they produced against him a letter from our governor, written to one of their commissioners in answer to a letter of his, wherein he had discovered the captain's proceeding in that matter. Soon after this the captain came by water into the bay to tender (as he said) satisfaction to the church. This was taken by some of the magistrates as a very presumptuous act, and they would have had him imprisoned, supposing that his safe conduct would not bear him out, having been once here and returned back again; but that counsel was not approved, because the time of his safe conduct was not expired, and it was thought very dangerous to our reputation to give the least occasion of reproach in this kind, seeing it might be objected against us to our great prejudice, where we should not have opportunity to clear our innocency. But the church, not being satisfied of his repentance, would not admit him to public speech. So, after one week, he returned home.

In this winter, in a close, calm day, there fell divers flakes of snow of this form *, very thin, and as exactly pointed as art could have cut them in paper, or, etc.

(1.) (*March*) 24.] The church of Boston sent three brethren, viz., Capt. Edward Gibbons, Mr. Hibbins, and Mr. Oliver the younger, with letters to Mr. Coddington and the rest of our members at Aquiday, to understand their judgments in divers points of religion, formerly maintained by all, or divers of them, and to require them to give account to the church of their unwarrantable practice in communicating with excommunicated persons, etc. When they came, they found that those of them, who dwell at Newport, had joined themselves to a church there newly constituted, and thereupon they refused to hear them as messengers of our church, or to receive the church's letters. Whereupon, at their return, the elders and most of the church would have cast them out, as refusing to hear the church; but, all being not agreed, it was deferred.[1]

18.] Mr. Norris was ordained teacher of the church of Salem, there being present near all the elders of the other churches, and much people besides.

21.] The *White Angel*, a small ship of Bristol, went from hence, and arrived there in twenty-four days; and, the same year, the *Desire*, a ship built at Marblehead, of one hundred tons, went from hence in the summer, and arrived at Gravesend, in the Thames, in twenty-three days.

Our neighbors of Plymouth had procured from hence, this

---

[1] Modern sympathy is with the moderate men in opposition to the harsh and repugnant policy of the elders.

The report of Oliver, quoted by Savage, says that "they denied our commission, and refused to let our letter be received; and they conceive, one church hath not power over the members of another church, and do not think they are tied to us by our covenant. So we were fain to take all their answers by going to their several houses. Mr. Hutchinson told us, he was more nearly tied to his wife than to the church: he thought her to be a dear saint and servant of God. We came then to Mrs. Hutchinson, and told her, that we had a message to do to her from the Lord and from our church. She answered, There are lords many, and gods many; but I acknowledge but one Lord. Which lord do you mean? We answered, we came in the name but of one Lord, and that is God. Then, saith she, so far we agree; and where we do agree, let it be set down. Then we told her, we had a message to her from the church of Christ in Boston. She replied, she knew no church but one. We told her, in scripture the Holy Ghost calls them churches. She said, Christ had but one spouse. We told her, he had in some sort as many spouses as saints. But for our church, she would not acknowledge it any church of Christ."

year, one Mr. Chancey, a great scholar, and a godly man, intending to call him to the office of a teacher;[1] but, before the fit time came, he discovered his judgment about baptism, that the children ought to be dipped and not sprinkled; and, he being an active man, and very vehement, there arose much trouble about it. The magistrates and the other elders there, and the most of the people, withstood the receiving of that practice, not for itself so much, as for fear of worse consequences, as the annihilating our baptism, etc. Whereupon the church there wrote to all the other churches, both here and at Connecticut, etc., for advice, and sent Mr. Chancey's arguments. The churches took them into consideration, and returned their several answers, wherein they showed their dissent from him, and clearly confuted all his arguments, discovering withal some great mistakes of his about the judgment and practice of antiquity. Yet he would not give over his opinion; and the church of Plymouth, (though they could not agree to call him to office, yet,) being much taken with his able parts, they were very loath to part with him. He did maintain, also, that the Lord's supper ought to be administered in the evening, and every Lord's day; and the church at Sandwich (where one Mr. Leveridge was minister) fell into the practice of it; but that being a matter of no great ill consequence, save some outward inconvenience, there was little stir about it. This Mr. Chancey was after called to office in the church of Scituate.

One Palmer, of Hingham, and two others, (being ancient and skilful seamen,) being in a shallop of ten tons, in an easterly wind, by Paddock's Island, were overset; yet one of them had

[1] Edward Norris and Charles Chauncy were both conspicuous divines; but the latter, becoming president of Harvard College, has a better hold on fame. Chauncy, to whom two professorships were offered at the English Cambridge, a marked token of appreciation, began his American career at Plymouth, going soon to Scituate. Though like his predecessor Dunster, held in Massachusetts to be unsound in his views as to baptism, he was trusted with the great educational responsibility, and made himself powerfully influential.

the sheet in his hand, and let fly; but it was too late, having but little ballast in her; yet it pleased God, there came by, soon after, a pinnace, which espied them sitting upon her side, yet deep in the water, and took them up, but the shallop was not heard of after.

Many men began to inquire after the southern parts; and the great advantages supposed to be had in Virginia and the West Indies, etc., made this country to be disesteemed of many; and yet those countries (for all their great wealth) have sent hither, both this year and formerly, for supply of clothes and other necessaries; and some families have forsaken both Providence and other the Caribbee Islands and Virginia to come live here. And though our people saw what meagre, unhealthful countenances they brought hither, and how fat and well liking they became soon, yet they were so taken with the ease and plenty of those countries, as many of them sold their estates here to transport themselves to Providence; among whom the chief was John Humfrey, Esq., a gentleman of special parts of learning and activity, and a godly man, who had been one of the first beginners in the promoting of this plantation, and had labored very much therein. He, being brought low in his estate, and having many children, and being well known to the lords of Providence,[1] and offering himself to their service, was accepted to be the next governor. Whereupon he labored much to draw men to join with him. This was looked at, both by the general court, and also by the elders, as an unwarrantable course; for though it was thought very needful to further plantation of churches in the West Indies, and all were willing to endeavor the same; yet to do it with disparagement of this country, (for they gave out that they could not subsist here,) caused us to fear, that the Lord was not with them in this way. And, withal, some considerations were propounded to them by the court, which diverted some of them, and made others to pause, upon three points especially: 1.

[1] See p. 228, note 1.

How dangerous it was to bring up an ill report upon this good land, which God had found out and given to his people, and so to discourage the hearts of their brethren, etc. 2. To leave a place of rest and safety, to expose themselves, their wives and children, to the danger of a potent enemy, the Spaniard. 3. Their subjection to such governors as those in England shall set over them, etc. Notwithstanding these considerations, divers of them persisted in their resolutions, and went about to get some ship or bark to transport them; but they were still crossed by the hand of God.

Mo. 3. (*May*) 17.] Joseph Grafton set sail from Salem, the 2d day in the morning, in a ketch of about forty tons, (three men and a boy in her,) and arrived at Pemaquid (the wind easterly) upon the third day in the morning, and there took in some twenty cows, oxen, etc., with hay and water for them and came to an anchor in the bay the 6th day about three after noon.

It came over by divers letters and reports, that the Lord Say did labor, by disparaging this country, to divert men from coming to us, and so to draw them to the West Indies; and, finding that godly men were unwilling to come under other governors than such as they should make choice of themselves, etc., they condescended to articles somewhat suitable to our form of government, although they had formerly declared themselves much against it, and for a mere aristocracy, and an hereditary magistracy to be settled upon some great persons, etc.

The governor also wrote to the Lord Say about the report aforesaid, and therein showed his lordship, how evident it was, that God had chosen this country to plant his people in, and therefore how displeasing it would be to the Lord, and dangerous to himself, to hinder this work, or to discourage men from supplying us, by abasing the goodness of the country, which he never saw, and persuading men, that here was no possibility of subsistence; whereas there was a sure ground for his children's faith, that, being sent hither by him, either he saw that the land was a good land, and sufficient to maintain them, or else he intended to make it such, etc. To this letter his lordship returned answer, (not denying that which was reported of him, nor the evidence of the Lord's owning the work, but) alleging, that this was a place appointed only for a present refuge, etc., and that, a better place being now found out, we were all called to remove thither.[1]

---

[1] Apparently New England was now in danger of being uprooted, though hardly yet fixed. It is not strange that Humfrey and Lord Saye and Sele thought the position too bleak and barren now that the advantages of Virginia and the West Indies were fully known. See Frank Strong, "A Forgotten Danger to the New England Colonies," in *Annual Report of the American Historical Association for* 1898, pp. 77–94.